A

OXFORDSHIRE

GLOUCESTERSHIRE

HEREFORD AND WORCESTER

SERIES EDITOR CATHERINE BAKER

·K·U·P·E·R·A·R·D·

Going Places

Going Places – the most comprehensive coverage in one volume of the leisure and sporting activities to be enjoyed in the cities, towns and villages of these adjoining counties. An invaluable source of information and ideas for visitors and residents alike, this guide offers all age groups the opportunity to pursue a favourite pastime or discover a new one regardless of the weather or season.

The activities section gives you detailed information on over sixty leisure activities, the names and addresses of their governing bodies and a list of all the places where you can enjoy them, arranged alphabetically under county headings. To find out more details look up the places in the second section of the guide.

The second section is a comprehensive gazetteer of one hundred places in the region. You will find a description, some local information and a detailed list of all the leisure activities with the telephone number, address or access information and any other interesting details. It couldn't be easier.

First published in the UK by:
Kuperard (London) Ltd,
30 Cliff Road,
London NW1 9AG

First published 1991
© Research and text
J & J Entertainment Ltd.
© Design and production
The Pen & Ink Book Company Ltd.

All rights reserved. No part of this work may be reproduced or transmitted by any means without permission.

ISBN 1-870668-58-8

The information contained in this Guide has been researched during 1990 and is as up-to-date as possible, it has been published in good faith and every effort has been made to ensure its accuracy. Neither the publishers nor the copyright holders can accept any responsibility for error or misinterpretation. All liability for loss, disappointment, negligence or other damage caused by reliance on the information contained in this Guide, or in the event of bankruptcy or liquidation or cessation of trade of any company, individual or firm mentioned is hereby excluded.

Design and production PEN & INK

Printed and bound in Great Britain

Acknowledgements

We are very grateful for the help we have received from the county, district and local councils, the tourist information centres and the individual establishments we have included in this guide. Every effort has been made to obtain accurate details at the time of going to press, however it is advisable that you telephone your destination before embarking on a long journey. Corrections, alterations or additional entries should be sent to The Editor, c/o The Publisher, for inclusion in a new edition.

We would like to thank the following for supplying the photographs included in this guide:

Abbey Stadium Sports Centre, Redditch; Cheltenham Art Gallery & Museums; Cheltenham Recreation Centre; Cheltenham Tourist Information Centre; Chris Ridgers; County Visuals, Kent County Council; Gloucestershire County Planning Department; The Heart of England Tourist Board; Hereford & Worcester County Council, Department of Engineering and Planning; Ian Meredith; Leominster District Council; The Norfolk Ski Club; Oxfordshire County Council; Redditch Borough Council; Solar Wings Ltd; South East England Tourist Board; South Herefordshire District Council; Tewkesbury Borough Council.

Contents

Introduction to

Activities

However you like to spend your time, whether ballooning or birdwatching, microlight flying or messing about in boats, playing a round of golf or soaking up the history and tradition found in historic houses, churches and castles, then these counties have much to offer and they are all listed in this section. Look up the leisure or sporting activity you are interested in, they are arranged alphabetically, and you will find a list of all the locations where you can pursue your interest, these are again listed alphabetically. To find out more details about these venues look up the town or village in the second section and under the relevant activity heading you will find the telephone number, address or access information and more details. It couldn't be easier and browsing through these pages you might even discover a new sport or activity to try, as well as a new appreciation and enjoyment of the leisure facilities offered in these counties.

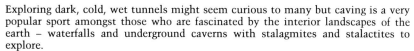

Caving

Exploring dark, cold, wet tunnels might seem curious to many but caving is a very popular sport amongst those who are fascinated by the interior landscapes of the earth – waterfalls and underground caverns with stalagmites and stalactites to explore.

The best way to learn caving techniques is to join a caving club, they will provide expertise, experience and equipment. For details of local clubs and information about caving contact the National Caving Association, their address is below.

National Caving Association
F S Baguley (Secretary)
White Lion House
Ynys Uchaf
Ystradgynlais
Swansea
☎ 0639 849519

GLOUCESTERSHIRE

Cheltenham: Gloucester Caving Club
Cinderford: Royal Forest of Dean
Caving Club
Coleford: Clearwell Caves Adventure

Clearwell Caves

HEREFORD & WORCESTER

Hagley: West Mercia Caving Club
Hay-on-Wye: Gagendor Caving Group

Hereford: Hereford Caving Club
Lydney: Marches Caving Club; Wye
Pursuits
Weobley: Worlds End Lodge

Climbing

There are some good opportunities for climbers to try out their skills and enjoy the breathtaking scenery around places such as the Wye Valley in Hereford and Worcester. Adventure and outdoor centres offer courses for both the beginner and the experienced climber whilst several sports centres throughout these counties have indoor climbing walls where the interested beginner can learn basic hand and footholds and the experienced climber can keep in shape.

The national body for climbing is given below and they will give advice on all aspects of mountaineering, climbing and mountain safety. They supply lists of clubs and courses on request.

British Mountaineering Council (BMC)
Crawford House
Precinct Centre
Booth Street East
Manchester
☎ 061 273 5835

HEREFORD & WORCESTER

Bromsgrove: Bromsgrove and Redditch
Mountaineering Club
Lydney: Wye Pursuits
Weobley: Worlds End Lodge

GLOUCESTERSHIRE

Tewkesbury: Tewkesbury Sports
Centre

OXFORDSHIRE

Banbury: Banbury Mountaineering Club
Didcot: Didcot Leisure Centre

Shooting

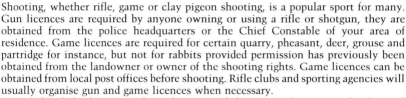

Shooting, whether rifle, game or clay pigeon shooting, is a popular sport for many. Gun licences are required by anyone owning or using a rifle or shotgun, they are obtained from the police headquarters or the Chief Constable of your area of residence. Game licences are required for certain quarry, pheasant, deer, grouse and partridge for instance, but not for rabbits provided permission has previously been obtained from the landowner or owner of the shooting rights. Game licences can be obtained from local post offices before shooting. Rifle clubs and sporting agencies will usually organise gun and game licences when necessary.

   More detailed information about shooting and clay pigeon shooting can be obtained from the associations listed below.

British Association for Shooting and Conservation
National Headquarters
Marford Mill
Clwyd
☎ 0244 570881

Clay Pigeon Shooting Association
107, Epping New Road
Buckhurst Hill
Essex
☎ 081 505 6221

GLOUCESTERSHIRE

Tewkesbury: Severn Sporting Agency Ltd

HEREFORD & WORCESTER

Hereford: Hereford Shooting School
Leominster: Leominster Gun Room

OXFORDSHIRE

Cropredy: Cropredy Gun Club
Deddington: Deddington and District Rifle and Revolver Club

Aerial Sports

Ballooning

The romantic appeal of hot air ballooning captivates many – if the idea of drifting through bright, clear skies appeals then this might be the pursuit for you. To gain your private pilot's licence tuition from a qualified pilot is necessary. A minimum of twelve hours flying experience and a test flight with a qualified examiner are the prerequisites necessary for you to make a solo flight. Additional examinations in navigation, meteorology, and air law will safely extend you ballooning skills.

   The British Ballooning and Airship Club is the governing body of the sport and they will provide information on ballooning meets and local clubs.

The British Ballooning and Airship Club
Barbara Green, Information Officer
P.O. Box 1006
Birmingham
☎ 021 643 3224

GLOUCESTERSHIRE

Cirencester: Ballooning in the Cotswolds

Gloucester: ACP Nationwide
Stonehouse: Jon Langley and Co, Aeronauts

HEREFORD & WORCESTER

Ross-on-Wye: Ross Ballons; Wye Valley Aviation
Stroud: John M Albury

7

Flying

To take to the skies has been man's aspiration for centuries and the appeal of flying never seems to diminish. To obtain a private pilot's licence requires a minimum of 40 hours flight training at a local flying club, five multiple-choice examinations in meteorology, aviation law, technical aspects, radio telephony and navigation and two flight tests with an examiner to observe both general handling and navigational skills. For anyone interested in taking up flying the Student Pilot Assocation, whose address is below, will supply both information and a list of flying schools on request.

For those who either own a plane or who might be interested in building a plane then the Popular Flying Association will be a valuable source of information, their address is below.

Student Pilots Association
30 Tisbury Road
Hove
East Sussex
☎ 0273 204080

Popular Flying Association
Terminal Building
Shoreham Airport
Shoreham-by-Sea
☎ 0273 461616

GLOUCESTERSHIRE

Cheltenham: Cotswold Aero Club
Gloucester: Cotswold Aero Club;
  Staverton Airport

HEREFORD & WORCESTER

Shobdon: Herefordshire Aero Club

OXFORDSHIRE

Kidlington: Oxford Air Training School

Gliding

Gliding is a graceful and exciting way to explore the skies. Learning to control a glider is easily and quickly mastered whilst learning to soar is the art every glider pilot seeks. A skilful pilot can cover over two hundred miles or climb to tens of thousands of feet.

Trial flights are available to give you a taste of the air and no age restrictions exist other than pilots under sixteen not being able to fly solo. Dual-control training gliders are used for training and an average of 50 take-offs and landings accompanied by a qualified instructor will take you to solo flying standard. To fly cross-country you must acquire your Bronze badge which will test not only your flying ability but also your knowledge of air law, meteorology and the theory of flight.

The governing body of gliding is the British Gliding Association, they will provide you with information about gliding and details of gliding clubs.

The British Gliding Association
Kimberley House
Vaughan Way
Leicester
☎ 0533 531051

GLOUCESTERSHIRE

Chalford: Cotswold Gliding Club
Nailsworth: Bristol and Gloucester
  Gliding Club

HEREFORD & WORCESTER

Shobdon: Herefordshire Gliding Club

Microlight Flying

Microlights are small aircraft that are great fun to fly. They are single or two seater hi-tech planes that have been flown as far afield as Africa and Australia and at speeds of over 100 mph. They are definitely not toy aeroplanes yet they need none of the facilities of a conventional aeroplane, your garage can be your hangar and any fair-sized field your aerodrome. If you are interested try an 'air experience' flight from one of the listed schools. Learning to fly then involves a training course to acquire your flying licence, this usually takes between one and six months. You need to be 17 and reasonably fit to fly your own microlight, patience and perseverance will enable you to learn the art of flying so you can escape into the air and enjoy this safe and exhilarating form of flying.

The British Microlight Association is the governing body of the sport and can be contacted for more information at the address below.

British Microlight Aircraft Association
Bullring
Deddington
Oxford
☎ 0869 38888

HEREFORD & WORCESTER

Shobdon: Microflight

OXFORDSHIRE

Deddington: British Microlight Aircraft Association

Aerial Sports

Parachuting

Parachuting is exciting, exhilarating and dynamic, it offers you the joy and freedom of the sky. You can experience the thrill of your first jump by static line parachuting where your parachute opens automatically as soon as you leave the aircraft, by accelerated free-fall (AFF) where your first descent is from 12,000 feet with two highly qualified instructors, or by tandem parachuting where you jump using a dual harness system with an instructor who controls your free-fall and landing – a quick and easy introduction to free-fall. You can progress from beginner to complete parachutist by one of two systems depending on how you made your first jump, and then go on to take up sport parachuting, a highly skilled sport offering many personal and competitive challenges.

The British Parachute Association is the governing body of the sport and will supply you with information both about the sport and courses offered by its affiliated clubs.

The British Parachute Association
Mr D Oddy (National Administrator)
5 Wharf Way
Glen Parva
Leicester
☎ 0533 785271

HEREFORD & WORCESTER

Shobdon: Herefordshire Aero Club

OXFORDSHIRE

Abingdon: Parachute Training Services
Witney: POPS UK

Indoor Sports

Badminton

Badminton is another of the racket sports that remains popular. There are plenty of opportunities to play in the many leisure and sports centres throughout the region. For information about badminton and details of local clubs contact the Badminton Association of England, their address is below.

Badminton Association of England
National Badminton Centre
Bradwell Road
Loughton Lodge
Milton Keynes
☎ 0908 568822

GLOUCESTERSHIRE

Bishops Cleeve: Cleeve Sports Centre
Cheltenham: Balcarras Sports Centre;
 Bournside Sports Centre;
 Cheltenham Recreation Centre
Cirencester: Cotswold Sports Centre
Dursley: Dursley Pool and Sports
 Centre
Tewkesbury: Tewkesbury Sports
 Centre

HEREFORD & WORCESTER

Bromsgrove: The Dolphin Centre
Droitwich Spa: Droitwich Spa Sports
 and Leisure Centre
Hereford: Herefordshire Badminton
 Association
Leominster: Leominster District
 Leisure Centre
Redditch: The Leys Sports Centre;
 St Augustines Sports Centre
Stourport-on-Severn: Stourport Sports
 Centre
Worcester: Nunnery Wood Sports
 Centre; Perdiswell Leisure Centre

Abingdon: Oxfordshire Badminton Association
Banbury: Banbury Badminton Club; Bodicote Badminton Club; Demag Badminton Club
Bloxham: Bloxham Badminton Club
Didcot: Didcot Leisure Centre
Henley: Henley Badminton Club

Oxford: Blackbird Leys Leisure Centre; East Oxford Sports Centre; Northway Centre Gymnasium
Thame: Swifts Badminton Club; Thame Badminton Club; Thame Sports and Arts Centre
Wallingford: The Regal Sports & Social Centre
Wheatley: The Park Sports Centre
Witney: Windrush Sports Centre

Leisure Centres

Excellent opportunities exist throughout the region to pursue a range of indoor sports options including the increasingly popular racket sports of squash and badminton as well as ice skating, roller skating and tenpin bowling. For the fit, not so fit and those who wish to relax are the more varied facilities offered by the sports and leisure centres listed, these include saunas, solariums, fitness centres, swimming pools, splash pools, badminton courts and bodybuilding gyms. The range of facilities offered by different leisure centres is so diverse that it would be advisable to contact individual centres to discover what they offer.

GLOUCESTERSHIRE

Bishops Cleeve: Cleeve Sports Centre
Cheltenham: Balcarras Sports Centre; Bournside Sports Centre; Cheltenham Recreation Centre; St Benedicts Sports Centre
Cirencester: Cotswold Sports Centre
Dursley: Dursley Pool and Sports Centre
Gloucester: Gloucester Leisure Centre
Stroud: Stratford Park Leisure Centre
Tewkesbury: Cascades; Tewkesbury Sports Centre
Wotton-under-Edge: Wotton-under-Edge Sports Centre

HEREFORD & WORCESTER

Bromsgrove: The Dolphin Centre
Droitwich Spa: Droitwich Spa Sports and Leisure Centre
Evesham: Evesham Sports Complex
Hagley: Old Helesonians Club
Hereford: Hereford Leisure Centre; Hereford Swimming Baths
Kidderminster: Wyre Forest Glades Leisure Centre
Leominster: Leominster District Leisure Centre
Redditch: Abbey Stadium Sports Centre; Arrow Vale Sports Centre; The Leys Sports Centre; St Augustines Sports Centre
Stourport-on-Severn: Stourport Sports Centre

Tenbury Wells: Leisure Centres
Worcester: Nunnery Wood Sports Centre; Perdiswell Leisure Centre; St John's Sports Centre; Worcester Swimming Pool and Fitness Centre

OXFORDSHIRE

Abingdon: The Old Gaol Leisure Centre
Banbury: Spiceball Park Sports Centre
Bicester: Bicester and Ploughley Sports Centre; Bicester Sports Club
Bloxham: Dewey Sports Centre
Chipping Norton: Greystones Sports Complex
Didcot: Didcot Leisure Centre
Faringdon: Faringdon Leisure Centre
Henley: Henley and District Sports Centre
Hook Norton: Hook Norton Sports and Social Club
Kidlington: Kidlington and Gosford Sports Centre
Oxford: Douglas Bader Sports Centre; Blackbird Leys Leisure Centre; East Oxford Sports Centre; Ferry Sports Centre; Northway Sports Centre; Oxrad Centre; Temple Cowley Pools
Thame: Thame Sports and Arts Centre
Wallingford: The Regal Sports & Social Centre
Wheatley: The Park Sports Centre
Witney: Windrush Sports Centre

Leisure Sports

ICE SKATING

OXFORDSHIRE

Oxford: Oxford Ice Rink

Squash

Squash is one of the racket sports that has flourished over the last twenty years, a popular sport for the busy executive or for the sports enthusiast who enjoys the challenge it provides and the fitness it requires. Squash courts are a prominent feature of most leisure and sports centres and many hotels offer squash facilities so it is unlikely that you will ever be far away from somewhere to play.

GLOUCESTERSHIRE

Bishops Cleeve: Cleeve Sports Centre
Cheltenham: Cheltenham Recreation Centre
Cinderford: Heywood Sports Centre
Cirencester: Cotswold Sports Centre
Dursley: Dursley Pool and Sports Centre
Gloucester: Gloucester Leisure Centre; Gloucestershire Squash Rackets Association
Stroud: Stratford Park Leisure Centre
Tewkesbury: Tewkesbury Sports Centre
Wotton-under-Edge: Wotton-under-Edge Sports Centre

HEREFORD & WORCESTER

Droitwich Spa: Droitwich Spa Sports and Leisure Centre
Evesham: Evesham Rowing Club
Hereford: Herefordshire Squash Rackets Association
Kidderminster: Wyre Forest Glades Leisure Centre
Ledbury: Feathers Hotel

Leominster: Leominster District Leisure Centre
Redditch: Abbey Stadium Sports Centre; Arrow Squash; Arrow Vale Sports Centre; The Leys Sports Centre
Stourport-on-Severn: Stourport-on-Severn; Worcestershire Squash Rackets Association

OXFORDSHIRE

Abingdon: Abingdon Squash Club
Banbury: Spiceball Park Sports Centre
Bicester: Bicester and Ploughley Sports Centre
Bloxham: Beauchamp Squash Club
Chipping Norton: The Regent Squash Club
Didcot: Didcot Leisure Centre
Faringdon: Faringdon Leisure Centre
Oxford: Ferry Sports Centre
Thame: North Street
Wallingford: Wallingford Sports & Social Club; Wallingford Squash Rackets Club
Wheatley: The Park Sports Centre

Adventure Centres

Choose from a wide range of sports and activities to build up your own programme at one of the special interest or multi-activity centres listed. The range of activities offered by multi-activity centres is diverse whilst special interest centres cater for one activity or type of activity. Accommodation and prices vary so send for a brochure to compare facilities before you make your choice.

The British Activity Holiday Association monitors instruction and safety standards, they offer a consumer advisory service that can be contacted via the address given below.

Special activity break packages for families are offered by many hotels and guesthouses, details of these have not been included but can be obtained from the local Tourist Information Centres.

British Activity Holiday Association
Norton Terrace
Llandrindod Wells
Powys
Wales
☎ 0597 823902

GLOUCESTERSHIRE

MULTI-ACTIVITY CENTRES

Bourton-on-the-Water: HF Holidays
Coleford: Forest Adventure
Gloucester: Gloucester Hotel and Country Club
St Briavels: Cinderhill House
Stow-on-the-Wold: Grapevine Hotel
Tewkesbury: Bell Hotel
Westonbirt: Hare and Hounds Hotel
Worcester: Severn Valley Sports

SPECIAL INTEREST CENTRES

Cheltenham: Badgeworth Riding Centre; Cotswold Collection Breaks; Prestbury Park Hotel
Chipping Campden: Seymour House Hotel
Cirencester: Steel-Away
Dursley: Uley Carriage Hire
Gloucester: Hatton Court
Stroud: Amberley Inn; Ashleigh House
Winchcombe: Thimble Cottage Craft Studio

HEREFORD & WORCESTER

MULTI-ACTIVITY CENTRES

Great Malvern: Montrose Hotel; Rainbow Action Holidays
Hereford: Acorn Activities; Western Adventure
Kington: Cantry Village Weekend Breaks
Lydney: Wye Pursuits
Much Marcle: Lower House Farm
Ross-on-Wye: PGL Adventure Ltd; PGL Drummonds Dub Watersports Centre
Stourport-on-Severn: Organisation Unlimited
Symonds Yat: Holly Barn
Weobley: Worlds End Lodge

SPECIAL INTEREST CENTRES

Bromyard: Straw Craft Holidays
Hope-under-Dinmore: Campus Centre
Ross-on-Wye: Pedalway; PGL Adventure
Symonds Yat: Wye Dean Canoe and Adventure Centre
Tenbury Wells: Fabric Craft Centre
Weobley: Bob Kilvert's Watercolour Weeks

OXFORDSHIRE

MULTI-ACTIVITY CENTRES

Worcester: Leisure Leaders Activity Holidays

SPECIAL INTEREST CENTRES

Banbury: Redkir Leisure
Carterton: Romany Caravan and Country Riding
Oxford: Art in Oxford; The Johnathon Markson Oxford Tennis Camp; Oxford Heritage Study Visits; Stained Glass Activities

Birdwatching

Birdlife in Britain is varied and birdwatching is an extremely popular activity as borne out by the current membership figures of the Royal Society for the Protection of Birds (RSPB) – over half a million. The RSPB have many reserves, often exceptionally beautiful locations where visitors can enjoy the relaxing atmosphere and observe the wealth of birds and wildlife from covered hides. The RSPB will supply information about their reserves, about bird watching holidays and their work on request from the address below.

The Royal Society for the Protection of Birds (RSPB)
The Lodge
Sandy
Bedfordshire
☎ 0767 680551

The Wildfowl and Wetlands Trust at Slimbridge

GLOUCESTERSHIRE

Coleford: Nags Head Nature Reserve
Slimbridge: The Wildfowl and Wetlands Trust
Upton-upon-Severn: Birdsmorton Waterfowl Sanctuary

HEREFORD & WORCESTER

Symonds Yat: Symonds Yat Rock
Shobdon: Pearl Lake; Shobdon Airfield
Weobley: Worlds End Lodge

Camping & Caravanning

Christchurch Camping Ground, Forest of Dean

Camping and caravanning have long been enjoyed by families and individuals of all ages as an inviting way of getting out into the countryside. The Camping and Caravanning Club will supply details about membership and their activities on request.

The Camping and Caravanning Club
Mr C A Smith (Director General)
Greenfield House
Westwood Way
Coventry
☎ 0203 694995

GLOUCESTERSHIRE

Bourton-on-the-Water: Folly Farm Camping and Caravan Park
Cheltenham: Stansby Caravan Park
Coleford: Cherry Orchard Farm; Christchurch Camping Ground; Forest of Dean; Rushmere Farm
Cotswold Water Park: Cotswold Hoburne
Upton-upon-Severn: Riverside Caravan Park

HEREFORD & WORCESTER

Bewdley: Little Lakes Holiday Park
Bromsgrove: Touring Caravans
Bromyard: Fir Tree Inn; Nether Court

Evesham: Leedons Park Broadway; Ranch Caravan Park Holiday Centre; Small Moors Holiday Park
Hay-on-Wye: Radnors End Campsite
Hereford: Hereford Racecourse Holiday Caravan and Campsite
Symonds Yat: Blackthorne Farm; Eastville Static Caravan Park; Symonds Yat East Campsite
Tewkesbury: Abbey Caravan Club Site

OXFORDSHIRE

Chipping Norton: Camping and Caravanning Club Site
Oxford: Cassington Mill Caravan Park; Oxford Camping International
Wallingford: Bridge Villa International Caravan and Camping Site; Maidboats Camping Site; Riverside Caravan and Camping Site
Witney: Hardwick Parks Ltd; Standlake Caravans; Swinford Farm
Woodstock: Diamond Farm

15

Cricket

Cricket conjures up images of English village greens on lazy Sunday afternoons in summer for people throughout the world. The tradition of county cricket in England is long and distinguished and can be appreciated and enjoyed by a visit to any of the county grounds. You might even be lucky enough to see some records shattered if the summers continue to be long and dry.

GLOUCESTERSHIRE

Gloucestershire: Gloucester County Cricket Club

HEREFORD & WORCESTER

Worcester: Worcester County Cricket Club

Cycling

Cycling is a wonderful way of exploring this region's rich and varied countryside. Cycles are often available for hire, several cycle shops are listed in this guide and others may be listed in leaflets available from the Tourist Information Centres who also produce maps and cycle routes for many areas. Some of the cycling holiday centres will provide a luggage porter and many offer cycling weekends to give you a taste of the 'cyclers' view of the countryside – a good introduction.

The Cyclists' Touring Club, listed below, will provide touring information, information about local cycling groups as well as technical and legal information.

The Cyclists' Touring Club
69 Meadrow
Godalming
Surrey
☎ 04868 7217

GLOUCESTERSHIRE

Nailsworth: Cycle Trail
Stroud: Stroud Valleys Cycle Trail

HEREFORD & WORCESTER

Bromsgrove: Beacon Road Cycling Club
Hereford: Coombes Cycles
Lydney: Riders of Lydney
Ross-on-Wye: Little and Hall; Pedalway

Worcester: Cadence Cycle Hire

OXFORDSHIRE

Abingdon: Mid Oxon Cycling Club
Bicester: Oxonian Cycling Club
Cropredy: Oxfordshire Cycleway
Deddington: Banbury Star Cyclists Club
Didcot: Cycling CTC; Phoenix Cycling
Oxford: Cycle Touring Club; Dentons Cycle Hire; Pennyfarthing Cycle Hire

Falconry

Birds of prey fascinate and thrill with their flight and swooping precision. The ancient art of keeping and training these proud birds to return from flight or to hunt quarry is equally fascinating and can be seen in practice at the falconry centres in this region. These centres are also interested in conservation as many species face dangers in the wild. The Newent centre has a captive breeding programme and receives pairs of endangered birds from many countries throughout the world. The best months to see the young birds are May and June. Guided tours and information about the breeding programme is available from the centres themselves.

GLOUCESTERSHIRE

Newent: The National Birds of Prey Centre

HEREFORD & WORCESTER

Hagley: The Falconry Centre

Fishing

Fishing in Britain is divided into coarse fishing, game fishing and sea fishing. Coarse fishing is very popular, the species usually caught are bream, carp, chub, dace, gudgeon, perch, pike, roach, rudd and tench. There are many fine opportunities for excellent coarse fishing in this region, the Rivers Severn, Thames, Trent and Wye being particularly good. The close season for coarse fishing is between March 15th and June 15th. Permission in the form of a rod licence is necessary from the water authority in charge of the water you are planning to fish, these are usually obtainable from local tackle shops and are issued by the National Rivers Authority for rivers and by the Regional Water Company for still waters such as lakes and reservoirs. After obtaining the rod licence permission must be obtained from the owner of the water, this might be an angling club in which case it is usual to pay a membership fee or it might mean buying a ticket, again local tackle shops are usually the best places to enquire about water ownership.

The region has one of the best game fishing rivers in the country within its boundaries – the River Wye in Hereford and Worcester. The close season for trout lasts from October 1st to March 24th and for salmon between November 1st and January 31st although these could vary depending on the different water authorities.

General information, licences and leaflets are available from the National Rivers Authority Thames and Severn-Trent regions, their addresses are given below. The National Anglers' Council will also provide information about fishing in the area.

**National Rivers Authority
Thames Region**
King's Meadow House
King's Meadow Road
Reading
☎ 0734 535000

**National Rivers Authority
Thames Region**
Denton House
Iffley Turn
Oxford
☎ 0865 749400

**National Rivers Authority
Severn-Trent Region**
Sapphire East
550 Streetsbrook Road
Solihull
☎ 021 711 2324

National Anglers' Council
Coarse Fishing ☎ 0332 362000
Game Fishing ☎ 071 283 5838
Sea Fishing ☎ 0626 331330

GLOUCESTERSHIRE

COARSE FISHING

Bibury: Bibury Trout Farm
Cheltenham: Cheltenham Angling Club; Ian Coley Ltd
Cinderford: Royal Forest of Dean Angling Club; Robert Sports
Cirencester: Abbey Lake; Ashton Keynes Angling Club

Coleford: River Wye; Cannop Ponds; Sport and Leisure
Cotswold Water Park: River Ray; South Cerney Angling Club
Fairford: River Coln; River Croft
Gloucester: Allsports; Gloucester United Anglers Association; River Severn at Wainlode; Tredworth Tackle
Leominster: Rivers Arrow and Trothy; Dinsley, Ridgemore, Humber and Duddleston Brooks
St Briavels: River Wye
Slimbridge: Sharpness and Avon Canal
Steeple Aston: River Cherwell; Oxford Canal
Stonehouse: Stroudwater Canal
Tewkesbury: River Avon; R Danter Tackle Shop
Upton-upon-Severn: River Severn

GAME FISHING

Cirencester: Lower Moor; River Churn
Cotswold Water Park: Horseshoe Lake; Manor Brook Lake; Rainbow Lake Trout Fishing Ltd
Stow-on-the-Wold: Donington Fish Farm

HEREFORD & WORCESTER

COARSE FISHING

Bewdley: Arley; John White Tackle; River Severn

18

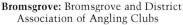

Fishing

Bromsgrove: Bromsgrove and District Association of Angling Clubs
Droitwich Spa: Droitwich and District Angling Society
Eardisland: River Arrow
Evesham: River Avon
Hay-on-Wye: G & B Sports; H R Grant & Son
Hereford: Hattons; Hereford and District Angling Association; Perkins of Hereford Ltd
Hope-under-Dinmore: River Lugg; Railway Inn
Kidderminster: Hurcott Pool; Kidderminster and District Angling Association; Ladies Pool
Lydney: Lydney and District Angling Club
Pembridge: Wick Grange; Kinver Freeliners Angling Club
Redditch: Arrow Valley Lake
Ross-on-Wye: River Wye
Shobdon: Pearl Lake; River Arrow
Stourport-on-Severn: John White Tackle
Tenbury Wells: River Teme
Worcester: Rivers Avon, Severn and Teme; Worcester Canal

GAME FISHING

Evesham: Black Monk Trout Lakes
Hay-on-Wye: Rivers Wye and Monnow; River Wye Information; Sportfish (Fly)
Hereford: Hereford Fly Fishing Club
Hope-under-Dinmore: River Lugg; Humber Brook; Marlbrook Water
Kington: Rivers Arrow and Trothy
Ross-on-Wye: River Wye; GB Sports
Tenbury Wells: River Teme

OXFORDSHIRE

COARSE FISHING

Abingdon: Abindgdon and District Angling Association
Banbury: Banbury and District Angling Association
Bampton: River Thames
Bicester: Bicester Angling Alliance; Bicester Angling Society
Bloxham: Adderbury Lakes; River Cherwell
Chipping Norton: River Evenlode; Salford
Cropredy: River Cherwell; Oxford Canal
Didcot: Didcot Angling Centre
Faringdon: River Thames; Turner's Tackle & Bait
Henley: The Boat Yard; Thames Conservancy
Islip: Rivers Cherwell and Ray
Kidlington: River Cherwell; Oxford Canal
Long Hanborough: River Evenlode
Oxford: National Federation of Anglers
Thame: Thame Angling Club
Wallingford: Jolly Anglers Club
Witney: River Windrush; Stanton Harcourt
Wroxton: Grimesbury Reservoir

GAME FISHING

Faringdon: Local ponds and lakes
Upton-upon-Severn: Clearwater Fish Farm

Football

Football has always been a popular sport both to play and to watch. This popularity has reached unparalleled proportions in recent years with professional players reaching the status previously accorded only to stars of the screen or the pop world. Always colourful and often exciting the league teams are worth a visit one Saturday afternoon – you might well be watching a soccer star of the future in action!

HEREFORD & WORCESTER

Hereford: Hereford United

OXFORDSHIRE

Oxford: Oxford United Football Club

Golf

Golf is a relaxing and increasingly popular sport for a wide range of people. The golf clubs listed welcome visitors but it is advisable that you contact the club in advance of playing in order to check if they have any restrictions – some require a handicap certificate or will only accept visitors who are members of another club. It is also worthwhile checking what the fees and hire charges are and what facilities are available. Most clubs have a pro-shop on the course where clubs and equipment can be hired and the professional will give tuition.

GLOUCESTERSHIRE

Bishops Cleeve: Cleeve Hill Municipal Course
Cheltenham: Cotswold Hills Golf Club; Lilleybrook Golf Club
Dursley: Stinchcombe Hill Golf Club
Minchinhampton: Minchinhampton Common Old Course; Minchinhampton Golf Club New Course
Painswick: Painswick Golf Club
Tewkesbury: Tewkesbury Park Hotel Golf and Country Club
Westonbirt: Westonbirt Golf Course
Worcester: Cotswold Edge Golf Course

HEREFORD & WORCESTER

Bewdley: Little Lakes Golf Club
Broadway: Broadway Golf Club
Bromsgrove: Bromsgrove Golf Centre; King's Norton Golf Club
Droitwich Spa: Droitwich Spa Golf & Country Club
Evesham: Evesham Golf Club
Hagley: Hagley Country Golf Club
Hereford: Belmont House Golf Club; Herefordshire Golf Club; Hereford Municipal Golf Course

Kington: Kington Golf Course
Leominster: Leominster Golf Club
Redditch: Abbey Park Golf & Country Club; Pitcheroak Municipal Golf Course; Redditch Golf Club
Ross-on-Wye: Ross-on-Wye Golf Club
Weobley: Herefordshire Golf Club
Worcester: Perdiswell Municipal Golf Club; Tolladine Golf Club; Worcester Golf and Country Club

OXFORDSHIRE

Abingdon: Frilford Heath Golf Club
Banbury: Cherwell Edge Public Course; Tadmarton Heath Golf Club
Bicester: Chesterton Country Golf Club
Chipping Norton: Chipping Norton Golf Club
Didcot: Haddow Hill Golf Club
Henley: Badgemore Park Country Club; Henley Golf Club, Huntercombe Golf Club
Hook Norton: Tadmarton Heath Golf Club
Kidlington: North Oxford Golf Club
Kingston Bagpuize: Frilford Heath Golf Club
Oxford: North Oxford Golf Club; Southfield Golf Course

Horse Racing

Horse racing is a sport enjoyed by many but riding is not always the way in which race lovers participate, watching and betting are very often the form their involvement takes. National hunt race lovers can enjoy their sport at the Cheltenham Racecourse which hosts the National Hunt Festival with its famous Gold Cup, run in March. A 'day at the races' can be enjoyed by all at any of the regions racecourses.

Cheltenham Racecourse

GLOUCESTERSHIRE

Cheltenham: Cheltenham Racecourse
Upton-upon-Severn: Fish Meadow

HEREFORD & WORCESTER

Broadway: Spring Hill
Hereford: Hereford Racecourse
Worcester: The Racecourse

Horse Riding

Riding is a very popular pursuit in Britain and there are many riding schools and equestrian centres throughout this region offering a range of facilities from residential instructional holidays to basic instruction and horse and pony hire. Some centres specialise in trail riding and pony trekking, some place a greater emphasis on horse care and stable management whilst others provide courses on a variety of equestrian skills such as show jumping, cross country and side saddle. The range of facilities provided may include an indoor school, a dressage ring or a cross country course. To discover more about the schools and riding in general you should contact the British Horse Society, their address is below, who will send you detailed information on request as well as a list of their many publications.

British Horse Society
British Equestrian Centre
Stoneleigh
Kenilworth
Warwickshire
☎ 0203 696697

GLOUCESTERSHIRE

Bourton-on-the-Water: Long Distance Riding Centre
Chalford: Camp Riding Centre

Cheltenham: Cheltenham Horse Riding Centre; Southam Riding School
Cirencester: The Talland School of Equitation
Coleford: Rushmere Farm Riding Stables
Cotswold Water Park: South Cerney Riding School
Newent: Huntley School of Equitation
Steeple Aston: Westfield Farm Riding Centre
Stow-on-the-Wold: Cromwell Stables
Wotton-under-Edge: Gin Saddlery

21

Bewdley: Crundalls Lane Stables
Bromsgrove: Seecham Equestrian Centre; Whitford Riding Stables
Droitwich Spa: Hunts Farm Stud and Stables
Evesham: Mayfield Riding School; Merrybroook Equestrian Centre; The Riding Stables
Great Malvern: The Avenue Riding Centre
Great Witley: Rockmoor Stables
Hagley: Lea Castle Equestrian Centre
Hereford: Greenbank Riding School
Inkberrow: Bradclose Farm
Kidderminster: Acre Farm, Far Forest Stables; Lea Castle Equestrian; Sokum Livery Stables; West Midlands Equitation Centre

Leominster: Meadow Bank Riding Centre
Lydney: Woodside Equestrian Centre
Ross-on-Wye: Lea Bailey Riding School
Stourport-on-Severn: Hartlebury Stables Ltd; Manor Farm Riding School
Weobley: Worlds Ends Lodge

OXFORDSHIRE

Burford: Barrington Stables
Carterton: Cotswold Equitation Centre
Didcot: Blewbury Riding and Trekking Centre Ltd
Faringdon: Oakfield Riding School
Henley: Turville Valley Stud Riding School
Hook Norton: Turpins Lodge
Oxford: British Horse Society; Field Study Riding Centre
Wallingford: Blenheim Riding Centre

Orienteering

Orienteering is a wonderful way to get out into the countryside no matter what your age or level of fitness. You can run, jog or walk as you read your map and choose your route to the red and white markers. You can go solo or share your experiences with friends and family – there's a course for everyone and groups of two and four are welcome on beginners courses. It costs very little and you can try it out at one of the permanent orienteering courses. If you like maps, fresh air and exploring the countryside then this could be the leisure activity for you. The British Orienteering Federation, their address is below, will supply you with details of clubs and future events as well as a list of the permanent orienteering courses around the country.

British Orienteering Federation
Riversdale
Dale Road North
Darley Dale
Matlock
Derbyshire
☎ 0269 673042

HEREFORD & WORCESTER

Hagley: Clent Course
Lydney: Wye Pursuits
Weobley: Worlds End Lodge
Worcester: Worcester Woods

OXFORDSHIRE

Oxford: South Central Orienteering Association
Witney: Thames Valley Orienteering Club

Tennis

Britain might not have produced a top-class tennis player in recent years but that cannot be attributed to lack of facilities. There are excellent indoor and outdoor courts, floodlit all-weather courts and expert tuition is also available. Complete beginners to experienced players concentrating on advanced techniques are catered for by the professional coaches in some of the coaching programmes. There are public tennis courts, usually hard, in most parks, recreation areas and leisure centres. You can hire them for a small fee and only have to turn up to play.

For anyone interested in lawn tennis the Lawn Tennis Association will supply you with information about their clubs and play opportunities if you approach them at the address below.

Lawn Tennis Association
J C U James (Secretary)
The Queen's Club
West Kensington
London
☎ 071 385 2366

Tennis and Rackets Association
Brigadier A D Myrtle (C.B., C.B.E.)
c/o The Queens Club
Palliser Road
London
☎ 071 381 4746

GLOUCESTERSHIRE

Bishops Cleeve: Cleeve Sports Centre
Cheltenham: Balcarras Sports Centre;
Bournside Sports Centre;
Montpellier Gardens; Pitville Park;
St Benedict's Sport Centre
Tewkesbury: Tewkesbury Sports
Centre

HEREFORD & WORCESTER

Bromsgrove: Bromsgrove Tennis Club;
Sanders Park
Droitwich Spa: Droitwich Lawn Tennis
Club
Evesham: Ashton-under-Hill Tennis
Club; Evesham Rowing Club
Great Malvern: The Manor Park Tennis
Club
Hereford: Whitecross Tennis Club;
King George V Playing Fields
Inkberrow: Inkberrow Tennis Club
Ledbury: Ledbury Lawn Tennis Club
Leominster: Leominster Tennis Club
Much Marcle: Woolhope Tennis Club
Pershore: Fladbury Tennis Club;
Pershore and District Sports Club
Redditch: Abbey Stadium Tennis Club;
Arrow Vale Sports Centre; Redditch
Tennis Club
Ross-on-Wye: Ross-on-Wye Tennis
Centre
Stourport-on-Severn: Stourport-on-
Severn Tennis Club
Tenbury Wells: Tenbury Tennis Club
Weobley: Three Counties Lawn Tennis
Club
Worcester: Gheluvelt Park; Nunnery
Wood Sports Centre; Worcester
Lawn Tennis Club

OXFORDSHIRE

Banbury: Banbury Sports Ground;
Banbury Tennis Club; People's Park
Deddington: Lawn Tennis and Squash
Club
Didcot: Didcot Lawn Tennis
Henley: Phyllis Court Club
Thame: Elms Park; Thame Sports Club
Wallingford: Bull Croft; Wallingford
Sports & Social Club
Witney: Witney Sports Centre

23

Walking & Rambling

Walking, rambling or, perhaps ambling will provide everyone, no matter what their age, with the opportunity to discover the charms of the countryside and the country inns that provide ideal stopping places for refreshments. The pace is entirely up to the walker and the route could be one selected from the OS map or one suggested in one of the innumerable books and leaflets of walks and nature trails. Many popular routes are signposted and footpaths, byways and bridlepaths have been linked in certain areas to form long distance routes which are well marked and easy to follow. The local Tourist Information Centres usually have a good selection of leaflets on local walks and if you would like to join a planned programme of walks the Ramblers' Association will provide you with details of their activities and club walks. The Long Distance Walkers Association will provide OS maps and guidebooks for recommended walks on request.

The Ramblers' Association
1/5 Wandsworth Road
London
☎ 071 582 6878

Long Distance Walkers Association
Mr P Dyson (Secretary)
30 Park Avenue
Roundhay
Leeds
West Yorkshire
☎ 0532 657029

GLOUCESTERSHIRE

Bishops Cleeve: Bishops Cleeve to Winchcombe; Cleeve Hill; The Cotswold Way
Bourton-on-the-Water: Circular Walks
Cheltenham: Circular Walks
Chipping Campden: Circular Walks
Cinderford: Forest Sculpture Trail; New Fancy Forest Walk; Soudley Ponds
Coleford: Bixslade Forest Walk; Christchurch Forest Walk; Waymarked Paths
Cranham: Barrow Wake Viewpoint
Dursley: Selsey Common
Newent: Forest Walks
Painswick: Cotswold Walks, The Cotswold Way
Ross-on-Wye: Circular Walk
St Briavels: Circular Walks; Offa's Dyke Path; Wye Valley Walk
Stanway: The Cotswold Way
Stonehouse: The Cotswold Way
Stroud: Circular Walks; Coaley Peak Picnic Site; Cotswold Way; Stroud Valleys Pedestrian Trail; Stroudwater Canal Towpath
Tewkesbury: Alleyways Walk; Battle Trail; Circular Walks
Westonbirt: Cotswold Rambling

Winchcombe: The Cotswold Way; Winchcombe Walks; The Wychavon Way
Wotton-under-Edge: Circular Walk; The Cotswold Way

HEREFORD & WORCESTER

Bewdley: Forest of Wyre; Nature Trail; The Worcestershire Way
Broadway: The Cotswold Way
Bromsgrove: Countrysiders; The Houseman Trail; The North Worcestershire Path; Bromsgrove Ramblers Association
Bromyard: Bringsty Common; Brockhampton Woodland Walk; Bromyard Downs
Droitwich Spa: Salwarpe Valley Nature Trail; The Wychavon Way
Evesham: Cleeve Hill
Great Malvern: The Elgar Trail; The Ramblers Association
Hay-on-Wye: The Offa's Dyke Path; Wye Valley Walk
Hereford: Hereford Visitor Trail; Nature Trails
Kington: The Offa's Dyke Path
Ledbury: Circular Trails
Leominster: Circular/Woodland Walks
Littledean: Blaize Bailey
Much Marcle: Dymock Daffodil Way; Poets Paths
Pershore: Riverside Walks; Spring Blossom Trail; Tiddesley Woods
Peterchurch: Golden Valley
Pontrilas: Golden Valley; Black Mountains
Redditch: Arrow Vale Countryside Group
Ross-on-Wye: Wye Valley Walk

Symonds Yat: Wye Valley Walk
Tenbury Wells: Local Walks; Tenbury
  Rambling Club
Weobley: Country Walks
Worcester: The Civil War Trail;
  Worcester Town Trail; The
  Wychavon Way

OXFORDSHIRE

Abingdon: Sutton Pools
Banbury: Banbury Rambling Club;
  Circular Walks; The Ramblers
  Association
Bampton: River Walk
Charlbury: Charlbury Circular Walk;
  The Oxfordshire Way
Faringdon: Circular Walks; Faringdon
  Town Trail; Folly Hill
Henley: Riverside Walks
Islip: The Oxfordshire Way
Stonor: Christmas Common; Icknield
  Way; Turvill Heath
Uffington: The Ridgeway
Wantage: The Ridgeway
Wallingford: Historic Town Walk; The
  Ridgeway; Riverside Walks
Wheatley: The Oxfordshire Way
Witney: Windrush Valley Walks
Wroxton: Rural Walks

Special Interests

Antiques

Paintings, furniture, porcelain, prints, decorative items, whatever you are particularly interested in from previous centuries – either as a serious collector or as an addicted browser – there are plenty of antique centres throughout the region. Many of them are housed in lovely buildings and situated in delightful, picturesque villages. For those who like the excitement of the auction room there are several auction rooms around the region where bargains might be found!

GLOUCESTERSHIRE

Coleford: Dean Forest Antiques
Gloucester: Gloucester Antique Centre
Moreton-in-Marsh: Anthony Sampson
Newent: The Mushrooms
Stow-on-the-Wold: Acorn Antiques;
  The Cotswold Antiques Centre;
  Lynn Greenwold Antiques; Stow
  Antiques
Tetbury: Brakespeare Antiques; Bristow
  Antiques; The Old George

HEREFORD & WORCESTER

Hereford: Antique Tea Shop; I and J L Brown; Stephen Cousins Antiques; Edwin Waring
Ledbury: John Nash Antiques; York House Antiques
Leominster: Jeffery Hammond Antiques; Hubbard Antiques
Ross-on-Wye: Trecilla Antiques
Worcester: Twenty antique dealers

OXFORDSHIRE

Abingdon: Hallidays Antiques
Burford: Antiques Centre
Chipping Norton: Chipping Norton Antiques Centre
Oxford: The Jam Factory; The Oxford Antique Trading Company
Thame: Peter of Thame
Wallingford: Summers
Witney: Robin Bellamy Ltd; Anthony Scaramanga; Witney Antiques
Woodstock: Fox House Antiques

Art Galleries

This region has some very distinguished galleries with internationally renowned collections of famous artists as well as many smaller galleries displaying the work of local artists capturing the colours and atmosphere of the surrounding countryside in their works.

GLOUCESTERSHIRE

Cheltenham: Cheltenham Art Gallery and Museum
Chipping Campden: Camperdene Gallery
Gloucester: Nature in Art International Centre for Wildlife Art
Stow-on-the-Wold: John Blockley Galleries; Fosse Gallery; Peppercorns House Gallery; Talbot Court Galleries
Tetbury: Long Street Gallery

HEREFORD & WORCESTER

Broadway: Bindery Gallery
Bromyard: Michael Oxenham Studio and Gallery
Droitwich Spa: Ombersley Gallery
Great Malvern: Lismore Gallery; Malvern Arts
Hay-on-Wye: The Kilvert Gallery; The Marches Gallery
Hereford: Hatton Gallery
Kington: Brobury House Gallery
Ledbury: The Biddulph Gallery; Collection Gallery; Shell House Gallery
Pembridge: Old Chapel Gallery
Tenbury Wells: Forge House Gallery
Worcester: Bevere Vivis Gallery and Pottery Shop; Framed

Cheltenham Art Gallery and Museum

OXFORDSHIRE

Bampton: The Art Gallery
Bloxham: H C Dickins
Chipping Norton: Manor House Gallery
Henley: The Barry M Keene Gallery; Bohun Gallery; Luxters Fine Art Gallery
Oxford: Christ Church Picture Gallery; Museum of Modern Art; Oxford Gallery
Wantage: Ardington Gallery

Arts & Crafts

Arts and crafts are richly represented in this area from traditional rocking horses to intricate doll's houses, hand-woven wool items to unusual painted silks. There are glass workshops to visit and potters to watch at work, silversmiths to see creating unusual jewellery and perfumes to sample – lots to see and try and enjoy at the various craft centres scattered throughout these counties.

GLOUCESTERSHIRE

Bourton-on-the-Water: Chestnut Gallery; The Cotswold Perfumery
Chalford: Dennis French Woodware
Cheltenham: The Rocking Horse Toyshop
Chipping Camden: Arts Society; Hart's Silversmiths
Cinderford: Coach House Crafts UK; W B Freeman; Victor Hugo Country Pots
Cirencester: Cirencester Workshops
Coleford: Country Theme; FODCA; Meadow Cottage Products; Peter Neale
Coleford: Prinknash Abbey and Pottery
Gloucester: Gloucester Pottery
Moreton-in-Marsh: Evenlode Pottery
Nailsworth: Stroud Valley Mills
Newent: Cowdy Glass Workshop; Newent Silver
St Briavels: McCubbins; St Briavels Pottery
Stow-on-the-Wold: Langston Priory Workshops and Showroom; Walton House Studio
Tewkesbury: Beckford Silk Ltd; Conderton Pottery; Tilly M's
Upton-upon-Severn: Arteria Galleries; Highway Gallery
Westonbirt: Hookhouse Pottery
Winchcombe: Winchcombe Pottery

HEREFORD & WORCESTER

Bewdley: Lax Lane Craft Centre; Old Bank Craft Studio
Bromsgrove: Avoncroft Art Society; Daub and Wattles Pottery
Bromyard: The Hop Pocket; Straw Crafts Centre
Evesham: Annard Woollen Mill
Great Malvern: The Doll's House Emporium; Malvern Workshop
Hanbury: The Jinney Ring Craft Centre
Ledbury: Homend Pottery; Ledbury Craft Centre
Leominster: The Lower Hundred Craft Workshop
Ross-on-Wye: Candlemakers
Tenbury Wells: Fabric Craft Centre
Weobley: The Forge Crafts Shop

OXFORDSHIRE

Abingdon: Abingdon Crafts Festival; Mary Holland Ltd; The Old Gaol
Burford: Burford Garden Centre
Carterton: Cotswold Woollen Weavers
Henley: Henley Arts and Crafts Guild; Henley Exhibition Centre
Hook Norton: Pottery and Craft Gallery
Oxford: Alice's Shop; Oxford Gallery Ltd
Thame: Thame Sports and Arts Centre
Wantage: Ardington Pottery
Wallingford: The Lamb Arcade; Roland Haycraft; Village Fabrics
Wheatley: Art in Action
Witney: Robert H Lewin; The Stable; Teddy Bears
Woodstock: Bladon Pottery; Craftsmen's Gallery; Woodstock Leathercraft Ltd

Corn dolly making

27

Country Parks

There has been a steadily growing awareness of the importance of retaining areas of countryside for recreational use and this has led to the designation of many areas of ancient and new woodland, downland, lakes, parkland and heathland as country parks. Ranging in size from under five to hundreds of acres, they offer country walks, fishing, horse rides, sailing, water sports, picnicking and nature reserves – plenty for everyone to enjoy.

GLOUCESTERSHIRE

Chipping Campden: Dovers Hill
Cirencester: Cirencester Park; Cotswold Water Park; Keynes Country Park; Neigh Bridge Country Park
Gloucester: Robinswood Hill Country Park
Moreton-in-Marsh: Batsford Park Arboretum
Stonehouse: Jardinerie Countryside Centre

HEREFORD & WORCESTER

Bewdley: Forest of Wyre; Visitor Centre
Broadway: Broadway Tower Country Park; Fish Hill
Bromsgrove: Lickey Hills Country Park; Sanders Park; Waseley Hills Country Park
Hagley: Clent Hills Country Park
Hope-under-Dinmore: Queenswood Arboretum and Country Park

Redditch: Arrow Valley Park; Morton Stanley Park
Stourport-on-Severn: Hartlebury Common and Leapgate Country Park

OXFORDSHIRE

Oxford: Shotover Country Park

Factory Tours

The processes involved in the production of many well-known objects, both large and small, are fascinating to see. Some factories allow visitors to tour and see the stages involved in the manufacture of the finished item. Enjoy watching and perhaps tasting the stages in cider-making or see the delicate craftsmanship that produces the fine porcelain for which Worcester is famous.

HEREFORD & WORCESTER

Hereford: Bulmers Cider
Worcester: Royal Porcelain Works

Farm Parks

Farm Parks will allow you to spend 'a day down on the farm' and see the farm at work. You can watch the cows being milked and the milk being pasteurised and bottled, see the calves, pigs, chickens and many rare breeds or wander around collections of farm machinery and horse-drawn waggons – a wonderful way to see the countryside in action.

GLOUCESTERSHIRE

Bourton-on-the-Water: Cotswold Farm Park
Dursley: Selsey Herb and Goat Farm
Frampton-on-Severn: St Augustine's Farm

HEREFORD & WORCESTER

Bromyard: Shortwood Working Dairy Farm
Symonds Yat: Wye Valley Farm Park

OXFORDSHIRE

Kingston Bagpuize: Millets Farm

Festivals & Fairs

The customs, traditions and history of the area live through the festivals and fairs that make the whole region a colourful, lively and fascinating world through the seasons. Everywhere are agricultural shows, county shows, flower festivals, fairs, traction-engine rallies, Morris dancing, regattas, raft races and music festivals. Many of the smaller events are more than worth a detour and a visit, they reveal much about the villages and towns that foster them and there are several events in this region, the Henley Royal Regatta or the Three Choirs Festival, for example, that draw international support and acclaim.

GLOUCESTERSHIRE

Bourton-on-the-Water: Six-a-Side Football
Cheltenham: Cheltenham Gold Cup; International Festival of Music; Cricket Festival; Festival of Literature
Chipping Camden: Cotswold Games; Scuttlebrook Wake
Frampton-on-Severn: Frampton Deer Roast; Elver Eating Contest
Gloucester: Gloucester Cricket Festival; Gloucester Carnival Festival; Barton Fair; Three Choirs Festival

Minchinhampton: Gatcombe Horse Trials
Nailsworth: Nailsworth Spring Festival
Northleach: Northleach Charter Festival; Northleach Steam and Stationary Engine Show
Painswick: Whit Sunday; Clipping Ceremony
Stow-on-the-Wold: May Fair; October Fair
Stroud: Stroud Show; Stroud Brass Band Festival; International Arts Festival; Half Marathon
Tewkesbury: Tewkesbury Mediaeval Fayre; Mop Fair

Upton-upon-Severn: Upton Folk Festival; Oak Apple Day Celebrations; Oliver Cromwell Jazz Festival; Upton Steam Rally; Water Carnival

HEREFORD & WORCESTER

Bromsgrove: Bromsgrove Music Festival; The Court Leet
Bromyard: Bromyard Folk Festival; Bromyard Gala; Multi Period Encampment
Droitwich Spa: Donkey Derby; Droitwich Carnival; Horticultural Show
Evesham: Countrywise Craft Fair; Flower Show; Lions Raft Regatta; Vale of Evesham Show
Great Malvern: The English Festival; Festival Fringe; Malvern Drama Festival; Three Counties Countryside Show
Hay-on-Wye: Jazz in the Hay; Vintage Rally
Hereford: Carnival Parade; Riverside Fete and Regatta; St Ethelberts Fair; Three Choirs Festival
Kington: Kington Eisteddfod; Kington Festival; Kington Horse and Agricultural Show
Ledbury: Carnival Day; Fayre and Folk Events
Leominster: Leominster Agricultural Show; Leominster Festival
Pembridge: Hiring Fair; Art and Craft Festival

Redditch: Water Fiesta; One Act Plays Festival; Redditch Carnival
Ross-on-Wye: 100-mile Raft Race; Ross Festival of the Arts; Steam Rally; Carnival Week; Ross Regatta
Stourport-on-Severn: Stourport-on-Severn Regatta; Carnival
Tenbury Wells: Tenbury Agricultural Show
Worcester: May Day Country Fair; Worcester Regatta

OXFORDSHIRE

Abingdon: Battle of Britain Open Day
Banbury: Michaelmas Fair
Bampton: Horse Fair; Morris Dancing
Charlbury: Street Fair
Chipping Norton: Street Fair
Didcot: Didcot Festival
Faringdon: Cheese Rolling; Mediaeval Fayre
Henley: Henley Festival of Music and the Arts; Henley Royal Regatta; Swan Upping at Cookham
Oxford: Torpids; Eights Week; May Morning; The Sherriff's Races; St Giles Fair; Morris Dancing
Thame: Carnival Week; Thame Agricultural Show; Show Fair; Autumn Charter Fair
Wallingford: Wallingford Regatta; Wallingford Carnival; Abbey Festival; Raft Race; Michaelmas Fair
Wheatley: Art in Action
Woodstock: Blenheim Horse Trials; Dressage Competition

The rich orchards and farmlands of these counties have produced some notable delicacies. There are famous Herefordshire ciders; vineyards with award-winning vintages to try, local ales that deserve a try, fresh ground flours, delicious cheeses such as Double Gloucester or a marmalade to remember – rich regional flavours to enjoy and savour.

GLOUCESTERSHIRE

Gloucester: Double Gloucester Cheese
Newent: St Annes Vineyard; Three Choirs Vineyard
Stow-on-the-Wold: Wye Organic Foods
Tetbury: Shiptons Stoneground Flour

HEREFORD & WORCESTER

Broadway: Barnfield Cider Mill
Bromyard: Bosbury Vineyards and Gardens; Hennerwood Oak Spring Water; Symonds Cider
Eardisland: The Elms
Great Malvern: Stocks Vineyard
Hope-under-Dinmore: Broadfield Vineyard
Ledbury: Bosbury Vineyards and Gardens

Much Marcle: Lyne Down Farm; Weston and Sons
Pembridge: Dunkertons Cider Company
Tenbury Wells: Hyde Farm Cheese
Weobley: Herefordshire Hamper

OXFORDSHIRE

Abingdon: Bothy Vineyard; Morland and Company

Berkeley: England Mills; Summers's Cider
Henley: Brakspears Brewery; Chiltern Valley Wines; The Hambledon Brewery
Hook Norton: Hookey Ales
Oxford: Frank Cooper Shop and Museum of Marmalade; Halls Oxford & West Brewery Company; Morrells Brewery
Thame: Le Manoir Aux Quatre Saisons

Forest Parks

Ancient and newly created woodland areas throughout this region are open to walk through and enjoy. Many, particularly those in the Forest of Dean, have nature trails, conservation centres and other interesting features for the visitor, details of these extra facilities is available from the Rangers at the individual locations.

GLOUCESTERSHIRE

Coleford: Puzzle Wood
Dursley: Dursley Woods

HEREFORD & WORCESTER

Great Malvern: Ravenshill Woodland Reserve
Redditch: Foxlydiate Woods and Pitcheroak; Oakenshaw Wood; Walkwood Coppice
Symonds Yat: Symonds Yat Rock
Worcester: Worcester Woods and Countryside Centre

Fun Parks

Whether it's waltzers, roller coasters, dodgems or big wheels all the fun of the fair can be enjoyed at permanent fun park sites. There are rides for the very young and amusements for the not-so-young too – entertainment for all the family. For those who enjoy the world in miniature the delightful replica of the village of Bourton-on-the-Water will be a real treat.

GLOUCESTERSHIRE

Bourton-on-the-Water: Model Village

HEREFORD & WORCESTER

Stourport-on-Severn: Shipleys Riverside Amusement Park

31

Gardens

Whether on a grand scale and landscaped by Capability Brown or tiny cottage gardens created by the love of successive inhabitants over the years, gardens are always places to inspire and revive the most weary of spirits. A constant tribute to the co-operation of man and nature, a natural painting using the richest possible palette, one that changes with the seasons, gardens satisfy all the senses whilst also harbouring a glorious array of wildlife. The eastern counties have many beautiful gardens, formal and grand, intricate and herbal, rambling and fragrant, open for you to explore.

GLOUCESTERSHIRE

Bibury: Barnsley House Garden
Chalford: Cowcombe Farm Herbs
Chipping Campden: Hidcote Manor Garden; Kiftsgate Court Gardens
Cinderford: Speech House Arboretum
Cranham: Miserden Park Gardens
Painswick: Painswick Rococo Garden
Steeple Aston: Rousham Landscaped Gardens
Stow-on-the-Wold: Abbotswood Garden
Westonbirt: Westonbirt Arboretum
Wotton-under-Edge: Alderley Grange Gardens

HEREFORD & WORCESTER

Bromyard: Stoke Lacy Herb Garden
Droitwich Spa: Clacks Farm
Great Malvern: Barnards Green House; The Picton Gardens
Great Witley: Sankyns Green
Hereford: Fragrant Garden; Redcliffe Gardens
Inkberrow: White Cottage Garden
Kidderminster: Stone House Cottage Gardens
Kington: Brobury House Gardens; Hergest Croft Gardens
Lydney: Lydney Park Gardens
Pershore: Bredon Springs; The Priory
Pontrilas: Abbey Dore Court Garden
Ross-on-Wye: The Hill Court Gardens; How Caple Court
Tenbury Wells: Burford House Gardens
Worcester: Cathedral Gardens; Spetchley Park Gardens

OXFORDSHIRE

Abingdon: Nag's Head Island
Kingston Bagpuize: Kingston House Garden
Oxford: Botanic Garden; Worcester College Gardens
Wheatley: Waterperry Gardens

Guided Tours

There are many experts to show you round the delights of this region. The major cities and towns in this region support Registered Guides who will have attended a training course sponsored by the various Tourist Boards, they can be identified by the 'Blue Badge' they wear. Some of these regional guides also have a regional endorsement, enquire when you are making your booking. Several of the individual historic houses, churches and museums offer their own guided tours, they will give full details of times and duration of tours on application. The Tourist Boards will provide information sheets on guiding activities, they are available from the addresses given below.

Heart of England Tourist Board
2–4 Trinity Street
Worcester
☎ 0905 29512

Thames & Chilterns Tourist Board
The Mount House
Witney
Oxfordshire
☎ 0993 778800

GLOUCESTERSHIRE

Cheltenham: Carriage Tours; Cheltenham Guided Tours
Cinderford: W B Freeman
Coleford: Timewalk
Minchinhampton: Pathfinder Tours
Tewkesbury: Intercounty Chauffeur Services

HEREFORD & WORCESTER

Hereford: Hereford Guild of Guides
Kidderminster: County Museum and Stone House Cottage Gardens; Royal Doulton Crystal and Harvington Hall
Lydney: Royal Forest of Dean and Wye Valley Educational Tours
Ross-on-Wye: Countryside Touring
Symonds Yat: Wyedean Archaeological Tours
Worcester: Faithful City Guides

OXFORDSHIRE

Henley: Country Ways
Oxford: Guide Friday; The Oxford Guild of Guides; Spires and Shires Minibus Tours; Whites of Oxford Ltd

Heritage

This region is rich in antiquities, it possesses monuments from the earliest periods in British history. There are Neolithic chambered tombs, Bronze Age remains, Iron Age hill forts and Roman villas. During Saxon times the most extensive linear earthwork in Britain, Offa's Dyke, was constructed, it runs for over a hundred miles from the mouth of the Wye to the Dee through Hereford and Worcester.

GLOUCESTERSHIRE

Cirencester: Cirencester Amphitheatre
Dursley: Uley Bury; Uley Tumulus
Gloucester: Bishop Hooper's Monument
Minchinhampton: Minchinhampton Bulwarks

Moreton-in-Marsh: Curfew Tower; Four Shires Stone
Newent: Chedworth Roman Villa
Painswick: Cooper's Hill; Haresfield Beacon
Pershore: Arthurs Stone; Snodhill Castle

Stow-on-the-Wold: Long Barrows; The Wells
Tewkesbury: Odda's Chapel; St Mary's Priory
Winchcombe: Belas Knap Long Barrow; St Peter's Church

Hereford: Chained Library; Mappa Mundi
Pershore: Bredon Hill; Pershore Bridge
Ross-on-Wye: Wilton Bridge
Shobdon: Sessile Oak
Symonds Yat: Goodrich Castle; Promontory Fort
Tenbury Wells: Saxon Preaching Cross
Yarpole: Croft Ambrey; Mortimer's Cross Battlesite; Richard's Castle

Abingdon: Abingdon Bridge; Ock Bridge
Bicester: Alchester
Chipping Norton: Castle; Rollright Stone Circle
Deddington: Deddington Castle
Faringdon: Radcot Bridge
Uffington: Blowing Stone; Dragon Hill; Uffington Castle; Wayland's Smithy; White Horse; White Horse Hill
Wallingford: The Bridge; Sinodun Hill Fort; Wallingford Castle
Witney: Buttercross; Grim's Dykes; North Leigh Roman Villa
Wroxton: Hornton Stone Quarry

Historic Buildings

The buildings of the region reflect the different influences that have affected the area over the centuries. The borderland castles are a reminder of the strategic importance of this area, the abbeys and priories show the strength of the monastic movement and the region's rich ecclesiastical past can be seen in its magnificent cathedrals at Hereford, Worcester, Gloucester and Cheltenham. The Middle Ages saw the wool traders become powerful merchants and their endowments produced the great wool churches of the Cotswolds, all built or remodelled in the perpendicular style, small-scale cathedrals with exquisite features – well worth a visit. Added to these are the exquisite college buildings of Oxford, the characteristic black-and-white timber-framed buildings of Hereford and Worcester, several notable tithe barns, mills and dovecotes, all of which make the area rich in architectural and historical interest.

Chipping Campden: Chipping Campden Church
Cirencester: Cirencester Church; Cirencester Lock Up; St Michael's Church
Cranham: Elkstone Church
Dursley: Woodchester Park Mansion
Fairford: Fairford Church
Gloucester: Blackfriars; Churches; Gloucester Cathedral; Gloucester Docks; Greyfriars; Llanthony Priory – Secunda; St Oswalds Priory
Minchinhampton: Market House
Northleach: Northleach Church
Painswick: St Mary's Church
St Briavels: St Briavels Castle; St Briavels Church
Stanway: Buckland Rectory; Hailes Abbey
Stonehouse: Frocester Tithe Barn
Stow-on-the-Wold: Lower Swell Parish Church; Parish Church of St Edward

Stroud: Mediaeval Hall; The Shambles; St Laurence's Church
Tetbury: Market Hall
Tewkesbury: Abbey Cottages; Black Bear Inn; House of Nodding Gables; King John's Bridge; Mythe Bridge; Old Baptist Chapel; Tewkesbury Abbey
Upton-upon-Severn: Dunstall Castle
Wotton-under-Edge: Kingswood Abbey Gatehouse; St Mary's Parish Church

Bewdley: Town Centre; St Anne's Church; St Leonard's Church; Tickenhill Manor
Broadway: Broadway Tower
Bromsgrove: Bromsgrove School; St John the Baptist Church
Bromyard: Edvin Loach Saxon Church; St Peter's Church
Droitwich Spa: Church of the Sacred Heart; St Peter's Church

Eardisland: Burton Court; Lucton Mill

Evesham: The Bell Tower; The Fleece Inn; Tythe Barn

Great Malvern: Holy Well; Little Malvern Court; Priory Church

Great Witley: Great Witley Church; Wichenford Dovecote

Hereford: Hereford Cathedral; The Old House

Inkberrow: Moat Farm Dovecote

Kidderminister: St George's Church; St Mary's Parish Church

Ledbury: Eastnor Castle; Old Grammar School

Leominster: Berrington Hall; Grange Court; Priory Church

Littledean: Littledean Hall

Pembridge: Church of St Mary; Market Hall; The New Inn

Pershore: Pershore Abbey; Tithe Barn; Wick Church

Peterchurch: Peterchurch Parish Church; Vowchurch Parish Church

Redditch: Bordesley Abbey

Ross-on-Wye: Brockhampton-by-Ross Church; How Caple Church; St Mary's Church

Shobdon: Shobdon Church; Shobdon Folly

Cirencester Church

Tenbury Wells: Newnham Bridge Watermill; Pump Rooms; The Royal Oak; Teme Bridge

Weobley: Cruck Barn; Dilwyn Church; Church of Mary Magdalene; Church of St Lawrence; Sarnesfield Church; Staunton-on-Wye Church; The Throne; Weobley Church

Worcester: Church of St Nicholas; Countess of Huntingdon's Hall; The Guildhall; Worcester Cathedral

Yarpole: Croft Castle

OXFORDSHIRE

Abingdon: Abbey Buildings; St Helen's Church; St Nicholas' Church; Upper Reaches Hotel

Banbury: Banbury Cross; Broughton Castle; Wroxton Abbey

Bampton: Pope's Tower; St Mary's Church

Berkeley: Berkeley Castle; Parish Church

Bicester: The Market Place; St Edburg's Church

Bloxham: Bloxham Church

Burford: High Street; St John the Baptist Church

Charlbury: Charlbury Station

Chipping Norton: St Mary's Church; Bliss Tweed Mill

Faringdon: Church of All Saints; Folly Tower; Great Coxwell Barn

Henley: The Chantry House; St Mary's Church

Hook Norton: Church

Long Hanborough: Church of St Lawrence; Combe Mill

Mapledurham: Mapledurham Watermill

Oxford: Oxford Colleges; Carfax Tower; Christ Church; Church of St Michael at the North Gate; Sheldonian Theatre; University Church of St Mary the Virgin

Stonor: Maharajah's Well

Thame: Brill Windmill; Church of the Blessed Virgin Mary; Long Crendon Courthouse; Rycote Chapel

Uffington: St Mary's Church; Holy Cross Church

Wantage: St Denys Church; Venn Mill

Wallingford: Dorchester Abbey; St Leonard's Church; St Mary's Church; St Mary's School; St Peter's Church; Town Hall

Wheatley: Conical Lock-up; St Mary's Church

Witney: Church of St Mary's; Old Blanket Hall; St Mary's Church; St Mary's Church; St Michael's Church

Wroxton: Horley Church; Hornton Church

Historic Houses

Over the centuries the fortunes of the country affected those of the regions and in turn were reflected in the style and grandeur of the houses built. Some included in this guide were the site of an historic event or the dwelling of a famous figure, others represent a family's prestige and a style of architecture. Most exhibit levels of workmanship and decoration that can be marvelled at and appreciated by all who see them.

GLOUCESTERSHIRE

Frampton-on-Severn: Frampton Court; Frampton Manor
Moreton-in-Marsh: Chastleton House; Sezincote House
Painswick: Castle Godwyn
Stanway: Snowshill Manor
Steeple Aston: Rousham House
Stow-on-the-Wold: Upper Swell Manor
Tetbury: Chavenage House
Wotton-under-Edge: Newark Park; Tolsey House

HEREFORD & WORCESTER

Bromyard: Lower Brockhampton
Great Malvern: Madresfield Court
Hagley: Hagley Hall
Hanbury: Hanbury Hall
Hay-on-Wye: Moccas Court
Hope-under-Dinmore: Dinmore Manor
Kidderminster: Harvington Hall
Littledean: Littledean Hall
Much Marcle: Hellen's
Pershore: Perrott House; Wick Manor

Pontrilas: Kentchurch Court; Pontrilas Court
Tenbury Wells: Burford House
Worcester: The Greyfriars; Nash House; The Old Palace

OXFORDSHIRE

Abingdon: Milton Manor House
Charlbury: Ditchley House
Chipping Norton: Chastleton House
Deddington: Leadenporch House
Faringdon: Buscot Park; Kelmscott Manor
Henley: Fawley Court; Greys Court
Kidlington: Church
Kingston Bagpuize: Kingston House
Stonehouse: Stonor Park
Thame: Prebendal House; Thame Park
Uffington: Ashdown House; Kingston Lisle Park
Wallingford: Newington House
Weobley: Butt House
Wheatley: Waterperry House
Witney: Minster Lovell Hall; Stanton Harcourt Manor
Woodstock: Blenheim Palace
Wroxton: Wroxton Abbey

Blenheim Palace

Museums

There are museums covering such diverse interests as packaging, historical instruments, agricultural bygones or cider making. Some record purely local history whilst others such as the Ashmolean Musem in Oxford, the oldest museum collection in Britain, are internationally famous. Whatever you might have a particular fascination for, there is probably a museum in this region to broaden your knowledge and feed your interest in the subject.

GLOUCESTERSHIRE

Bibury: Arlington Mill Museum
Bourton-on-the-Water: Cotswold Motor Museum
Chalford: Oakridge Village Museum
Cheltenham: Cheltenham Art Gallery and Museum; Gustav Holst Birthplace Museum; Pittville Pump Room Museum
Chipping Campden: Woolstapler's Hall Museum
Cinderford: Dean Heritage Centre
Cirencester: Corinium Museum
Coleford: Clearwell Caves; Great Western Railway Museum
Gloucester: Gloucester Cathedral Treasury; Gloucester City Museum and Art Gallery; Gloucester Folk Museum; The House of the Tailor of Gloucester; National Waterways Museum; Robert Opie Collection; Regiments of Gloucester; Transport Museum
Newent: The Shambles

The Shambles, Newent

Northleach: Cotswold Countryside Collection; Keith Harding's World of Mechanical Music
Stanway: Hailes Abbey Museum
Stroud: Stroud (Cowle) Museum; Lansdown Hall
Tetbury: Tetbury Police Bygones Museum
Tewkesbury: The Little Museum; John Moore Museum; Tewkesbury Museum

Upton-upon-Severn: Upton Heritage Centre
Winchcombe: Simms International Police Collection; Winchcombe Folk Museum; Winchcombe Railway Museum and Garden

HEREFORD & WORCESTER

Bewdley: Bewdley Museum
Bromsgrove: Avoncroft Musum of Buildings; Bromsgrove Museum
Bromyard: Bromyard Heritage Centre
Droitwich Spa: Droitwich Heritage Centre
Evesham: Almonry Museum
Great Malvern: Boehm Studios; Malvern Museum
Hereford: The Broomy Hill Engines; The Bulmer Railway Centre; Churchill Gardens Museum; Cider Museum; Hereford City Museum and Art Gallery; St John Mediaeval Museum
Kidderminster: Hereford and Worcester County Museum
Kington: Kington Museum
Ledbury: Butcher Row House Museum
Leominster: Leominster District Folk Museum
Lydney: Dean Forest Railway; Lydney Park Museum
Peterchurch: Clothiers Farm
Redditch: Midland Bus and Transport Museum; Forge Hill Museum
Ross-on-Wye: The Lost Street Museum
Symonds Yat: Herefordshire Rural Life Museum
Worcester: City Museum and Art Gallery; The Commandery; Dyson Perrins Museum; Elgar's Birthplace Museum; The Guildhall; Tudor House Museum

OXFORDSHIRE

Abingdon: The County Hall and Museum
Banbury: Banbury Museum

Berkeley: Jenner Museum
Bloxham: Bloxham Village Museum
Burford: Tolsey Musuem
Carterton: Swinford Museum
Charlbury: Charlbury Museum; Stonesfield Museum and Slate Mine
Chipping Norton: Chipping Norton Museum
Cropredy: Edge Hill Battle Museum; Granary Museum
Didcot: Champs Chapel Museum
Long Hanborough: Oxford Bus Museum Trust
Oxford: Ashmolean Museum; Bate Collection of Historical Instruments; Bodleian Library; Museum of the History of Science; Museum of Modern Art; Museum of Oxford; The Oxford Story; Pitt Rivers Museum; University Museum
Tenbury Wells: Tenbury Museum
Uffington: Tom Brown's School Museum
Wantage: Champs Chapel Museum; Vale and Downland Museum Centre
Wallingford: Benson Veteran Cycle Museum; Dorchester Abbey Museum; Wallingford Museum
Witney: Cogges Manor Farm Museum
Woodstock: Oxfordshire County Museum

Natural History

The region is scattered with nature reserves that often have trails, hides and information centres, some also have guides. There are also several animal sanctuaries, unusual animal collections in natural surroundings and conservation centres that are fascinating to visit.

GLOUCESTERSHIRE

Cinderford: Soudley Ponds; Speech House Woodland
Coleford: Nags Head Nature Reserve
Cranham: Prinknash Bird Park
Minchinhampton: Rodborough and Minchinhampton Commons
Newent: Betty Daw's Nature Reserve; Newent Butterfly and Natural World Centre
Painswick: Cooper's Hill; Frith Wood Nature Reserve
Steeple Aston: BBONT Reserve
Stroud: Coaley Park Nature Reserve; Elliot Nature Reserve

HEREFORD & WORCESTER

Bewdley: Shatterford Lakes
Broadway: Broadway Gravel Pit
Evesham: Cleeve Prior Nature Reserve; Windmill Hill Nature Reserve
Great Malvern: Knapp and Paper Mill Nature Reserve
Ledbury: Ledbury Naturalists Field Club
Redditch: Ipsley Alders Nature Reserve; Mill Pond
Yarpole: Bircher Common; Fishpool Valley

OXFORDSHIRE

Banbury: The Water Fowl Sanctuary

Bloxham: Adderbury Lakes; BBONT Reserve
Charlbury: Wychwood Forest
Hook Norton: BBONT Reserve
Islip: Otmoor
Oxford: Aston Eyot; BBONT; Chilswell Valley; Lye Valley Nature Reserve; Port Meadow; Raleigh Park; Rock Edge
Thame: Boarstall Duck Decoy
Wheatley: Waterperry Wood

Ornamental Parks

Ornamental parks provide colourful, fragrant recreational areas where you can take a stroll or take a seat and watch the world go by. They vary in size, elaboration and theme from town to town but always provide pleasure to those passing through them and to the wildlife who make them their habitat.

GLOUCESTERSHIRE

Cheltenham: Hatherley Park; Hesters Way Park; Imperial Gardens; Montpellier Gardens; Oxford and Priory Gardens; Pittville Park; The Promenade; Sandford Park; Winston Churchill Memorial Gardens
Chipping Campden: Ernest Wilson Memorial Garden
Gloucester: The Park
Stroud: Stratford Park

HEREFORD & WORCESTER

Droitwich Spa: St Peter's Fields
Evesham: Abbey Gardens; Crown Meadows; Workman Gardens
Great Malvern: Priory Park
Pershore: Abbey Park
Ross-on-Wye: The Prospect
Stourport-on-Severn: Riverside Meadows
Worcester: Cripplegate Park; Fort Royal Park; Gheluvelt Park; Pitchcroft

OXFORDSHIRE

Abingdon: Abbey Meadow; Albert Park
Henley: Mill Meadow Park
Oxford: Bury Knowle Park; Cutteslowe Park; Florence Park; Headington Hill Park; Hinksey Park; South Park
Thame: Elms Park

Railways

Very few of us fail to respond to the delights of steam railways, entwined as they are with tales of our childhood. The heartening hoots they make as they puff by bring storybook pictures alive – book up for one of their special rides!

GLOUCESTERSHIRE

Bourton-on-the-Water: Model Railway
Coleford: Great Western Railway Museum
Stanway: Gloucestershire and Warwickshire Railway
Winchcombe: Gloucestershire and Warwickshire Railway

HEREFORD & WORCESTER

Bewdley: Severn Valley Railway
Kidderminster: Severn Valley Railway

OXFORDSHIRE

Burford: Cotswold Wildlife Park
Didcot: Didcot Railway Centre
Wallingford: Cholsey & Wallingford Railway

39

Safari Parks

Safari parks, a revolution in animal management when first introduced in this country in the 1960s, give the animals a more natural environment within which to roam free whilst giving visitors an appreciation and understanding of their behaviour in the wild.

HEREFORD & WORCESTER

Bewdley: West Midlands Safari and Leisure Park

Theatres

The region has an interesting selection of theatres and arts centres which produce many innovative and acclaimed productions as well as the more familiar and much loved classics.

GLOUCESTERSHIRE

Cheltenham: Everyman Theatre; Playhouse Theatre; Shaftesbury Theatre
Dursley: Prema Arts Centre
Gloucester: Guildhall Arts Centre; The Kings Theatre; The New Olympus Theatre
Stroud: The Cotswold Playhouse
Tewkesbury: Roses Theatre

HEREFORD & WORCESTER

Droitwich Spa: Norbury Theatre
Evesham: Evesham Arts Centre

Great Malvern: Malvern Festival Theatre
Hereford: The New Hereford Theatre
Kidderminster: Rose Theatre
Redditch: The Palace Theatre
Worcester: Swan Theatre; Worcester Arts Workshop

OXFORDSHIRE

Chipping Norton: The Theatre
Oxford: Apollo Theatre; Burton Taylor Theatre; The Old Fire Station Arts Centre
Wallingford: The Corn Exchange; Kinecroft Theatre

Wildlife Parks

Many people have directed their love of animals and wildlife into the collection and breeding of often rare and exotic species. This has over recent years led to the opening of their collections to the public. Set in acres of ground the wildlife are kept in pleasant surroundings and the parks often have amenities for children such as pets corners, adventure playgrounds and picnic sites.

GLOUCESTERSHIRE

Bourton-on-the-Water: Birdland; Folly Farm
Great Malvern: Malvern Hills Animal and Bird Gardens

HEREFORD & WORCESTER

Evesham: The Domestic Fowl Trust; Twyford Country Centre
Pershore: Delamere Bird Garden
Symonds Yat: Symonds Yat Bird Park

OXFORDSHIRE

Burford: Cotswold Wildlife Park
Wallingford: Wellplace Bird Farm

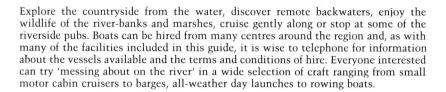

Boat Hire

Explore the countryside from the water, discover remote backwaters, enjoy the wildlife of the river-banks and marshes, cruise gently along or stop at some of the riverside pubs. Boats can be hired from many centres around the region and, as with many of the facilities included in this guide, it is wise to telephone for information about the vessels available and the terms and conditions of hire. Everyone interested can try 'messing about on the river' in a wide selection of craft ranging from small motor cabin cruisers to barges, all-weather day launches to rowing boats.

GLOUCESTERSHIRE

Cheltenham: Pitville Park Boating Lake
Steeple Aston: Black Prince

HEREFORD & WORCESTER

Bromsgrove: Alvechurch Boat Centre; Black Prince Holidays Ltd
Evesham: Evesham Marina; Fenmatch Ltd
Redditch: Arrow Valley Park Lake
Symonds Yat: Kingfisher River Trips
Worcester: Pitchcraft Boating Station

OXFORDSHIRE

Abingdon: Abingdon Boat Centre; Red Hire Cruisers
Deddington: Anglo Welsh
Henley: Hobbs & Sons Ltd; JS Hooper; Salter Bros Ltd
Oxford: Boat Enquiries; The Thames Hire Cruiser Association
Wallingford: Maidboats

Boat Trips

For those who have no wish to captain their own vessel there are several organised boat trips to enjoy. There is a craft to suit everyone, steamer, pleasure barge or motor launch – whatever appeals. All sorts of refreshments and entertainments are available on the larger boats for individuals or groups.

GLOUCESTERSHIRE

Gloucester: National Waterways Museum
Tewkesbury: Tolsey Lane
Upton-upon-Severn: Severn Leisure

HEREFORD & WORCESTER

Droitwich Spa: Droitwich Marina
Stourport-on-Severn: Severn Steamboat Company
Worcester: Ferry Crossing; North and South Quays

OXFORDSHIRE

Didcot: Thames Cruises
Faringdon: Thames Cruises
Henley: Salter Bros Ltd
Oxford: Salter Bros Ltd
Witney: Pinkhill Lock

Canoeing

Canoeing appeals to a wide cross-section of people as you can choose between expeditions on calm waters or the challenge of pitting yourself against the wilder waters found in rivers with rapids and in the sea. Types of water are classified by the British Canoe Union and they range from placid water, white water Grades I to III and river, estuary, harbour through to sea and surf. To begin canoeing it is wise to seek expert guidance to learn the simple techniques and safety measures. There are many approved centres and the Canoe Union will supply a list on request from the address given below. Interestingly very few people learn to 'canoe' as canoes are open boats propelled by a single-bladed paddle whereas most people learn to 'kayak' in kayaks where they sit right inside propelled by a doubled-bladed paddle.

British Canoe Union
Adbolton Lane
West Bridgford
Nottingham
☎ 0602 821100

GLOUCESTERSHIRE

Cotswold Water Park: Spinerd Sailboards
Tewkesbury: Croft Farm Leisure and Water Park

HEREFORD & WORCESTER

Hereford: Hereford Kayak Club
Lydney: Wye Pursuits

Redditch: Arrow Valley Park Lake
Ross-on-Wye: PGL Adventure
Symonds Yat: Monmouth Canoe Hire; Wyedean Canoe and Adventure Centre
Tenbury Wells: Teme Bridge

OXFORDSHIRE

Cropredy: Banbury and District Canoe Club
Oxford: Riverside Canoe Club

Canoeing on the River Wye

Dinghy Sailing

Walking on water is not possible for most of us but sailing on it certainly is. Young and old, individuals and families have found great enjoyment in sailing over the years and continue to do so. Family sailing holidays provide lots of fun and there are many centres and schools recommended by the Royal Yachting Association (RYA) where it is possible to learn to sail and follow their Dinghy Sailing Scheme. Dinghy sailing can be enjoyed far from the sea anywhere there are stretches of water and seasonal or residential courses are available at many of the centres listed. For more information contact the RYA at the address below.

Royal Yachting Association
Romsey Road
Eastleigh
Hampshire
☎ 0703 629962

GLOUCESTERSHIRE

Tewkesbury: Tewkesbury Marinas
Cotswold Water Park: Cotswold Sailing Club; South Cerney Sailing Club; Whitefriars Sailing Club

OXFORDSHIRE

Banbury: Banbury Cross Sailing Club; Banbury Sailing Club
Henley: Henley Sailing Club
Oxford: Oxford Sailing Club
Witney: Hardwick Leisure Park
Wroxton: Grimsbury Reservoir

Diving

Treasure troves beneath the sea whether old galleons or brilliant and bizarre underwater sea creatures attract many people to take up diving. Modern equipment is extremely light compared with the diving suits once worn so anyone who can swim and who is reasonably fit can try out an introductory diving course. The British Sub-Aqua Club (BSAC), the governing body of the sport, are known for the high standards they set and by following a course at a diving school or by joining one of the BSAC clubs it should be possible to attain their Novice Diver standard over three to six months. Continuing on to obtain their Sport Diver status will equip a diver to dive anywhere in the world in the company of other qualified divers. Underwater photography in tropical waters or exploring wrecks can begin with trying out an aqualung in a swimming pool. For more information contact the BSAC at the address given.

British Sub-Aqua Club (BSAC)
Talfords Quay
Ellesmere Port
Cheshire
☎ 051 357 1951

HEREFORD & WORCESTER

Hereford: Hereford Sub-Aqua Club

OXFORDSHIRE

Banbury: Banbury Sub Aqua Club
Oxford: British Sub-Aqua Southern Region

45

Inland Waterways

What better way to discover a different aspect of the countryside than to glide peacefully through its waterways. British Waterways were built during the Industrial Revolution to transport goods between cities and now they are owned or managed by the British Waterways Board and nearly all are open to leisure cruising. Peaceful relaxed cruising, exploring the backwaters, enjoying the waterside pubs, meeting new people and observing the wildlife in the hedgerows and banks – what better way to spend some time.

Modern narrow boats are fully equipped and there are many options for hire. For some help in making your decision about which way to go, the Inland Waterways Association might be able to help, they will provide information and have produced a guide to the inland waterways that could prove very useful, contact them at the address given here.

The Inland Waterways Association
114 Regents Park Road
London
☎ 071 387 9302

GLOUCESTERSHIRE

Berkeley: Gloucester & Sharpness Canal
Steeple Aston: Oxford Canal
Stonehouse: Stroudwater and Thames-Severn Canal
Stroud: Stroudwater Canal

HEREFORD & WORCESTER

Bromsgrove: Worcester and Birmingham Canal
Stourport-on-Severn: Staffordshire and Worcestershire Canal

OXFORDSHIRE

Banbury: Oxford Canal
Berkeley: Gloucester & Sharpness Canal
Kidlington: Oxford Canal
Oxford: Oxford Canal

Jet-Skiing

Jet-skiing is another exciting watersport for the adventure seeking water lover. There are only a few places that offer opportunities to pursue this sport in this region at present but many of the numerous watersports centres will no doubt be including it in the near future.

GLOUCESTERSHIRE

Cotswold Water Park: Cotswold Jet Ski
   Club Ltd

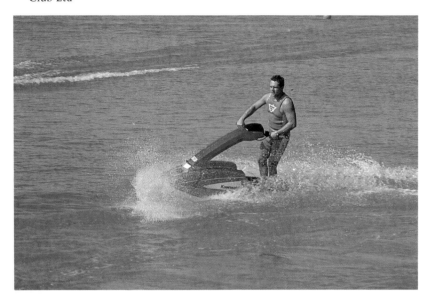

Punting

Punts seem to effortlessly glide along, no intrusive noise of an engine to disturb enjoyment of the river, no complicated controls to master, but anyone who has tried to punt will know that punting is a skill and one that can give rise to much hilarity in the learning. If you feel like the challenge then there are punts to hire but if you wish to enjoy the river then you can choose to be only a passenger.

OXFORDSHIRE

Henley: Henley Riverside
Oxford: Salter Bros Ltd

Rowing

Rowing, whether for pleasure or to take part in competition races, is a route to becoming and remaining extremely fit – a physically demanding sport with great rewards, not least the enjoyment of the river and its surrounds. For information and details of clubs contact the Amateur Rowing Association at the address below.

Amateur Rowing Association
Ivan Pratt (Executive Secretary)
6 Lower Mall
Hammersmith
London
☎ 081 748 3632

HEREFORD & WORCESTER

Evesham: Evesham Rowing Club
Hereford: Hereford Rowing Club
Worcester: River Severn Rowing Club

OXFORDSHIRE

Henley: Henley Rowing Club
Oxford: Oxon Rowing Association
Wallingford: Wallingford Rowing Club

Swimming

Swimming remains one of the most enjoyable and therapeutic of the watersports. The leisure centres throughout the region often have very exotic pool surrounds and include aquaslides, whirlpools and inflatables to provide extra fun in the water.

Cascades, Tewkesbury

GLOUCESTERSHIRE

Cheltenham: Cheltenham Recreation Centre; Sandford Pools
Cinderford: Heywood Sports Centre
Cirencester: Cirencester Open-Air Swimming Pool; Cotswold Sports Centre
Dursley: Dursley Pool and Sports Centre
Gloucester: Gloucester Leisure Centre

HEREFORD & WORCESTER

Bromsgrove: The Dolphin Centre
Droitwich Spa: Droitwich Lido Park; Droitwich Spa Brine Baths
Great Malvern: The Splash
Hereford: Hereford Swimming Baths
Kidderminster: Wyre Forest Glades Leisure Centre
Ledbury: Ledbury Swimming Pool
Pershore: Pershore Indoor Swimming Pool
Redditch: Hewell Road Swimming Pool; The Leys Swimming Pool
Ross-on-Wye: Ross-on-Wye Swimming Pool

Stourport-on-Severn: Stourport Sports Centre
Tenbury Wells: Tenbury Swimming Pool
Tewkesbury: Cascades
Worcester: Worcester Swimming Pool and Fitness Centre

OXFORDSHIRE

Abingdon: Abbey Meadow; The Old Gaol Leisure Centre
Banbury: Banbury Open-air Pool; Banbury Swimming Club; Spiceball Park Sports Centre
Carterton: Carterton Swimming Pool
Chipping Norton: Chipping Norton Swimming Pool
Didcot: Didcot Pool
Henley: Henley & District Sports Centre
Kidlington: Kidlington and Gosford Sports Centre
Oxford: Blackbird Leys Pool; Ferry Sports Centre; Temple Cowley Swimming Pools
Wallingford: Wallingford Swimming Pool
Witney: Windrush Sports Centre
Woodstock: Woodstock Swimming Pool

Water-skiing is an exhilarating sport and can be safely pursued at one of the clubs affiliated to the British Water Ski Federation. Basic equipment is usually provided and there are opportunities to develop the skill and confidence necessary to progress to jumps and competitions. For information and a list of clubs with details of their facilities contact the British Water Ski Federation at the address given below.

British Water Ski Federation
390 City Road
London
☎ 071 833 2855/6

GLOUCESTERSHIRE

Cirencester: Cirencester Water Ski Club; Cotswold Water Ski Club

OXFORDSHIRE

Kingston Bagpuize: Standlake Barefoot Ski Club

Windsurfing

Windsurfing or boardsailing as it is also known has become very popular and the colourful sails and characteristic silhouettes of the windsurfers are a familiar sight on many lakes and off many beaches. The relative ease with which windsurfers can be transported makes it a fairly flexible sport to pursue. To learn to windsurf it is advisable to approach a school approved by the Royal Yachting Association, most will supply boards, sails and wetsuits. You will be taken through the techniques involved on dry land before taking to the water and then over a couple of days you will learn how to sail a course, how to rig a board and how to observe the rules of safety for yourself and other water users. A beginners course does not involve a huge outlay and it might introduce you to an exciting new sport. Contact the Windsurfing Information Centre at the Royal Yachting Association for more details.

The Windsurfing Information Centre
Royal Yachting Association
Romsey Road
Eastleigh
Hampshire
☎ 0703 629962

GLOUCESTERSHIRE

Cirencester: Keynes Park Windsurfing Club
Cotswold Water Park: Spinerd Sailboards
Tewkesbury: Croft Farm Leisure and Water Park

HEREFORD & WORCESTER

Redditch: Arrow Valley Park Lake
Ross-on-Wye: Hartleton Lake

OXFORDSHIRE

Oxford: Hinksey Park Lake
Witney: Hardwick Leisure Park

Skiing

Ski-lovers can enjoy their sport on dry slopes and to find out more information about skiing in Britain should contact the British Ski Federation at the address below.

British Ski Federation
258 Main Street
East Calder
West Lothian
☎ 0506 884343

GLOUCESTERSHIRE

Gloucester: Gloucester Ski Slope

HEREFORD & WORCESTER

Hereford: Hereford Ski Club

Introduction to

Places

Discover Gloucestershire, Oxfordshire, Hereford and Worcester. Despite being easily accessible from London and the Midlands this region remains peaceful and its rich diversity of landscapes, sports and activities is relatively unexplored. There are honey-coloured Cotswold stone villages, picturesque black-and-white, half-timbered houses, cathedral cities with long histories and many treasures. Cider apple orchards and rolling farmland contrast with the spectacular scenery of the Wye Valley – a centre for many adventure sports. There is much to do and plenty to see.

Select the city, town or village you wish to visit, they are arranged alphabetically, and you will find a description, local information including population figures where available, and a detailed list of leisure activities with the telephone number, address or access information and any other interesting details. If you want to know more about a particular activity look it up in the activities section where you will find general information about it, the name and address of the governing body plus a list of all the places in the region where you can enjoy the activity. You might find a familiar place has unexpected opportunities to enjoy a favourite pursuit or an unfamiliar place is much more exciting than you expected!

Guide to symbols

i	tourist information centre (✳ Not open all year)
▶₁₈	18-hole golf course
▶₉	9-hole golf course
P	car parking
†	abbey, cathedral, church of interest
⌂	historic building, historic house, historic property
⌂	museum, art gallery
⇌	BR station
⊛	leisure centre, sports centre, swimming pool
→	one-way streets

The River Thames near Abingdon

The Clent Hills

Henley-on-Thames

Abingdon, situated on the banks of the Thames, has been an important and prosperous market town for over 900 years. The Abbey was the sixth richest in England at the time of the dissolution of the monasteries and the foundations discovered beneath the Abbey Grounds indicate that the abbey church must have been magnificent. The town bridge, built in the 15th century, added to the town's importance as a river crossing and to its prosperity. Abingdon was once the county town of Berkshire and many of the buildings still bear the name 'county' in their titles. The town was incorporated into Oxfordshire in 1974. It was in Abingdon that the famous MG cars were made for fifty years until production ceased in 1980. The familiar octagonal badge bore the letters MG, which stood for Morris Garages.

The town offers attractive riverside walks, the opportunity to cruise along the river or fish from its banks or to take a boat trip to Oxford or beyond. The converted Napoleonic prison now provides an impressive arts and leisure centre to add to the town's recreational facilities.

i Ground Floor
The Old Gaol
Bridge Street
☎ 0235 522711

Market days Monday, Saturday
Early closing Thursday
Population 30,000

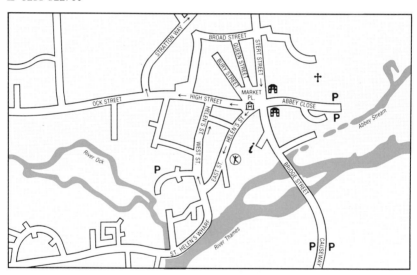

Aerial Sports

PARACHUTING

Parachute Training Services
Doug Peacock, 11 Godwyn Close
☎ 0235 529570

Indoor Sports

BADMINTON

Oxfordshire Badminton Association
For details contact Mrs D Newton.
☎ 0235 521484

LEISURE CENTRES

The Old Gaol Leisure Centre
Bridge Street
Health suite with a sauna and whirlpool, many sporting and leisure facilities. Bar and cafeteria. Arts centre and Tourist Information Centre in the same building.
☎ 0235 522806

SQUASH

Abingdon Squash Club
North Court Road
Members club, clubhouse and bar.
☎ 0235 530374

53

Outdoor Leisure

CYCLING

Mid Oxon Cycling Club
D Aitken, 33 Clevelands

FISHING

Coarse Fishing
For permits and information contact the
National Rivers Authority.
☎ 0734 535000

**Abingdon and District Angling
Association**
Details of fishing on the Thames from
R Bateman, 16 The Gap, Marcham.
☎ 0865 391809

GOLF

Frilford Heath Golf Club
4 miles west of Abingdon
☎ 0865 390864

WALKING AND RAMBLING

Sutton Pools
2 miles south-east at Sutton Courtenay,
access is from the path at the Wharf.
Exceptionally lovely walk from one of
the prettiest villages in the area. George
Orwell and Herbert Asquith are buried
here.

Special Interests

ANTIQUES

Hallidays Antiques
East of Abingdon on the A423 at
Dorchester
One of England's largest antique
showrooms specialising in 18th century
furnishings, panelling and fireplaces.
Housed in a magnificent Georgian
building.
☎ 0865 340028

ARTS AND CRAFTS

Abingdon Crafts Festival
The Abbey Buildings, Thames Street
Contact the Abingdon Crafts Festival
Office, PO Box 43 for details.

Mary Holland Ltd
Organises crafts and antiques fairs.
☎ 0235 521873

The Old Gaol
Arts centre open daily; housed in a 19th
century gaol built by Napoleonic
prisoners of war.
☎ 0235 533633

FESTIVALS AND FAIRS

September
Battle of Britain Open Day - held at RAF
Abingdon.

FOOD AND DRINK

Bothy Vineyard
Frilford Heath
Tours of the vineyard and tastings.
Asparagus, red and white currants and
honey in farm shop.
☎ 0491 681484

Morland and Company
Established in the 18th century with a
brewing tradition of over 250 years it
serves over 300 pubs in several counties
with draught and speckled beers.
☎ 0235 553377

GARDENS

Nag's Head Island
Public gardens with a good vantage point
for watching the River Thames activity.

HERITAGE

Abingdon Bridge
The bridge crosses the Thames and is
over 550 years old, it is listed as an
ancient monument.

Ock Bridge
A small iron bridge over the River Ock,
built in 1824 by the Wilts and Berks
Canal Company.

HISTORIC BUILDINGS

Abbey Buildings
The remains of England's third-largest
abbey and some of the adjacent buildings
give an idea of Abingdon's origins which
date from AD 675. The remaining Abbey
Gateway is impressive.
☎ 0235 525339

St Helen's Church
East Saint Helen Street
The church is wider than it is long,
108 feet wide, and dates from the 13th
century. Notable for its candelabra and
the painted ceiling in the Lady Chapel.
The Long Alley Almshouses behind the
church date from the 15th century.

St. Nicholas' Church
Abbey Close
Built in the 12th century for the use of
the lay servants of Abingdon Abbey.
Until recently loaves were placed on the
tomb of John and Jane Blacknall each
month and then distributed to the poor.
This custom had been carried out since
1684 in accordance with their will.

Upper Reaches Hotel
The site of a monastic watermill which can still be seen inside the hotel. The millwheels are incorporated into the terrace garden.

Milton Manor House
3 miles south of Abingdon
17th century house believed to have been built by Inigo Jones; Strawberry Hill Gothic Library and chapel, enlarged by the addition of Georgian wings. Set in 20 acres of gardens beside a lake. Collections of teapots, visiting card cases and musical boxes.
☎ 0235 831871/831287

MUSEUMS

The County Hall and Museum
Market Place
History of Abingdon displayed in the 17th century County Hall built by one of Christopher Wren's masons.
☎ 0235 523703

ORNAMENTAL PARKS

Abbey Meadow
Through the Abbey Gateway beside the Thames
A garden, golf course, pitch and putt and swimming pool set in a recreational area.

Albert Park
300 yards north of Ock Street
19th century formal garden with tennis courts and a bowling green.

Water Sports

BOAT HIRE

Abingdon Boat Centre
Nag's Head Island
Cruisers and smaller boats; week and day hire.
☎ 0235 521125

Red Hire Cruisers
Ferry Boat House, Wilsham Road
Hire cruisers.
☎ 0235 521562

CANOEING

Kingfisher Canoe Club
Details from Richard Beveridge
☎ 0993 700073

SWIMMING

Abbey Meadow
Open-air swimming pool.

The Old Gaol Leisure Centre
Bridge Street
☎ 0235 522806

Culham Lock, near Abingdon

Bampton is an attractive small Oxfordshire town well known for its magnificent parish church set in a cathedral-like close and as the home of the famous Morris men. The old town is now the venue for frequent art exhibitions and the Thames offers good fishing and pleasant riverside walks.

Outdoor Leisure

FISHING

Coarse Fishing
Good fishing in the waters of the River Thames. For information and permits, contact the National Rivers Authority.
☎ 0865 749400

WALKING AND RAMBLING

River Walks
Walks along the banks of the River Thames.

Special Interests

ART GALLERIES

The Art Gallery
Market Square
Frequent exhibitions.

FESTIVALS AND FAIRS

Spring Bank Holiday
Morris dancing in the streets.

August
Horse Fair dating from the reign of Edward I held.

HISTORIC BUILDINGS

St Mary's Church
Magnificent exterior, 13th century spire, stands in cathedral-like close.

Pope's Tower
Stanton Harcourt
Part of a once great manor, home of the Harcourt family, where Alexander Pope completed part of his translation of The Iliad in 1718.

Banbury, a Saxon settlement in the 6th century, is now Oxfordshire's second largest town. It has prospered as a regional market town and, from the 13th century, as a wool centre. During the 17th century fire and the Civil War destroyed much of the mediaeval town leaving only a few old buildings, notably inns. Tradition continues in the annual Michaelmas Fair and the weekly street market which has been held for over 800 years.

Banbury is perhaps most famous for its nursery rhyme cross and Banbury cakes, spiced-fruit pastry, enjoyed here since Tudor times. The original cross was destroyed in an upsurge of Puritanism three centuries ago and was replaced in the 19th century by the present one. The cakes are still available in the town even though the original Banbury cake shop has disappeared.

i Banbury Museum
8 Horsefair
☎ 0295 259855

Market days Thursday, Saturday
Early closing Tuesday
Population 38,588

Adventure Sports

CLIMBING

Banbury Mountaineering Club
For details contact either Brian Holmes or Paul Elliott.
☎ 0295 720850   ☎ 0295 253301

Indoor Sports

BADMINTON

Banbury Badminton Club
For details contact P Buzzard,
38 Springfield Avenue.
☎ 0295 252110

Bodicote Badminton Club
For details contact I Robson, 30 Burns
Road.
☎ 0295 252876

Demag Badminton Club
For details contact M W Dutton,
228 Chatsworth Drive.
☎ 0295 256960

LEISURE CENTRES

Spiceball Park Sports Centre
Multigym, practice halls, sauna,
solarium, pools and squash courts. Bar
and cafeteria.
☎ 0295 257522

SQUASH

Spiceball Park Sports Centre
☎ 0295 257522

Multi-Activity Holidays

SPECIAL INTEREST CENTRES

Redkir Leisure
Trelawn House, 37 North Bar
Falconry breaks.
☎ 0295 253389/266545

Outdoor Leisure

FISHING

**Banbury and District Angling
Association**
Fishing on the River Cherwell and the
Oxford Canal, contact Mr Geoffrey
Bradbeer, 7 Bentley Close.
☎ 0295 268047

GOLF

Cherwell Edge Public Course ⛳₁₈
Chacombe
☎ 0295 711591

Tadmarton Heath Golf Club ⛳₁₈
5 miles west of Banbury off the B4035 at
Wigginton
☎ 0608 737649

TENNIS

Banbury Sports Ground
Public tennis courts.

Banbury Tennis Club
Horton View Sports Ground, Horton
View
Facilities for tennis and squash;
clubhouse. Open to all ages and abilities;
competitive playing in local leagues.
Contact Mr J R Marshall.
☎ 0295 254185

People's Park
Public tennis courts.

WALKING AND RAMBLING

Banbury Rambling Club
Contact Mrs E Ruck for details.
☎ 0295 263528

Circular Walks
For details of all walks, guided and
unguided in the Cherwell District
contact The Chief Recreation Officer,
Cherwell District Council, Bodicote
House, Bodicote.
☎ 0295 252535 extn 193

The Ramblers Association
For the Cherwell group contact Charles
Wooland.
☎ 0295 712094

Special Interests

FESTIVALS AND FAIRS

October
Michaelmas Fair – three day event with
street stalls and fairs. Held since 1554,
originally a Hiring Fair where
farmworkers and maidservants gathered
to find their next year's employment.

HISTORIC BUILDINGS

Banbury Cross
The original cross of nursery rhyme fame
was one of three crosses in Banbury in
the Middle Ages, all had been destroyed
by the 17th century. The present cross
was erected to celebrate the wedding of
Queen Victoria's eldest daughter.

Broughton Castle
2 miles west of Banbury at Broughton
Moated Elizabethan manor house
originally built in 1306. Interesting
mediaeval chapel and gatehouse and
civil war relics. Home of the Fiennes
family for the last 600 years.
☎ 0295 812027

Wroxton Abbey
West of Banbury at Wroxton St Mary
17th century mansion with exceptional
plasterwork, panelling and tapestries
built on the site of an Augustinian
priory. Set in a recently restored 18th
century park.

MUSEUMS

Banbury Museum
8 Horsefair
History of Banbury and district and
regular temporary exhibitions housed in
a restored Edwardian building.
☎ 0295 259855

NATURAL HISTORY

The Water Fowl Sanctuary
Wigginton Heath
Wildife and rare breeds; over two
thousand birds and animals on view.
☎ 0608 730252/677391

Water Sports

DINGHY SAILING

Banbury Cross Sailing Club
14-foot or smaller dinghys on Grimsby
reservoir. For details contact the
Commodore, Roy Dilsaver.
☎ 0295 254495

Banbury Sailing Club
Based at Beddington reservoir; members
have continual access to the water;
regular racing.
☎ 0327 60960

DIVING

Banbury Sub Aqua Club
Spiceball Park Sports Centre
Mill Club
For details contact Johnathon Irwin.
☎ 0295 788284

INLAND WATERWAYS

Oxford Canal
90-mile inland waterway, built in the
1780s, running from Oxford and
Coventry. Bridges, locks, wharves and
warehouses along its route are original.
For details and craft licences contact the
British Waterways Board.
☎ 0923 226422

SWIMMING

Banbury Open-air Pool
☎ 0295 262742

Banbury Swimming Club
For details contact G Hughes.
☎ 0295 254806

Spiceball Park Sports Centre
☎ 0295 257522

Berkeley is a tranquil town in the centre of the Vale of Berkeley which stretches for 15 miles on the eastern bank of the Severn and encompasses thousands of acres of flat land crossed by watercourses with stone hump-backed bridges and little lanes that pass through meadows of peacefully grazing cows. A seventeen mile canal passes through the Vale linking Gloucester with the sea at nearby Sharpness. It once provided a vital commercial link and is now enjoyed as a venue for fishing and sailing.

Special Interests

FOOD AND DRINK

England Mills
Sea Mills
Stone ground millers providing a variety of flours; organic, country seeded, mueslis, whites, malted grain, pastry and cake. Also provide a range of wholefoods.
☎ 0453 811150

Summers' Cider
Slimbridge Lane, Halmore
Cider and perry makers using traditional and modern techniques.
☎ 0453 811218

HISTORIC BUILDINGS

Berkeley Castle
12th century castle occupied continuously for 800 years by the Berkeley family. King Edward II was murdered here in the dungeons in 1327. Set in parkland with red and fallow deer, wild geese and a butterfly house.

Berkeley Castle

Parish Church
Notable east window of nine lights depicting Christ healing the sick – a memorial to Edward Jenner, who was born in Berkeley.

MUSEUMS

Jenner Museum
The Chantry, Church Lane, High Street
Medical museum in the house of Doctor Edward Jenner, who discovered the vaccination against smallpox. Beautiful Georgian gardens.
☎ 0453 810631

Jenner Museum

Water Sports

INLAND WATERWAYS

Gloucester & Sharpness Canal
17-mile waterway linking Gloucester with the sea at Sharpness near Berkeley.

Bewdley stands on the edge of the Wyre Forest beside the River Severn. It is a gracious old town with a conservation area of fine 18th century houses at its centre; quays and narrow side streets provide a reminder of its past as a river port. Railway enthusiasts will enjoy the Severn Valley Railway which has its administrative headquarters here; it runs through the Severn Vale between Bridgnorth and Kidderminster. There are places for the sports enthusiast to ride, walk, fish and play golf and the safari park here offers an adventure for all the family.

Market day Saturday
Early closing Wednesday
Population 86,027

Outdoor Leisure

CAMPING AND CARAVANNING

Little Lakes Holiday park
Little Lakes, Lye Head
100-acre holiday complex with many amenities.
☎ 0299 266400

FISHING

Coarse Fishing
There is good fishing in the River Severn.

Arley
Two meadows with coarse fishing in the River Severn. Permits from the Harbour Inn.
☎ 0299 401204

John White Tackle
Stourport
☎ 02993 71735

Game Fishing
Fishing for salmon in the River Severn.

GOLF

Little Lakes Golf Club ♌
Little Lakes Holiday Park, Lye Head
Green fees on weekdays.
☎ 0299 266385

HORSE RIDING

Crundalls Lane Stables
Crundalls Lane
☎ 0299 404045

WALKING AND RAMBLING

Forest of Wyre
Callow Hill
Information on various walks in the forest available from the Visitor Centre.
☎ 0299 266302

Nature Trail
3½-mile nature trail starting near the Duke William Inn.

The Worcestershire Way
Passes through Bewdley en route from Kingsford Country Park to the Malvern Hills.

Special Interests

ARTS AND CRAFTS

Lax Lane Craft Centre
Lax Lane
Various craft studios and workshops. Part of the Bewdley Museum.
☎ 0299 403570 extn 20

Old Bank Craft Studio
9 Severnside South
Variety of arts and crafts; original paintings.
☎ 0299 402028

FOREST PARKS

Forest of Wyre
Near Bewdley
Extensive woodlands; waymarked trails; walks; visitor centre and picnic areas.
☎ 0299 266302

Visitor Centre
Callow Hill
Obtain information here on all walks and history of the forest.
☎ 0299 266302

HISTORIC BUILDINGS

Town Centre
Load Street
Conservation area of 18th century houses, noted for its Georgian elegance.

St Anne's Church
Load Street
Grade II Georgian listed church; it forms
the focal point of the town's outstanding
conservation area.
☎ 0299 402275

St Leonard's Church
Ribbesford
Grade I listed sandstone church with
Norman foundations.
☎ 0299 402275

Tickenhill Manor
Hill above the town
Remains of Tudor royal palace with a
brick facade added in 1738.

MUSEUMS

Bewdley Museum
Load Street
Industrial history and crafts associated
with the Wyre Forest. Craft studios;
brass foundry and ropewalk.
☎ 0299 403573

NATURAL HISTORY

Shatterford Lakes
Bridgnorth Road, Shatterford
Nature park with deer, trout lakes, many
breeds of birds and a wealth of wildlife.
☎ 029 97 403

RAILWAYS

Severn Valley Railway
The Railway Station
The administrative headquarters of the
Severn Valley Railway which runs from
Bridgnorth to Kidderminster, and is
operated mainly by volunteer members.
Fine model railway called 'Wribbenhall
Junction.' Souvenir shop and restaurant.
☎ 0299 403816

SAFARI PARKS

West Midlands Safari and Leisure Park
Spring Grove
195 acres of countryside with animal
reserves; leisure area with various
amusements and refreshments.
☎ 0299 402114

GLOUCESTERSHIRE / Bibury / GLOUCESTERSHIRE

Bibury, with its honey-coloured stone buildings, old-world charm and peaceful
atmosphere, represents the 'magic' of the Cotswolds – it might have a distinctly
familiar air as it is one of the Cotswold villages that most often appears on calendars
and book covers.

Outdoor Leisure

FISHING

Bibury Trout Farm
Working farm with rainbow trout and
wildlife. Farm shop and picnic area.
Tackle provided for fishing.
☎ 028 574 215

Special Interests

GARDENS

Barnsley House Garden
2 miles south-west of Bibury at Barnsley

Established garden with 18th century
summerhouse. Rare shrubs, trees and
plants.
☎ 028 574 281

MUSEUMS

Arlington Mill Museum
17th century corn mill with working
machinery and seventeen rooms
showing rural life; Edwardian and
Victorian period rooms; Arts and Crafts
movement and William Morris items.
☎ 028 574 368

Bicester is a lively market town and agricultural centre as it has been since the Middle Ages when it was granted various licences for festivals and fairs. Seven annual fairs were held here in the 18th century including the annual August fair specialising in leatherwork, a locally established industry as were wool-combing, chair-making, bell-casting and, in the 19th century, straw-plaiting.

Old Bicester can still be found in the half-timbered 16th and 17th century buildings around the market place and the church which has some notable early English features.

Market day Friday
Early closing Thursday
Population 18,827

Indoor Sports

LEISURE CENTRES

Bicester and Ploughley Sports Centre
Queens Avenue
Sports hall, activity hall, sunbeds, spa and sauna, swimming pool, squash courts and leisure suites.
☎ 0869 253914

Bicester Sports Club
Oxford Road
☎ 0869 241000

SQUASH

Bicester and Ploughley Sports Centre
☎ 0869 253914

Outdoor Leisure

CYCLING

Oxonian Cycling Club
Club participates in all forms of cycling; road racing and time trials. For details contact J E Vallis, 11 Turnberry Close.

FISHING

Bicester Angling Alliance
☎ 0869 243871

Bicester Angling Society
Fishing in the lake. No tickets required. For details contact Mr Isles.
☎ 0869 243871

GOLF

Chesterton Country Golf Club ⁊₁₈
Chesterton
☎ 0869 241204

Special Interests

HERITAGE

Alchester
1¹/₂ miles south of Bicester
Site of Roman town and junction of several Roman roads including Akeman Street that linked London to St Albans and Cirencester. The site is now farmland but the contours of the town can be discerned.

HISTORIC BUILDINGS

The Market Place
Two old coaching inns (now public houses) the King's Arms and the Swan. Several half-timbered 16th and 17th century houses.

St Edburg's Church
15th century church with earlier Saxon arch, early English font and ancient wooden screen; pinnacled tower.

Bishops Cleeve is situated on the Cotswold escarpment near Cheltenham and offers some enjoyable walks with panoramic views of the Severn Valley. It has a sports centre with a good selection of facilities as well as a golf course.

Indoor Sports

BADMINTON

Cleeve Sports Centre
☎ 0242 673581

LEISURE CENTRES

Cleeve Sports Centre
Two Hedges Road
Fitness centre, activities hall, climbing wall, badminton, tennis and squash facilities; outdoor courts.
☎ 0242 673581

SQUASH

Cleeve Sports Centre
☎ 0242 673581

Outdoor Leisure

GOLF

Cleeve Hill Municipal Course ⌐18
Cleeve Hill
☎ 0242 672592

TENNIS

Cleeve Sports Centre
☎ 0242 673581

WALKING AND RAMBLING

Bishops Cleeve to Winchcombe
Circular walk up the Cotswold scarp from Bishops Cleeve to Winchcombe via Postlip and Cleeve Common. Contact the Cotswold Warden Service for details.
☎ 0452 425674

Cleeve Hill
Circular waymarked walk around the Cotswold Scarp. Contact the Tewkesbury Tourist Information Centre for a free leaflet.
☎ 0684 295027

The Cotswold Way
Cleeve Hill is the highest point on the 97-mile long distance footpath, panoramic views.

Bloxham is a large thatch and ironstone village that retains most of its mediaeval street plan, as well as several 16th and 17th century cottages, intact. It offers a variety of sports facilities, interesting reserves for the naturalist to explore, an art gallery and stained glass by William Morris to enjoy.

Indoor Sports

BADMINTON

Bloxham Badminton Club
Competitive club playing at Warrener School. For details contact C Leyburn.
☎ 0295 720777

LEISURE CENTRES

Dewey Sports Centre
Bloxham School
Various clubs organised in the sports hall.
☎ 0295 721707

SQUASH

Beauchamp Squash Club
Beauchamp Centre
☎ 0295 720988

Outdoor Leisure

FISHING

Coarse Fishing
Fishing on the River Cherwell and the
Adderbury Lakes. For details contact the
local angling club.
☎ 0295 710488

Special Interests

ART GALLERIES

H C Dickins
High Street
Nineteenth and twentieth century
English sporting and landscape painting
☎ 0295 721949

HISTORIC BUILDINGS

Bloxham Church
200-foot spire, Norman Stonework,
15th century font and rood screen.
Stained glass by William Morris and
Edward Burne-Jones.

MUSEUMS

Bloxham Village Museum
The Court House, Church Street
Collection of local bygones relating to
the history of the village housed in 17th
century court house.
☎ 0295 720283

NATURAL HISTORY

Adderbury Lakes
Adderbury
Remaining tracts of an estate laid out by
Capability Brown for the Dukes of
Argyll; being developed as a reserve. Two
lakes, waterfall, islands, variety of
wildlife including muntjac deer and
kingfishers.
☎ 0295 870312

BBONT Reserve
Reserve incorporates disused railway
line; wide range of habitats.
☎ 0865 775476

GLOUCESTERSHIRE / **Bourton-on-the-Water** / GLOUCESTERSHIRE

Bourton-on-the-Water, a picturesque Cotswold village situated on the banks of the
Windrush river, has many attractions including a replica of itself in miniature, a
model railway, a vintage car museum, two notable bird collections and a farm park
for the whole family to enjoy.

Population 2932

Multi-Activity Holidays

MULTI-ACTIVITY CENTRES

HF Holidays
Harrington House
Countryside discovery, walking, sports,
arts and crafts and music holidays based
at Harrington House.
☎ 081 905 9556

Outdoor Leisure

CAMPING AND CARAVANNING

Folly Farm Camping and Caravan Park
Free access to wildfowl and animal park.
☎ 0451 20285

HORSE RIDING

Long Distance Riding Centre
Fosseway
General tuition and hacking.
☎ 0451 21101

WALKING AND RAMBLING

Circular Walks
Six Cotswold walks around the town,
4 to 12 miles in length. For a leaflet
contact the Cotswold Warden Service.
☎ 0452 425674

Special Interests

ARTS AND CRAFTS

Chestnut Gallery
High Street
Small, privately owned gallery
specialising in ceramics and blown glass.
Woodcarvings, prints and local scenes in
watercolours.
☎ 0451 20017

The Cotswold Perfumery
Exhibition of perfumery; watch
manufacturing processes; audio-visual
show; history of perfume exhibits;
quizzes; perfume garden and shop.
☎ 0451 20698

FARM PARKS

Cotswold Farm Park
5 miles north-west at Guiting Power
Unique collection of rare and historic
breeds of farm animals in a natural

Cotswold Farm Park

setting. Farm nature trail, adventure
playground, pets corner, shop, picnic
area and café. Disabled access.
☎ 0451 850307

FESTIVALS AND FAIRS

August
Six-a-side football played to FA rules in
the River Windrush on the late summer
Bank Holiday Monday.

FUN PARKS

Model Village
Garden of the Old New Inn, High Street
A replica of the village, built 50 years ago
in local stone to a scale of one-ninth
with miniature trees and rivers.
☎ 0451 20467

Model Village

65

Cotswold Motor Museum
The Old Mill
30 vintage cars, over 800 period
advertising signs and large collection of
motor memorabilia. Village Life
Exhibition with reconstructions of
rooms, shops and workshops. Also shop
selling toys and trains.
☎ 0451 21255

RAILWAYS

Model Railway
Box Bush, High Street
Approximately 400 square feet of scenic
model railway, with over 40 British and
continental trains running on three main
displays. Large shop with toys, trains and
accessories.
☎ 0451 20686

WILDLIFE PARKS

Birdland
Riverside
Unique collection of endangered species
of birds of the world; every year rare
breeds are bred for the first time in
captivity. Unique penguin rookery.
Tropical house.
☎ 0451 20480

Folly Farm
Duckpool Valley
Conservation centre for rare and
endangered breeds of domestic wildfowl.
Series of lake and natural environments.
Handfeed the ducks and other friendly
animals.
☎ 0451 20285

HEREFORD & / Broadway / WORCESTER

Broadway, set in delightful countryside on the edge of the Vale of Evesham, is a
village of great architectural note. Its long High Street is lined with fine Georgian,
Stuart and Tudor buildings, the grandest, perhaps, is the Lygon Arms Hotel, a former
Manor house reputed to have been the resting place of both Charles I and Oliver
Cromwell during the Civil War.

i ✳ 1 Cotswold Court
☎ 0386 852937

Early closing Thursday
Population 3125

Outdoor Leisure

GOLF

Broadway Golf Club ⛳
Willersey Hill
Members of other clubs with a handicap
are welcome.
☎ 0386 853683/883275

HORSE RACING

Spring Hill
Point to point racing, an annual event.
For details contact the Tourist
Information Centre.
☎ 0386 852937

WALKING AND RAMBLING

The Cotswold Way
97-mile trail that passes through
Broadway on its path from Chipping
Campden to Bath following the scarp
slope of the Cotswolds.

Special Interests

ART GALLERIES

Bindery Gallery
69 High Street
Fine art dealers specialising in 16th to
20th century paintings.
☎ 0386 852649

COUNTRY PARKS

Broadway Tower Country Park
Off the A44
Over 30 acres; woodland walk,
picnicking, nature trails and historic
folly tower.
☎ 0386 852390

Fish Hill
Off the A44
12-acre site, nature trail and picnic area
with access to the Cotswold Way.
Woodland walk from the top of Fish Hill
with views overlooking the village.

FOOD AND DRINK

Barnfield Cider Mill
Near Broadway on the Childswickham
road
Home produced cider and wines,
tastings; farm cheeses, honey, jam, eggs,
homemade cakes.
☎ 0386 853145

HISTORIC BUILDINGS

Broadway Tower
2 miles south-east of Broadway off
the A44
18th century folly built by the sixth Earl
of Coventry, 65-foot tower gives
spectacular views over twelve counties.
Adventure park and nature trails in
surrounding country park.

St Eadburgha's Church
Norman church set amongst trees below
Broadway Hill.

NATURAL HISTORY

Broadway Gravel Pit
Man-made site with semi-natural
habitats for a wide range of flora and
fauna.

HEREFORD & / Bromsgrove / WORCESTER

Bromsgrove can be found south of the Clent and Lickey hills, pleasant walking
country rising to 1000 feet. An old market town with several fine Georgian timber-
framed and gabled buildings, it was an important centre for nail-making for 300 years
until machine-made nails were introduced. There is plenty to do and see in the
undulating countryside around the town.

i 47–49 Worcester Road
☎ 0527 31809

Market days Tuesday, Friday, Saturday
Early closing Thursday
Population 38,155

Adventure Sports

CLIMBING

**Bromsgrove and Redditch
Mountaineering Club**
Written enquiries for information to
D Humphrys, 58 Lingen Close,
Winyates, West Redditch.

Indoor Sports

BADMINTON

The Dolphin Centre
☎ 0527 72923/77123

LEISURE CENTRES

The Dolphin Centre
School Drive
Sports hall, weight training, sunbeds,
badminton, swimming pool, keep-fit
suites, refreshments.
☎ 0527 72923/77123

Outdoor Leisure

CAMPING AND CARAVANNING

Touring Caravans
Chapel Lane, Wythall
Site with good facilities.

CYCLING

Beacon Road Cycling Club
☎ 021 443 3272

FISHING

Coarse Fishing
Fishing in the local reservoirs and lakes.
For details or permits contact the
National Rivers Authority.
☎ 021 711 2324

**Bromsgrove and District Association of
Angling Clubs**
For details contact D Pennels, 5 Burcott
Lane.

GOLF

Bromsgrove Golf Centre
Stratford Road
41 floodlit bays, golf shop.
☎ 0527 575885

King's Norton Golf Club ⛳
Brockhill Lane, Weatheroak, Alvechurch
Professionals shop, catering. Visitors by
appointment.
☎ 0564 826789/826706

HORSE RIDING

Seecham Equestrian Centre
Rowney Green Lane, Alvechurch
Tuition, advanced and beginners.
☎ 021 445 2333

Whitford Riding Stables
Whitford Bridge, Stoke Pound
Lessons and hacking, residential courses
in the summer.
☎ 0527 32005

TENNIS

Bromsgrove Tennis Club
St Godwalds Road, Aston Fields
☎ 0527 78252

Sanders Park
Kidderminster Road
Public courts.
☎ 0527 32148

WALKING AND RAMBLING

Countrysiders
☎ 021 445 2523

The Houseman Trail
A motoring and pedestrian route around
the properties associated with the poet
A E Houseman.
☎ 0527 74136

The North Worcestershire Path
26-mile waymarked path linking four
country parks from Kniver to the Forhill
Picnic area to Wythall.
☎ 0527 31809

Bromsgrove Ramblers Association
☎ 0527 71988

Special Interests

ARTS AND CRAFTS

Avoncroft Art Society
Avoncroft Art Centre, Stoke Heath
Classes in many subjects for adults and
children.
☎ 0527 32592

Daub and Wattles Pottery
5 Windsor Street
Wide variety of original pottery;
watches, clocks, mirrors, lamps and
bowls being made in a building that has
hardly altered since 1821.
☎ 0527 79979

COUNTRY PARKS

Lickey Hills Country park
North of Bromsgrove off the B4096
Woodland, pond; picnic sites, good
views.

Sanders Park
West of Bromsgrove on the
Kidderminster road
40 acres through which Battlefield Brook
flows. Tennis courts.

Waseley Hills Country Park
North of Bromsgrove off the M5
Windmill Hill, 900 foot, gives
spectacular views over the Severn
Valley and the Blade Country.
☎ 0562 710025

FESTIVALS AND FAIRS

May
Bromsgrove Music Festival – a two
week festival including a wide range of
entertainment from jazz to orchestral
concerts, features international artists.

June
The Court Leet – a colourful procession
with local court and bailiff in full regalia;
ale tasting and bread weighing.
Bromsgrove Carnival.

HISTORIC BUILDINGS

Bromsgrove School
Dates from the 1500s with parts of its
17th century structure remaining. The
Old Chapel and Hall were added in the
19th century.

St John the Baptist Church
Norman church built on the site of a
Saxon Chapel, restored in 1858; retains a
12th century nave, 13th century chancel
and a tall elegant spire.

MUSEUMS

Avoncroft Museum of Buildings
Off the Bromsgrove bypass at Stoke Heath
7 centuries of history recorded in rescued and restored buildings on 15-acre site. Shop, café and picnic area.
☎ 0527 31886/31363

Bromsgrove Museum
Exhibits of local industries and crafts of the Bromsgrove Guild; costumes; haberdashery and Victorian/Edwardian toy shop windows. Craft, toy and model shop.
☎ 0527 77934

Water Sports

BOAT HIRE

Alvechurch Boat Centre
Scarfield Wharf, Alvechurch
☎ 021 445 2909

Black Prince Holidays Ltd
The Wharf, Hanbury Road, Stoke Prior
2-12 berth boats for hire on the Birmingham and Worcester Canal for 3 days or more.
☎ 0527 78289

INLAND WATERWAYS

Worcester and Birmingham Canal
Passes east of the town climbing the Lickey Hills via a long flight of locks. Large marina at Alvechurch. Fishing and cruising on the canal or walking along the towpaths.

SWIMMING

The Dolphin Centre
25-metre pool, learner pool, aquasplash waterflume and tuition.
☎ 0527 72923/77123

/| ____
HEREFORD & /// **Bromyard** / WORCESTER /
|/ |/

Bromyard is a market town rich in architectural styles, from the black-and-white timber-framed buildings – a notable example being the Falcon Inn where the Royal Mail Coach once made its daily call – to Georgian style mansions such as the Old Vicarage. The area around has much to offer including a well known herb farm, the Symonds Cider factory, a working farm, a straw crafts centre, delightful walks and some interesting churches to visit before sampling the local spring water or wine.

i Rowberry Street
☎ 0885 482038 ✳
☎ 0885 482341

Early closing Tuesday
Population 6000

Multi-Activity Holidays

SPECIAL INTEREST CENTRES

Straw Craft Holidays
Straw Craft Centre, The School House, Much Cowarne
Residential courses offered in all straw crafts including marquetry and furniture; week-long courses in summer, and some weekends in winter.
☎ 0432 820317

Outdoor Leisure

CAMPING AND CARAVANNING

Fir Tree Inn
Much Cowarne
4-acre orchard in the grounds of a public house.
☎ 053 186 619

Nether Court
Stoke Lacy
Simple amenities on family farm; room for tents and five carvans.
☎ 0432 820247

WALKING AND RAMBLING

Bringsty Common
East of Bromyard
Gorse and bracken moorland, ideal for walking.

69

Brockhampton Woodland Walk
On the main A44 Worcester to
Leominster road
Circular trails through young
plantations and mature oak woodland.
Details and leaflets are available from
the Tourist Information Centre.
☎ 0885 482341

Bromyard Downs
Open hill area 800 feet high with
panoramic views in all directions from
the many walks.

Special Interests

ART GALLERIES

Michael Oxenham Studio and Gallery
The Square
☎ 0885 482231

ARTS AND CRAFTS

The Hop Pocket
New House, Bishops Frome
Exhibition of traditional local crafts and
British Wool Collection; topiary garden
and tours of hop kilns by arrangement.
☎ 053186 323

Straw Crafts Centre
The School House, Much Cowarne
All straw crafts practised including corn
dollies, rick finials, straw marquetry,
hats and furniture. Residential courses
in summer and some winter weekends.
☎ 0432 820317

FARM PARKS

Shortwood Working Dairy Farm
Shortwood, Pencombe
Various farm animals that can be fed and
touched; hand milking. Woodland, cider
orchard and farm trail.
☎ 0885 400205

FESTIVALS AND FAIRS

July
Bromyard Gala – fair organs and vintage
vehicles from showmen's engines to
farm implements, ten days in early July.
☎ 0885 483378

September
Bromyard Folk Festival – weekend in
mid-September.
☎ 053 16 70279

Multi Period Encampment – annual
Renaissance time warp on Bromyard
Downs involving costumes, archery and
pistol shootings.

December
Victorian Festival – town goes back in
time to the Victorian era; locals dress in
period costume, many events over four
days in mid-December.

FOOD AND DRINK

Bosbury Vineyards and Gardens
The Slatch, Bosbury
9-acre English vineyard selling English
wine. Rose garden.
☎ 053186 226

Hennerwood Oak Spring Water
Hennerwood Oak, Hazeley, Pencombe
Spring water for sale. Farm open daily.
☎ 088 55 603/245

Symonds Cider
Stoke Lacy
Visitor centre, shop.
☎ 0885 490411

GARDENS

Stoke Lacy Herb Garden
Herb nursery and garden established in
1939; wide variety of culinary, medicinal
and fragrant herbs.
☎ 0432 820232

HISTORIC BUILDINGS

Edvin Loach Saxon Church
4 miles north of Bromyard, off an
unmarked road on the B4203
Remains of an early Romanesque
Church.

St Peter's Church
Late Norman parts of building with
evidence of earlier Saxon building; three
Norman doorways, and the 'Bromyard
Bushel' a massive metal bowl
representing the standard measure as
stated in the 1670 Act of Parliament.

HISTORIC HOUSES

Lower Brockhampton
3 miles east of Bromyard on the A44
Late 14th century half-timbered moated
manor house with a balustered minstrel
gallery, 15th century chapel and the
ruins of a 12th century chapel set in
parkland. National Trust.

MUSEUMS

Bromyard Heritage Centre
1 Rowberry Street
Stable block of the vicarage converted to
exhibit various artefacts showing the
history of the town; it also houses the
Tourist Information Centre.
☎ 0885 482038 summer
☎ 0885 482341 winter

Burford is one of the Cotswolds' most beautiful small towns. An ancient and historic coaching town, its characteristically honey-coloured stone buildings sweep gracefully down to a little bridge over the Windrush river. An important centre for the antiques trade, the town offers much of interest to explore and nearby is the Cotswold Wildlife Park with its roaming animal collection.

i Sheep Street
☎ 0993 82 3558

Market day Friday
Early closing Wednesday
Population 1724

Outdoor Leisure

GOLF

Burford Golf Club 🏌
Members only at weekends.
☎ 0993 82 2344

HORSE RIDING

Barrington Stables
Home Farm, Little Barrington
General instruction in riding and jumping; riding holidays with full board and accommodation; hacking, schooling and livery.
☎ 045 14 479

Special Interests

ANTIQUES

Antiques Centre
Burford is an important centre for the antique trade with a wonderful variety of shops to browse.

ARTS AND CRAFTS

Burford Garden Centre
Working craft centre, adventure playground and garden centre.
☎ 0993 82 3117

HISTORIC BUILDINGS

High Street
Beautiful street of mediaeval Cotswold stone architecture.

St John the Baptist Church
Church dates from Norman times, remodelled in the 15th century; elaborate south porch and 15th century brasses. Place of imprisonment of 400 Levellers (rebels against Cromwell) during the Civil War; three were executed in the churchyard.

MUSEUMS

Tolsey Museum
High Street
16th century merchants' meeting place and court house now a museum housing local exhibits: the town's archives, a Regency doll's house made by local craftsmen and the history of coopering and ropemaking.
☎ 0993 82 3647

RAILWAYS

Cotswold Wildlife Park
Narrow-gauge railway.
☎ 0993 82 3006

WILDLIFE PARKS

Cotswold Wildlife Park
Set in 120 acres of garden and parkland around a Gothic style manor house; contains a large and varied collection of animals from all over the world including leopards, a white rhino, zebras, ostriches and the red panda. Many species roam in the open separated from visitors by open ditches.
Brass rubbing, narrow-gauge railway, train rides, aquarium and butterfly centre, pony rides, adventure playground, refreshments.
☎ 0993 82 3006

71

Carterton is a bustling south Oxfordshire town of more recent origins than many of the neighbouring towns and villages, it is the home of RAF Brize Norton. Nearby is a working weaving mill and a rural museum and for the romantic amongst you there is a centre hiring out Romany caravans for touring holidays – an ideal way to see the unexplored Oxfordshire Cotswolds!

Market day Thursday
Early closing Wednesday
Population 13,000

Multi-Activity Holidays

SPECIAL INTEREST CENTRES

Romany Caravan and Country Riding
Oxleaze Farm, Filkins
Organisers of activity holidays including trail riding, hunting and horse-drawn caravan tours.
☎ 036 786 489

Outdoor Leisure

HORSE RIDING

Cotswold Equitation Centre
93 Shilton Road
Student courses, livery and schooling for competitions.
☎ 0993 842262

Special Interests

ARTS AND CRAFTS

Cotswold Woollen Weavers
South-west of Carterton at Filkins
Working weaving mill in an 18th century barn, traditional skills and machinery at work, exhibition gallery and mill shop.
☎ 036 786 491

MUSEUMS

Swinford Museum
Filkins
Domestic and rural trade and craft tools of the mid-19th century.

Water Sports

SWIMMING

Carterton Swimming Pool
Open-air, heated, seasonal.

Chalford

Chalford clings to the steep, wooded Cotswold hillside, it resembles an Alpine village with its houses rising tier by tier above the Golden Valley. The lanes of this picturesque village are extremely narrow and not for the faint-hearted motorist!

Aerial Sports

GLIDING

Cotswold Gliding Club
Aston Down Airfield
Mini courses, weekly courses and gliding holidays.
☎ 0285 76473
☎ 0452 614596 mini courses
☎ 0242 231031 weekly courses and gliding holidays

Outdoor Leisure

HORSE RIDING

Camp Riding Centre
Camp
Indoor facilities; hacking available.
☎ 028 582 219

Special Interests

ARTS AND CRAFTS

Dennis French Woodware
The Craft Shop, Brimscombe Hill, Brimscombe
Craft shop selling own woodwork and good variety of well-finished products.
☎ 0453 883054

GARDENS

Cowcombe Farm Herbs
Gipsy Lane
Herb and wildflower nursery; specialising in cottage garden species.
☎ 0285 76 544

MUSEUMS

Oakridge Village Museum
Off the A419 at Oakridge
Collection of local items; photographs of historical interest.
☎ 0285 76438

73

Charlbury stands in the Evenlode Valley close to the Wychwood Forest. It was first mentioned in the 7th century as the burial place of the first Bishop of Lichfield. The village has had connections with prosperous Quakers in its past, as well as a tradition of glove-making. A visit to Ditchley House or a tour around a slate mine count amongst its attractions.

Outdoor Leisure

WALKING AND RAMBLING

Charlbury Circular Walk
Details from the West Oxfordshire District Council.
☎ 0993 702941

The Oxfordshire Way
Long-distance footpath passes through the village and along the Evenlode Valley.

Special Interests

FESTIVALS AND FAIRS

September
Street Fair

HISTORIC BUILDINGS

Charlbury Station
Railway station designed by Brunel.

HISTORIC HOUSES

Ditchley House
2 miles from Charlbury on the B4437 Designed by James Gibb and completed in 1722 on the site of an earlier historic house; elegant mouldings and marble fire place. Used as a planning centre for D-day by Churchill. Set in parkland landscaped by Capability Brown. Parties by prior arrangement.
☎ 0608 677346

MUSEUMS

Charlbury Museum
Market Street
Recollections of the town's past – key obtainable from the pharmacy opposite.

Stonesfield Museum and Slate Mine
Witney Lane, Stonesfield
History of Stonesfield roofing slate; artefacts and old tools. Trips down the mine by appointment.
☎ 0993 891600

NATURAL HISTORY

Wychwood Forest
Once a royal hunting area as large as the New Forest, now much reduced in size. Interesting flora and fauna.

Cheltenham, an elegant Regency spa town sited on the edge of the Cotswold Hills, is a lively centre for education, music, art and commerce. The discovery of the only alkaline spring waters in Britain transformed it from a Cotswold village to a fashionable spa town that enjoyed the patronage of the Royal Family and British and European nobility. The legacy of this period can be enjoyed today in the town's excellent art gallery and museum and in its wide spacious tree-lined avenues, beautiful gardens and elegant buildings. The spa waters can still be enjoyed at the Pittville Pump Room which, with its colonnade and dome, is perhaps Cheltenham's most beautiful building.

The Cheltenham Music Festival was started in 1944. It was hoped that it would encourage contemporary British music and since then it has been the venue of first performances of works by Benjamin Britten, Malcolm Arnold and many other British composers.

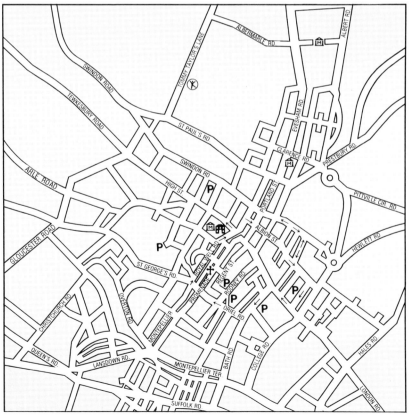

i Municipal Offices
The Promenade
☎ 0242 522878

Market day Thursday
Early closing Wednesday
Population 87,500

Adventure Sports

CAVING

Gloucester Caving Club
For details contact M Green, 29 Limber
Hill, Wymans Brack.

Aerial Sports

FLYING

Cotswold Aero Club
☎ 0452 713924

Indoor Sports

BADMINTON

Balcarras Sports Centre
☎ 0242 510182

Bournside Sports Centre
☎ 0242 239123

Cheltenham Recreation Centre
☎ 0242 528764

LEISURE CENTRES

Balcarras Sports Centre
East End Road, Charlton Kings
Joint-use centre collaborating with
St Benedicts and Bournside. Sports hall,
gym and outdoor facilities.
☎ 0242 510182

Bournside Sports Centre
Warden Hill Road
Weight training, sunbed, sports hall,
gym and outdoor facilities.
☎ 0242 239123

Cheltenham Recreation Centre
Tommy Taylor's Lane
Pool, sauna, spa pool and sunbeds.
☎ 0242 528764

St Benedicts Sports Centre
Arle Road
Sports hall, gym and outdoor facilities.
☎ 0242 226299

SQUASH

Cheltenham Recreation Centre
☎ 0242 528764

Multi-Activity Holidays

SPECIAL INTEREST CENTRES

Badgeworth Riding Centre
Cold Pool Lane, Upper Hatherley
☎ 0452 713818

Cotswold Collection Breaks
Breaks focussed around walking or
horses, based in Cheltenham.
☎ 0242 517110

Prestbury Park Hotel
Jaqueline Gorrie, The Burgage, Prestbury
Walking holidays.
☎ 0242 529533

Outdoor Leisure

CAMPING AND CARAVANNING

Stansby Caravan Park
The Reddings
30 pitches, facilities, dogs by
arrangement.
☎ 0452 712168

CYCLING

Crabtrees
50 Winchcombe Street
☎ 0242 515291

FISHING

Coarse Fishing
Fishing in Pittville Lake in Pittville Park
in the town centre. For details and
permits contact the National Rivers
authority.
☎ 021 711 2324

Cheltenham Angling Club
For details contact A Cox, 4 Ewens Road.

Ian Coley Ltd
444 High street
☎ 0242 522443

GOLF

Cotswold Hills Golf Club ⚐
Ullenwood
☎ 0242 525201

Lilleybrook Golf Club ▶18
Cirencester Road, Charlton Kings
☎ 0242 525201

HORSE RACING

Cheltenham Racecourse
Steeplechase Company Ltd, Prestbury
Park
A left-handed, 1 mile 3 furlong oval
course which hosts 16 national hunt
days each year. It is the home of national
hunt racing.
☎ 0242 513014

Cheltenham Races

HORSE RIDING

Cheltenham Horse Riding Centre
Noverton Farm, Noverton Lane,
Prestbury
☎ 0242 570824

Southam Riding School
Southam
☎ 0242 242194/244527

TENNIS

Balcarras Sport Centre
☎ 0242 510182

Bournside Sports Centre
☎ 0242 239123

Montpellier Gardens
Hard and grass courts.
☎ 0242 583711

St Benedict's Sport Centre
☎ 0242 226299

Pittville Park
Hard courts.
☎ 0242 584393

WALKING AND RAMBLING

Circular Walks
There are several circular walks in and
around Cheltenham. Contact the
Tourist Information Centre for details.
☎ 0242 522878

Special Interests

ART GALLERIES

Cheltenham Art Gallery and Museum
Clarence Street
Internationally important Arts and
Crafts Movement collection of furniture,
textiles, paintings and sculpture; noted
17th century Dutch paintings.
☎ 0242 237431

ARTS AND CRAFTS

The Rocking Horse Toyshop
32 Winchcombe Street
Extensive range of hand-made rocking
horses and quality toys including doll's
houses.
☎ 0242 580000

FESTIVALS AND FAIRS

March
National Hunt Festival – at
Cheltenham Racecourse during which
the Gold Cup race is run.

July
Cheltenham International Festival of
Music – a fortnight of music from world
class orchestras to street buskers.

Cheltenham Cricket Festival

Cricket Festival held at Cheltenham
College.

October
Festival of Literature – two weeks of
drama, comedy, poetry readings and
exhibitions.

Festival of Literature

GUIDED TOURS

Carriage Tours
Pittville Pump Rooms
Tours of Regency Cheltenham in a
Landau carriage. Contact the Tourist
Information Centre for details.
☎ 0242 522878

Cheltenham Guided Tours
Details from the Tourist Information
Centre.
☎ 0242 522878

MUSEUMS

Cheltenham Art Gallery and Museum
Local history and archaeology
collections. Art gallery and exhibitions.
☎ 0242 237431

Gustav Holst Birthplace Museum
4 Clarence Road, Pittville
Regency-style house with period rooms
items belonging to the Holst family.
☎ 0242 524846

Pittville Pump Room Museum
Pittville Park
Regency building in own park, housing
Gallery of Fashion where exhibits show
major fashion changes between 1760 and
1960. Changing exhibitions.
☎ 0242 512740

ORNAMENTAL PARKS

Hatherley Park
Off Bournside Road
Lake and play area.

Hesters Way Park
Off Princess Elizabeth Way
Rose garden.

Imperial Gardens
Off Victoria Walk
Floral gardens and fountain.

Montpellier Gardens
Off Montpellier Walk and adjacent to
Imperial Gardens
Tennis courts and putting green.
☎ 0242 523406

Oxford and Priory Gardens
Berkeley Place
Floral gardens.

Pittville Park
Aboretum, ornamental and boating
lakes; 18 hole pitch and putt golf, tennis
courts, playground, nature trails. Bands
play in summer.

The Promenade
Long gardens; Neptune's fountain.

Sandford Park
Off Keynsham Road
Floral gardens, play area and recreation
ground by the River Chelt.

Winston Churchill Memorial Gardens
Off the High Street
Gardens and play area.

THEATRES

Everyman Theatre
Regent Street
Professional repertory company with a
mixed programme including West End
productions.
☎ 0242 572573

Playhouse Theatre
Bath Road
☎ 0242 522852

Shaftesbury Theatre
St Georges Place
☎ 0242 222795

Water Sports

BOAT HIRE

Pittville Park Boating Lake
☎ 0242 584393

SWIMMING

Cheltenham Recreation Centre
Main, diving and teaching pools; sauna;
solarium and other facilities.
☎ 0242 528764

Sandford Pools
Keynsham Road
Two open-air heated pools.
☎ 0242 524430

Chipping Campden, set in a bowl of hills near the Cotswold escarpment, is a particularly fine Cotswold centre. It has a perfectly preserved curving High Street with many of its beautiful buildings dating from mediaeval times when it was a prosperous wool centre. Its 'wool' church is magnificent and its history and traditions are displayed in the Woolstapler's Hall. The surrounding countryside can be enjoyed by following any of the circular walks around the town and Hidcote Manor Garden north-east of the town is delightful, not to be missed.

i ✳ Woolstapler's Hall Museum
High Street
☎ 0386 840289

Population 2010

Multi-Activity Holidays

SPECIAL INTEREST CENTRES

Seymour House Hotel
High Street
Activity breaks including interests such as music, antiques, the wool trail, wine, painting and churches.
☎ 0386 840429

Outdoor Leisure

WALKING AND RAMBLING

Circular Walks
For details of six walks from 2½ to 5 miles long around Chipping Campden, contact the Cotswold Warden Service
☎ 0452 425674

Special Interests

ART GALLERIES

Camperdene Gallery
Camperdene House, High Street
Exhibitions of local work.

ARTS AND CRAFTS

Arts Society
Broad Campden Village Hall
Lectures and practical sessions covering many types of arts and crafts.

Hart's Silversmiths
The Old Silk Mill, Sheep Street
Silversmiths Workshop (C R Ashbee's Guild of Handicraft) where the Hart family have been making silverware since 1908.
☎ 0386 841100

COUNTRY PARKS

Dovers Hill
1 mile north-west of Chipping Campden
Natural amphitheatre on a spur of the Cotswolds with panoramic views; waymarked trail. National Trust.

FESTIVALS AND FAIRS

June
Cotswold Games – at Dovers Hill, created in the 17th century as the Olympics of rural sports such as cudgel and shin-kicking.
Scuttlebrook Wake – follows the games with fancy dress floats and a fair.
☎ 0386 840289

GARDENS

Hidcote Manor Garden
Hidcote Bartrim
Famous modern garden with many rare trees, shrubs and plants separated by walls and hedges of different species.
☎ 0386 438333

Kiftsgate Court Gardens
4 miles north of Chipping Campden
Gardens with many unusual plants, shrubs, old fashioned and species roses set in the grounds of a private house.
☎ 0386 438777

HISTORIC BUILDINGS

Church
15th century church with a 14th century chancel and stately 120-foot high tower; fine brasses.

MUSEUMS

Woolstapler's Hall Museum
High Street
14th century Wool Hall contains eleven rooms with exhibits of domestic items, cameras, medical equipment, period costumes and an exhibition of the wool industry. Also houses the Tourist Information Centre.
☎ 0386 840289

ORNAMENTAL PARKS

Ernest Wilson Memorial Garden
Leysbourne High Street
Garden commemorating work of Ernest Wilson, born here, particularly his study of Chinese and Japanese botanical specimens.
☎ 0386 840289

Chipping Norton, at 650 feet, is the highest town in Oxfordshire and is a favourite stopping off point for visitors. It is mentioned in the Domesday Book as Norton; 'Chipping', meaning 'market', was not added to the name until the 13th century. Once a prosperous wool town it remains a busy Cotswold centre with plenty to explore both within the town and in the countryside around including the fascinating Neolithic stone circle nearby.

i 5 Middle Row
☎ 0608 644379

Market day Wednesday
Early closing Thursday
Population 5230

Indoor Sports

LEISURE CENTRES

Greystones Sports Complex
Home of several sports clubs.

SQUASH

The Regent Squash Club
New Street
4 squash courts, coaching available. Sauna, jacuzzi, solarium; social club.
☎ 0608 642384

Outdoor Leisure

CAMPING AND CARAVANNING

Camping and Caravanning Club Site
Chipping Norton Road, Chadlington
75 pitches for tents, trailer tents, caravans and motor caravans; many facilities.
☎ 0608 641993

FISHING

Coarse Fishing
Fishing in the River Evenlode. For permits and information contact the National Rivers Authority.
☎ 0865 749400

Salford
Facilities for the disabled to fish in the River Evenlode.

GOLF

Chipping Norton Golf Club ⛳
Visitors welcome; tuition available.
☎ 0608 642383

Special Interests

ANTIQUES

Chipping Norton Antiques Centre
Ivy House, 1 Middle Row, Market Square
Good selection of quality and decorative 1900 dateline stock.

ART GALLERIES

Manor House Gallery
West Street
Wide selection of watercolours, original prints and etchings; emphasis on local artists.
☎ 0608 642620

FESTIVALS AND FAIRS

September
Street Fair – present form of the Mop Fair which was held to hire servants.

HERITAGE

Castle
Remains of castle built by Norman barons can be seen as mounds near the church.

Rollright Stone Circle
3 miles north-east between Great and Little Rollright
Late Neolithic stone circle containing seventy stones including the 'King' stone and the four 'Whispering Knights'; thought to be constructed about 1500 BC and as important as Avebury and Stonehenge.

HISTORIC BUILDINGS

St Mary's Church
Fine 15th century nave, decorated windows and brasses. The nearby almshouses are delightful.

Bliss Tweed Mill
18th century weaving mill that dominates the town, ceased operation in the 1980s, now being converted to a private residence.

HISTORIC HOUSES

Chastleton House
Barton-on-the-Heath
Jacobean mansion built for a Royalist wool merchant. 17th century topiary garden.
☎ 060874 355

MUSEUMS

Chipping Norton Museum
Rear of Baptist Chapel, New Street
Displays of Old Hitchman Brewery; collection of items from Bliss Tweed Mill; Edwardian dairy and kitchen; shop with old postcards and history books for sale.
☎ 0608 642754

THEATRES

The Theatre
2 Spring Street
☎ 0608 642350

Water Sports

SWIMMING

Chipping Norton Swimming Pool
Fox Close
Open air, seasonal.

GLOUCESTERSHIRE / **Cinderford** / GLOUCESTERSHIRE

Cinderford is the largest town in the Forest of Dean, an enchanting area of ancient woodland between the Wye and the Severn rivers. It is an area of distinctive cultural and natural history that can best be appreciated by exploring its network of footpaths and trails on foot or by horse and carriage. A visit to the Dean Heritage Centre will explain many of the Foresters' traditions and privileges. Disputes between the Foresters who lived by woodcutting and poaching and the iron-founders who moved into the Forest in the 17th century were settled by the Verderers' Court, a court held in Speech House. The house is now a hotel but the court still uses a room there ten times a year for official sitting of the court.

i 12 Belle Vue Road
☎ 0594 823184

Adventure Sports

CAVING

Royal Forest of Dean Caving Club
Contact K Stacey, 85 Church Road for details.

Indoor Sports

LEISURE CENTRES

Heywood Sports Centre
Causeway Road
Sports hall, gym, weight training, squash and pool.
☎ 0594 824008

81

SQUASH

Heywood Sports Centre
☎ 0594 824008

Outdoor Leisure

FISHING

Coarse Fishing
Carp, chubb, roach, rudd, perch and
tench can be found in the pools in the
Forest of Dean.

Robert Sports
Licences, permits and maps of the pools
supplied.
☎ 0594 823905

Royal Forest of Dean Angling Club
The club owns Lightmoor Pool, Steam
Mills Lake, Waterloo Screens and many
other pools.
☎ 0594 824413

WALKING AND RAMBLING

Forest Sculpture Trail
Access at Beechenhurst off the B4226
Sculptures are sited in the woodland, the
artists having derived inspiration from
the forest setting. An innovative way to
explore the forest along a 4-mile trail.

New Fancy Forest Walk
Access at site of former New Fancy
Colliery
2½-mile trail along disused railway
tracks and paths through the forest.

Soudley Ponds
Access at the Dean Heritage Centre
1¼-mile flat walk around a series of
small lakes. Suitable for the disabled.

Special Interests

ARTS AND CRAFTS

Coach House Crafts UK
Oakfield House, Hawthorns Cross, Dry
Brook
Woodcraft; woodturning
demonstrations by prior arrangement.
☎ 0594 543018

W B Freeman
Forest Vale Lodge, 86 Valley Road
Woodcarvings and sticks.
☎ 0594 824614

Victor Hugo Country Pots
Dean Heritage Centre, Soudley
Terracotta hand-thrown pots for all
seasons.
☎ 0594 822170

GARDENS

Speech House Arboretum
South-west of Cinderford on the B4226
Collection of conifers and broadleaved
trees planted from 1916 onwards,
interesting walk.

Speech House, Forest of Dean

GUIDED TOURS

W B Freeman
Forest Vale Lodge, 86 Valley Road
Rides in the Forest of Dean by horse and
carriage.
☎ 0594 824614

MUSEUMS

Dean Heritage Centre
Camp Mill, Soudley
Portrayal of the Forest of Dean's natural
and man-made heritage: social,
industrial and natural history displays;
reconstructed cottage and mine. Craft
workshops, craft shop, picnic sites and
playground.
☎ 0594 822170

NATURAL HISTORY

Soudley Ponds
Near the Dean Heritage Centre
Series of small lakes constructed as fish
ponds in the 19th century, now a Site of
Special Scientific Interest.

Speech House Woodland
South-west of Cinderford on the B4226
Mature oak trees with a picnic site.

Water Sports

SWIMMING

Heywood Sports Centre
☎ 0594 824008

Cirencester

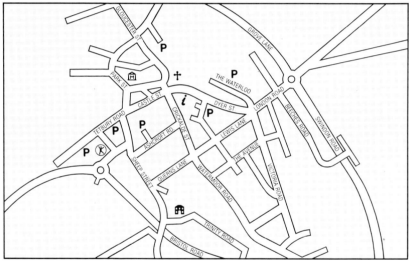

Cirencester was founded by the Romans as an administrative centre for the southern area of the Cotswold hills and was second only to London in size and importance. The old town, Corinium, was built on the site of a military camp located at the crossroads of three major Roman roads – this site has been excavated and has produced many exciting finds that can be seen in the Corinium Museum.

Cirencester is now a thriving market town, its colourful market place is dominated by the magnificent cathedral-like parish church – one of the famous 'wool' churches of the Cotswolds. There are a variety of interesting attractions in the town and ample facilities for leisure activities both indoor and outdoor including a wide range of water sports facilities provided by the nearby Cotswold Water park.

i Corn Hall
Market Place
☎ 0285 654180

Population 16,230

Aerial Sports

BALLOONING

Ballooning in the Cotswolds
36 Cheltenham Road, Rencamb
☎ 028 583 515

Indoor Sports

BADMINTON

Cotswold Sports Centre
☎ 0285 654057

LEISURE CENTRES

Cotswold Sports Centre
Tetbury Road
Sports hall, sauna and solarium, roller
skating, weights room, table tennis,
pools and refreshements.
☎ 0285 654057

SQUASH

Cotswold Sports Centre
☎ 0285 654057

Multi-Activity Holidays

SPECIAL INTEREST CENTRES

Steel-Away
Bothy Cottage, The Butts, Poulton
1 or 2 day mountain bike tours
☎ 0285 851356

Outdoor Leisure

FISHING

Coarse Fishing
There are several good fishing stations in
the area. Contact the National Rivers
Authority.
☎ 021 711 2324

Abbey Lake
Access via Market Square or footpath
from Spitalgate Lane or Corinium Gate
into Abbey Grounds. Permits from D & J
Sports.
☎ 0285 652227

Ashton Keynes Angling Club
The club controls lakes 32, 34 and 56 in
the Cotswold Water Park. Day tickets
are available from the Rangers Office,
Keynes Country Park, no night fishing.
☎ 0285 861459

Game Fishing
Lower Moor
Day and season tickets for fly fishing are
available from Lower Moor Farm for
fishing lakes 52 and 53 of the Cotswold
Water Park.

River Churn
Permits from J & D Sports.
☎ 0285 652227

HORSE RIDING

The Talland School of Equitation
Church Farm, Siddington
General instruction in riding and
jumping to BHS exam standard. Hacking
in the Cotswold Hills.
☎ 0285 652318

Special Interests

ARTS AND CRAFTS

Cirencester Workshops
Brewery Court, Cricklade Street
17 independent craft businesses in a
former brewery building; leatherworks,
textiles, bookbinders and a blacksmith.
☎ 0285 651566

Cirencester Workshops

COUNTRY PARKS

Cirencester Park
3000 acres of park and woodland with
trails; polo played every Sunday in the
summer months.
☎ 0285 653135

Cirencester Park

Cotswold Water Park
South of Cirencester
Two large collections of lakes created from flooded gravel pits, facilities for all types of watersports; birdwatching and lakeside walks.
☎ 0285 861459

Keynes Country Park
Lakes 31, 32 and 34 of Cotswold Water Park. Walks, picnic sites, information, playground and nature reserve. Day tickets for windsurfing and angling.
☎ 0285 861459

Neigh Bridge Country Park
Lake 56 Cotswold Water Park
Walks, picnic site, parking, information, playground. Day tickets for angling from Keynes Country Park.

Corinium Museum

HERITAGE

Cirencester Amphitheatre
Next to bypass on the west of Cirencester
Roman amphitheatre, one of the largest and best preserved in Britain, dates from the 2nd century.
☎ 0272 734472

HISTORIC BUILDINGS

Cirencester Church
A great Cotswolds wool church; 15th century pulpit, superb tower, three storied fan-vaulted porch and brasses.

Cirencester Lock Up
Cotswold District Council Offices, Trinity Road
Two-celled lock up built in 1804 and moved to its present site in 1837; display panels give the history of lock-ups and their uses, the history of the building and the Cirencester workhouse.
☎ 0285 655611

St Michael's Church
Duntisbourne Rouse
Tiny church in delightful valley setting; Saxon nave, small crypt chapel reached by external steps.

MUSEUMS

Corinium Museum
Park Street
Award-winning museum with fine collection of antiquities from Roman Britain; reconstructions of rooms in Roman Cirencester. Displays from prehistory to mediaeval times.
☎ 0285 655611

Water Sports

JET-SKIING

Cotswold Jet Ski Club Ltd
Lake 11, Spine Road, Cotswold Water Park
☎ 0285 861345

SWIMMING

Cirencester Open-Air Swimming Pool
Riverside Walk, Thomas Street
Built in 1869 – one of the oldest outdoor pools in England.
☎ 0285 653947

Cotswold Sports Centre
Main and learner pool; slipstream ozone plant water treatment to reduce chlorine irritation pioneered here.
☎ 0285 654057

WATER SKIING

Cirencester Water Ski Club
Lake 37, Cotswold Water Park
Private members club; courses run by prior arrangement, slalom, jump, two trick courses; tournaments.
☎ 028 586 1776

Cotswold Water Ski Club
Greatmoor Lake, South Cerney
Slalom and jump.
☎ 027 264 2057

WINDSURFING

Keynes Park Windsurfing Club
Keynes Country Park, Lake 32, Cotswold Water Park
Temporary membership available; tuition and board hire.
☎ 0285 861202

Coleford

Coleford is an attractive small town in the Forest of Dean. This ancient woodland area has plenty to offer as a walking, caving, climbing, birdwatching, camping and adventure centre. Its ancient iron mines have miles of caves to explore and nearby open iron workings offer a maze of paths in a unique environment unchanged since it was first developed in the 1800s. There are forest and woodland walks, nature reserves with unusual birds and wildlife and local guides to introduce you to the history, both natural and human, of the Forest of Dean.

The crafts of the Royal Forest of Dean Craftworkers are available here, and there is a blacksmith to watch at work. For railway enthusiasts there is the Great Western Railway Museum to enjoy; it runs special steam days and houses many fascinating exhibits.

i Market Place
☎ 0594 36307

Coleford Town Centre

Adventure Sports

CAVING

Clearwell Caves Adventure
Ancient iron mines with over 2 square miles of caves and mine systems to explore; caving trips organised.
☎ 0594 32535

Multi-Activity Holidays

MULTI-ACTIVITY CENTRES

Forest Adventure
Instruction at introductory and advanced levels in rock-climbing, abseiling, caving and canoeing.
☎ 0594 34661

Outdoor Leisure

BIRDWATCHING

Nags Head Nature Reserve
Off the B4431
The oak trees of the Cannop Valley support a number of unusual birds including the Pied Flycatcher. RSPB.

CAMPING AND CARAVANNING

Cherry Orchard Farm
Newland
Natural landscaped field – minimal facilities on a working farm.
☎ 0594 32212

Christchurch Camping Ground
Forestry Commission, Christchurch
Complex of 3 sites, many facilities; camp shop, telephones, playground.
☎ 0594 33376

Forest of Dean
Details of the Biblings campsite in the Forest are available from the Forestry Commission, Crown Offices, Bank St.
☎ 0594 33057

Rushmere Farm
Crossways
Small select site on the forest edge; riding available.

FISHING

Coarse Fishing
Fishing in the River Wye and Cannop Ponds.

Sport and Leisure
Market Place
Permits, licences, information and tackle.
☎ 0594 33559

HORSE RIDING

Rushmere Farm Riding Stables
Crossways
Riding and driving tuition, novices
welcome.
☎ 0594 35319

WALKING AND RAMBLING

Bixslade Forest Walk
Access at Cannop Ponds off the B4226
4-mile circular walk round stone
quarries and old coal mines.

Christchurch Forest Walk
Access from Biblins car park off the
B4432
3¹/₄-mile trail offering good views, relics
of charcoal burning and drift mining can
be observed.

Waymarked Paths
A Ramblers Association leaflet of
waymarked rambles and other walks in
the Forest of Dean is available from the
Tourist Information Centre.
☎ 0954 36307

Special Interests

ANTIQUES

Dean Forest Antiques
The Corner House, Berry Hill Pike
Antiques, commemorative ware and
memorabilia.
☎ 0594 33211

ARTS AND CRAFTS

Country Theme
11 Gloucester Road
China, glass, pottery, tags, cards, frames,
local crafts and souvenirs; also
photography gallery.
☎ 0594 36961

FODCA
Crafts Shop, Parkend
Quality craftwork made locally by the
Royal Forest of Dean Craftworkers
Association.
☎ 0594 564222

Meadow Cottage Products
15 Gloucester Road
Cottage industry producing a range of
designer sewn products; goods made to
order; shop and workshop open to view.
☎ 0594 33444

Peter Neale
Scatterford Smithy, Newland
Blacksmith producing quality hand-
forged ironwork; restorations and period
reproductions; workshop.
☎ 0594 37309

FOREST PARKS

Puzzle Wood
Perrygrove Road
Open iron workings in a woodland
setting; maze of paths with unique
wooden seats and bridges; unaltered
since first transformed in the 1800s.
Souvenir shop, refreshments.
☎ 0594 33187

GUIDED TOURS

Timewalk
13 Meadow Walk, Sling
Guided walks of the Royal Forest of
Dean by local guides.
☎ 0594 33544

MUSEUMS

Clearwell Caves
Near Coleford
Ancient iron mines with a system of
underground tunnels and chambers;
displays show how iron has been mined
for over 2500 years.
☎ 0594 32535/23700

Great Western Railway Museum
1883 Coleford GWR goods building
houses the museum; collection includes
full size and model exhibits and other
train memorabilia. Special steam days.
Railway walk.
☎ 0594 33569

NATURAL HISTORY

Nags Head Nature Reserve
Off the B4431
Wealth of wildlife in old oaks of Cannop
valley. Forest Nature Reserve trail.
Forestry Commission and RSPB
management.

RAILWAYS

Great Western Railway Museum
☎ 0594 33569

Cotswold Water Park

The Cotswold Water Park is situated in the Upper Thames Valley around two areas of lakes that have been formed as a result of gravel extraction around the settlements of Cerney Wick, South Cerney, Ashton Keynes and Lechlade. A total of nearly 100 lakes offer a variety of recreational water-based activities including jet-skiing and windsurfing together with nature reserves, walks, fishing venues, riding and cycling routes. Walks around the area provide an insight into the wetlands and flora which are nationally important for nature conservation while passing by characteristic Cotswold villages of historic and architectural interest.

Outdoor Leisure

CAMPING AND CARAVANNING

Cotswold Hoburne
Static holiday caravans and 300 pitches for caravans and tents around lakes 21 and 22 of Cotswold Water Park; plenty of facilities: restaurant and bar, swimming pools, tennis, playground, angling and boating.
☎ 0285 860216

FISHING

Coarse Fishing
Good fishing in the River Ray and the Cotswold Water Park itself.

South Cerney Angling Club
Tickets and day membership available for lakes 16 and 26 Cotswold Water Park from self service kiosks at the lakeside; facilities for disabled at lake 16.

Game Fishing
For licences and permits contact the National Rivers Authority, Thames region.

Horseshoe Lake
Lake 3 Cotswold Water Park
Facilities for the disabled.
☎ 0285 861006

Manor Brook Lake
Lake 59 Cotswold Water Park
Day tickets and season tickets available at the lakeside; coarse fishing tickets also available.
☎ 0453 822286

Rainbow Lake Trout Fishing Ltd
Wildmoorway Lane, South Cerney
☎ 0285 861133

HORSE RIDING

South Cerney Riding School
Cerney Wick Farm, Cerney Wick
Hacking and tuition; accommodation available.
☎ 0793 750151

Water Sports

CANOEING

Spinerd Sailboards
Lake 10 Cotswold Water Park
☎ 0285 861555

South Cerney

SAILING

Cotswold Sailing Club
Lake 9 Cotswold Water Park, Ashton
Keynes section
Day membership available on Sundays.
☎ 0793 751551

South Cerney Sailing Club
Lake 16 Cotswold Water Park, Ashton
Keynes section
Temporary 10-day membership available
from the clubhouse.
☎ 0285 860062

Whitefriars Sailing Club
Lake 26 Cotswold Water Park, Ashton
Keynes section
Day membership available for boat
owners at weekends.
☎ 0285 861670

JET-SKIING

Cotswold Jet Ski Club
Lake 11 Cotswold Water Park
Jet-ski hire by the half hour, equipment
and tuition included.
☎ 0285 861345

WINDSURFING

Spinerd Sailboards
Lake 10 Cotswold Water Park
Day membership for board owners, hire
of boards and canoes, tuition. Shop,
angling day tickets, picnicking and
swimming.
☎ 0285 861555

Cranham

Cranham is surrounded by magnificent beech woods covering the steep hillsides
where Henry VIII and Anne Boleyn hunted during a stay at Gloucester in 1535. They
were entertained by the Bishop of Gloucester at the nearby 14th century abbey which
has had a modern abbey built upon its foundations by Benedictine monks who moved
here from Caldy Island in 1928. The Abbey pottery and gardens are open to the public
but only male visitors may visit the monastery itself.

Outdoor Leisure

WALKING AND RAMBLING

Barrow Wake Viewpoint
Off the Birdlip bypass
Extensive views over the Vale of
Gloucester.
☎ 0452 425675

Special Interests

ARTS AND CRAFTS

Prinknash Abbey and Pottery
Pottery set in ground of modern
Benedictine abbey built on the site of a
shooting lodge of Henry VIII; tours, shop,
refreshments and children's play area.
☎ 0452 812239

GARDENS

Miserden Park Gardens
Miserden
Spring bulbs, rose garden and perennial
borders; woodland trail.
☎ 0285 82303

HISTORIC BUILDINGS

Elkstone Church
Elkstone
12th century Norman church with an
unusual tympanum and chancel arch
and a first floor dovecote.

NATURAL HISTORY

Prinknash Bird Park
Prinknash Abbey
Collection of birds and waterfowl, deer,
pygmy goats and a trout pool in 9 acres of
parkland and lakes.
☎ 0452 812727

Prinknash Abbey

Cropredy

Cropredy, tucked away in North Oxfordshire, was the site of a famous Royalist victory in June 1644 – helmets, bayonets, cannonballs and other battle relics are on display in the church. The area with its grassy meadows, cornfields, ancient hedgerows, quiet streams and clumped trees gives little indication of its turbulent past and, despite its strategic commercial location, it remains very rural. Cropredy lies beside the River Cherwell and the Oxford Canal both of which offer good fishing and pleasant water-side walks as well as opportunities for a quiet day's fishing or boating. North Oxfordshire life in Victorian times is depicted in a museum nearby and, for the more energetic explorer, the Oxfordshire cycleway passes this way.

i Country Crafts
The Green
☎ 0295 758203

Adventure Sports

SHOOTING

Cropredy Gun Club
Clay pigeon shoot every Sunday.
☎ 0327 61051

Outdoor Leisure

CYCLING

Oxfordshire Cycleway
Circular route around Oxfordshire.

FISHING

Coarse Fishing
Fishing in the River Cherwell and Oxford Canal. For details contact the National Rivers Authority.
☎ 0865 749400

MUSEUMS

Edge Hill Battle Museum
Farnborough
Arms, armour, costumes and models.
☎ 029 589 593

Granary Museum
Butlin Farm, Claydon
Housed in farm buildings; the museum illustrates life in North Oxfordshire in Victorian times.
☎ 029 589 258

Water Sports

CANOEING

Banbury and District Canoe Club
Meet at Cropredy Bridge Club House.
Contact W Weir for details.
☎ 0295 710962

Deddington was once an important market town as reflected by its large central square, town hall, period houses and imposing church. It is now home to the British Microlight Aircraft Association, the governing body of microlight flying, an exciting and popular sport. Nearby is a boat hire centre which offers an ideal way of discovering the beauty of the Oxfordshire countryside – via its waterways and rivers, discovering the secrets of its backwaters.

Adventure Sports

SHOOTING

Deddington and District Rifle and Revolver Club
For details contact M Powell.
☎ 0295 810571

Aerial Sports

MICROLIGHT FLYING

British Microlight Aircraft Association
Bullring
The governing body of the sport, they can be contacted for infomation about the sport and locations offering instruction and microlight flying facilities.
☎ 0869 38888

Outdoor Leisure

CYCLING

Banbury Star Cyclists Club
For details of weekly events contact P Broadgate.
☎ 0869 38535

TENNIS

Lawn Tennis and Squash Club
Meadow View, Adderbury
☎ 0295 810877/55403

Special Interests

HERITAGE

Deddington Castle
Mediaveal castle, now a grassy mound.

HISTORIC HOUSES

Leadenporch House
14th century house where Sir Thomas Pope, founder of Trinity College, Oxford, was born in 1534.

Water Sports

BOAT HIRE

Anglo Welsh
Aynho
Holiday launches and cruisers.
☎ 0869 38483

Didcot is a fairly modern town that expanded with the coming of Brunel's Great Western Railway (GWR) and it is the Railway Centre on the site of the GWR's main steam locomotive depot, beside the railway station, that is the town's main attraction. It has a splendid collection of engines and rolling stock of all kinds covering over 100 years of railway history, it has a regular programme of steam days and a re-created period station to greet the visitor.

   The town has a wide selection of leisure facilities – you can play golf, go riding or fishing, play tennis, badminton or squash, swim, join a cycling club or take a narrowboat cruise on the river.

Adventure Sports

CLIMBING

Didcot Leisure Centre
Climbing wall.
☎ 0235 811250

Indoor Sports

BADMINTON

Didcot Leisure Centre
Four badminton courts.
☎ 0235 811250

LEISURE CENTRES

Didcot Leisure Centre
Mereland Road
Sports hall, conditioning, table tennis
and bar.
☎ 0235 811250

SQUASH

Didcot Leisure Centre
Four courts, coaching for beginners and
improvers.
☎ 0235 811250

Outdoor Leisure

CYCLING

Cycling CTC
☎ 0235 814359

Phoenix Cycling
☎ 0235 813571

FISHING

Coarse Fishing
Fishing for usual coarse fish. Contact the
National Rivers Authority for details.
☎ 0865 749400

Didcot Angling Centre
For details about licences and locations.
☎ 0235 817005

GOLF

Haddow Hill Golf Club ⛳
☎ 0235 510410

HORSE RIDING

**Blewbury Riding and Training Centre
Ltd**
Basselsway, Blewbury
General instruction, and show centre.
☎ 0235 851016

TENNIS

Didcot Lawn Tennis
☎ 0235 812032

Special Interests

FESTIVALS AND FAIRS

October
Didcot Festival – amateur productions,
music, jazz and folk for one week.
☎ 0235 811250

MUSEUMS

Champs Chapel Museum
Chapel Square, East Hendred
Displays of local interest in a 15th
century chapel.
☎ 0235 833312

RAILWAYS

Didcot Railway Centre
Great Western Society Ltd
Recreation of the golden age of the Great
Western Railway; restored locomotives,
passenger carriages and freight wagons;
reconstruction of Brunel's original broad
gauge trackwork. Regular programme of
steam days.
☎ 0235 817200

Water Sports

BOAT TRIPS

Thames Cruises
2–4 Frilsham Street, Sutton Courtenay
Trips from Radcot Bridge in a 48-seater
narrow boat.
☎ 0235 848879

SWIMMING

Didcot Pool
Newlands Avenue
Outdoor pool.

Droitwich Spa

Droitwich Spa was visited by first the Saxons and later the Romans who came here to produce salt from the water which is ten times stronger than sea water. Once a spa town popular throughout Europe it is only recently that the town's famous Brine Baths have been completely rebuilt to be opened once again to the public.

The town has a new canal marina set in parkland at its centre and a Heritage Centre documenting the town's development. There is good shopping and several interesting buildings including a church with a magnificent mosaic covering its entire interior – plenty to do and see in and around this Wychavon town.

i St Richards House, Victoria Square
☎ 0905 774312

Population 18,227

Indoor Sports

BADMINTON

Droitwich Spa Sports and Leisure Centre
☎ 0905 771212

LEISURE CENTRES

Droitwich Spa Sports and Leisure Centre
Sports hall, fitness room, outdoor facilities.
☎ 0905 771212

SQUASH

Droitwich Spa Sports and Leisure Centre
☎ 0905 771212

Outdoor Leisure

FISHING

Coarse Fishing
Droitwich Canal and River Avon.

Droitwich Tackle
27 High Street
☎ 0905 770848

GOLF

Droitwich Spa Golf & Country Club ⓖ
Westford House, Spa Lane
☎ 0905 770129

HORSE RIDING

Hunts Farm Stud and Stables
Crowle
☎ 0905 60221

TENNIS

Droitwich Lawn Tennis Club
☎ 0905 775111

WALKING AND RAMBLING

Salwarpe Valley Nature Trail
Details from the Tourist Information Centre.
☎ 0905 774312

The Wychavon Way
40-mile route from the River Severn at Holt to Winchcombe; winds through attractive countryside and villages.

Special Interests

ART GALLERIES

Ombersley Gallery
Church Terrace, Ombersley
Paintings and collectable craft.
☎ 0905 620655

FESTIVALS AND FAIRS

June
Donkey Derby – at Droitwich Lido Park.

July
Droitwich Carnival

August
Horticultural Show

GARDENS

Clacks Farm
Boreley, Ombersley
Site of a television gardening programme.
☎ 0905 620250

HISTORIC BUILDINGS

Church of the Sacred Heart
Magnificent mosaic interior of multi-coloured Venetian glass depicting the life of the 13th century St Richard of Droitwich.

St Peter's Church
14th century tower; 750-hole dovecote in nearby St Peter's Manor.

MUSEUMS

Droitwich Heritage Centre
Local history exhibits showing town's
development from Saltings to Spa town.
Exhibitions.
☎ 0905 774312

ORNAMENTAL PARKS

St Peter's Fields
Open parkland with newly established
arboretum.

THEATRES

Norbury Theatre
A varied programme of plays and
musicals.
☎ 0905 770154

Water Sports

BOAT TRIPS

Droitwich Marina
Town centre
New marina on the Droitwich canal.

SWIMMING

Droitwich Lido Park
Open-air salt water pool using natural
Droitwich brine; heated indoor pool.
☎ 0905 772006

Droitwich Spa Brine Baths
St Andrew's Road
Spa bathing pool, warm waters,
hydrotherapy.
☎ 0905 794894

GLOUCESTERSHIRE / **Dursley** / **GLOUCESTERSHIRE**

Dursley is a charming, traditional town where William Shakespeare is reputed to
have stayed. The town had borough status from 1471 until 1883 and whilst it is
now a manufacturing centre and the second largest town in the Stroud district it has
remained relatively unspoiled. Its Market House, supported by stone pillars with an
attractive bell turret, is both elegant and decorative. Alleyways nearby surprise the
strolling visitor by their secret charms, they have streams running alongside them.
There are ancient sites, historic buildings, delightful walks and various leisure
facilities to enjoy in the area nearby. This thriving town has for many years been the
home to engineering innovation as the site for Lister-Petter and Mawdsleys, major
engineering firms.

Indoor Sports

BADMINTON

Dursley Pool and Sports Centre
☎ 0453 546441

LEISURE CENTRES

Dursley Pool and Sports Centre
Castle Street and Rednock Drive
Indoor pool, squash, badminton.
☎ 0453 546441

SQUASH

Dursley Pool and Sports Centre
☎ 0453 546441

Multi-Activity Holidays

SPECIAL INTEREST CENTRES

Uley Carriage Hire
Weavers House, Uley
7-day horse-drawn caravan holidays.
☎ 0453 860288

Uley village

Outdoor Leisure

GOLF

Stinchcombe Hill Golf Club ⓝ
Visitors welcome, coaching available.
☎ 0453 543878

WALKING AND RAMBLING

Selsey Common
2 miles south-west of Stroud
Walks through woods and open
grassland; good views.

Special Interests

FARM PARKS

Selsley Herb and Goat Farm
Water Lane
4 acres with formal herb gardens, over
200 varieties of herb plants for sale; goats
and other animals.
☎ 0453 766682

FOREST PARKS

Dursley Woods
Acres of woodland criss crossed with
footpaths and bridleways.

HERITAGE

Uley Bury
1 mile north-east at Uley
Ancient hill fort.

Uley Tumulus
2 miles north-east of Dursley
Chambered long barrow, 120 feet,
known as Hetty Peglers Tump. Keys
from nearby house.

HISTORIC BUILDINGS

Woodchester Park Mansion
At the bottom of a Cotswold valley; an
unfinished masterpiece in stone. Visits
by appointment only.
☎ 0453 860531

THEATRES

Prema Arts Centre
Uley
Regular exhibitions, arts, crafts and
performance workshops.
Visiting companies at weekends.
☎ 0453 860703/860800

Water Sports

SWIMMING

Dursley Pool and Sports Centre
☎ 0453 546441

Eardisland is a pretty village on the banks of the River Arrow with many fine black-and-white Herefordshire timber-framed buildings. The village on the southern bank of the river is a haven for wildfowl and differs distinctly from the open, bright and neatly tended part of the village on the northern bank.

Outdoor Leisure

FISHING

Coarse Fishing
Fishing in the River Arrow.

Special Interests

FOOD AND DRINK

The Elms
Traditional cream and farmhouse teas.
☎ 054 47 405

HISTORIC BUILDINGS

Burton Court
14th century Great Hall with dovecotes, costume exhibitions, childrens' model fairground and pick your own fruit. Open during the season from Wednesday to Sunday.
☎ 054 47 231

Lucton Mill
Mortimer's Cross
18th century watermill last used in 1940. Open on Thursday afternoons and by appointment.

Evesham lies at the centre of the Vale of Evesham and is the bustling market town for the famous fruit and market garden produce of the area – the countryside is a beautiful sight during the blossom time in spring. The town has a long history; the site of an 8th century abbey and a mediaeval pilgrimage place, it has a museum and many interesting buildings. There are nature reserves and wildlife parks to visit nearby and town parks and meadows lead down to the River Avon in the town centre where the marina offers a wide range of water sports options from windsurfing to narrow boat hire.

i Almonry Museum
Abbey Gate
☎ 0386 44 6944

Market days Tuesday to Saturday
Early closing Wednesday
Population 15,123

Indoor Sports

LEISURE CENTRES

Evesham Sports Complex
Davies Road
Four pools, sauna, solarium, weight training, pools, squash and badminton.
☎ 0386 47542

SQUASH

Evesham Rowing Club
☎ 0386 446131

Outdoor Leisure

CAMPING AND CARAVANNING

Leedons Park Broadway
Childswickham Road
Touring and camping pitches; modern and comprehensive facilities; cafe, restaurant and childrens play area.
☎ 0386 852423

Ranch Caravan Park Holiday Centre
Honeybourne
Established family run park with outdoor swimming pool, laundry, licensed club and shop.
☎ 0386 830744

Small Moors Holiday Park
Anchor Lane, Harvington
Quiet site near the River Avon.
☎ 0386 870446

FISHING

Coarse Fishing
Fishing in the Avon for perch, carp, roach and bream; a stretch of the river at Evesham is reserved for the disabled.

Game Fishing
Trout fishing at lakes in the area.

Black Monk Trout Lakes
Lenchwick
Two spring-fed lakes stocked with trout set in 10 acres.
☎ 0386 870180

GOLF

Evesham Golf Club ♿
Craycombe Links, Fladbury Cross
Visitors with a handicap or members of another club welcome during the week.
☎ 0386 860395

HORSE RIDING

Mayfield Riding School
South Littleton
Hacks, road work, bridleways; private and group lessons, training, livery service and riding holidays.
☎ 0386 830207

Merrybrook Equestrian Centre
Haselor Lane, Evesham
Hacking, indoor schooling; cross country course.
☎ 0386 860830

The Riding Stables
Clarks Hill, Hampton
Livery service; hacks up to a full day; beginners lessons; horse transport.
☎ 0386 443385

TENNIS

Ashton-Under-Hill Tennis Club
Conker Corner, Cornfield Way, Ashton-Under-Hill
☎ 0386 881848

Evesham Rowing Club
Abbey Park
☎ 0386 446131

WALKING AND RAMBLING

Cleeve Hill
Footpath from South Littleton to Marlcliff, along the ridge-top overlooking the River Avon.
☎ 0386 44 6944

Special Interests

ARTS AND CRAFTS

Annard Woollen Mill
Handgate Farm, Church Lench
Working woollen mill and mill workshop; farm animals.
☎ 0386 870270

River Avon at Evesham

FESTIVALS AND FAIRS

May
Lions Raft Regatta on the River Avon.

June
Vale of Evesham Show
Countrywise Craft Fair at Crown
Meadow.

August
Flower Show at the Public Hall.

HISTORIC BUILDINGS

The Bell Tower
Magnificent 110-foot tower, the remains
of Evesham's Benedictine monastery
founded in 714 and once rich and
powerful; destroyed during the
dissolution.

The Fleece Inn
Bretforton
Traditional mediaeval pub; little
changed 17th century interior. National
Trust.

Tythe Barn
Middle Littleton
14th century, 40-foot long barn.
National Trust.

MUSEUMS

Almonry Museum
Abbey Gate
Local Romano-British, Anglo-Saxon,
mediaeval and monastic remains.
☎ 0386 446944

NATURAL HISTORY

Cleeve Prior Nature Reserve
Cleeve Prior
Areas of scrub grassland and limestone
above the River Avon on a steep wooded
bank.

Windmill Hill Nature Reserve
$2^1/_2$ miles north-east of Evesham off the
B4510
15 acres of limestone grassland with
views across the Avon Valley. Contact
the Worcestershire Nature Conservancy
Trust.
☎ 0905 773031

ORNAMENTAL PARKS

Abbey Gardens
Municipal park and gardens, tennis
courts and children's play area.

Crown Meadows
Riverside meadow and tree-lined
avenue.

Workman Gardens
Ornamental garden and lime avenue
beside the river.

THEATRES

Evesham Arts Centre
Victoria Avenue
300-seat theatre, music, drama, dance
and musicals.
☎ 0386 442589

WILDLIFE PARKS

The Domestic Fowl Trust
Honeybourne Pastures, Honeybourne
All old pure breeds of hens, ducks, geese
and turkeys displayed in 10 acres of
breeding paddocks; children's farm and
adventure playground.
☎ 0386 833083

Twyford Country Centre
Twyford Farm
Wildlife and falconry centre; crafts
centre with workshops, garden centre,
miniature railway and fishing.
☎ 0386 446108

Water Sports

BOAT HIRE

Evesham Marina
Town centre
Rowing boats and narrow boats for hire.

Fenmatch Ltd
Evesham Marina, Kings Road
1-2 week boat hire for holidays along
the River Avon; narrow boats ranging
from 2 to 12 berths.
☎ 0386 47813

ROWING

Evesham Rowing Club
Abbey Park
Competitive rowing section; squash and
tennis courts, cricket and snooker
teams; coaching available for all sports,
large clubhouse with bars and lounge.
Open to all ages.
☎ 0386 446131

WINDSURFING

Evesham Windsurfing Ltd
Stratford Road, Norton
☎ 0527 852883

Fairford is a pretty village in eastern Gloucestershire renowned for the unique set of 28 stained glass windows that can be found in its splendid perpendicular-style 'wool' church. The windows date from the 15th century and tell the story of the Bible. To the rear of the High Street are the open meadows on the banks of the Rivers Coln and Croft. They give the village an appealing sense of spaciousness and both are good fishing rivers.

West window, Fairford church

Outdoor Leisure

FISHING

Coarse Fishing
Fishing in the Rivers Coln and Croft. For information and permits contact the National Rivers Authority.
☎ 021 711 2324

Special Interests

HISTORIC BUILDINGS

Fairford Church
Perpendicular church built in the late 15th century by John Tame. Famous for its complete set of stained glass windows.

Faringdon, a rural town in south-west Oxfordshire, has an interesting history. Evidence exists of the inhabitance of Prehistoric man, the Romans, Saxons, Vikings and Normans and, during the Civil War, this was a Royalist stronghold. There are many fine inns dating from the era when this was an important stop on the coaching route. There is plenty to see both in and around the town – nearby you will find the oldest bridge to span the Thames, one of the largest tithe barns in the country and the home of William Morris, a key figure in the Pre-Raphaelite Brotherhood – just a few of the delights of this area.

i ✳ The Pump House
5 Market Place
☎ 0367 242191
Population 4730

Indoor Sports

LEISURE CENTRES

Faringdon Leisure Centre
Fernham Road
Large sports hall, squash courts, roller skating, fitness room, sauna and sunbed, lounge bar and social area.
☎ 0367 241755

SQUASH

Faringdon Leisure Centre
☎ 0367 241755

Outdoor Leisure

FISHING

Coarse Fishing
Fishing along the Thames and its tributaries.

Turner's Tackle & Bait
☎ 0367 241044

Game Fishing
Local fly-fishing ponds and lakes, for details contact the Tourist Information Centre.
☎ 0367 242191

HORSE RIDING

Oakfield Riding School
Oakfield, Great Coxwell
Specialise in child tuition, novice adults and hacking.
☎ 0367 240126

WALKING AND RAMBLING

Circular Walks
Leaflets available from Oxfordshire County Council.
☎ 0865 810226

Faringdon Town Trail
4-mile trail; contact the Tourist Information Centre for a leaflet.
☎ 0367 242191

Folly Hill
$\frac{1}{2}$-mile walk from the town centre, beautiful views from what was once a Celtic camp.

Special Interests

FESTIVALS & FAIRS

May
Mediaeval Fayre on Bank Holiday Monday.

July
Cheese Rolling – rolling cheeses down White Horse Hill.

HERITAGE

Radcot Bridge
North of Faringdon
Oldest bridge to span the Thames; Prince Rupert won a battle here in the Civil War.

HISTORIC BUILDINGS

Church of All Saints
Late 12th century, with Norman features, scrolled ironwork and brasses.

Folly Tower
Built by Lord Berners in 1935, 140 feet high with marvellous views.

Great Coxwell Barn
2 miles south off the A420
Monastic stone barn built by the Cistercians in the 13th century, one of the largest tithe barns in the country. National Trust.

HISTORIC HOUSES

Buscot Park
Off the A417
1780 Adam-style house, home of the Faringdon collection of paintings and furniture set in landscaped park with extensive water gardens. National Trust.
☎ 0367 240786

Kelmscott Manor
North-west of Faringdon off the B4449
Elizabethan manor house with gardens down to the river. William Morris, 19th century artist, designer and craftsman lived there from 1871 until his death in 1896. The Pre-Raphaelite Brotherhood and Arts and Crafts Movement flourished here. Works by Morris and others in the Brotherhood including carpets, wallpapers and tapestries.
☎ 0367 52486

Water Sports

BOAT TRIPS

Thames Cruises
Radcot
Cruises in a narrow boat.
☎ 0235 848879

Frampton-on-Severn

Frampton-on-Severn lies in the Severn Vale between the River Frome and the canal. It boasts the largest village green in England – twenty acres! The village has a pretty 14th century church with an unusual two-storey porch and the green, overlooked by two beautiful houses, Frampton Court and Frampton Manor Farm, is the site of the annual elver eating contest where baby eels, for centuries regarded as a poor man's food and now a delicacy, are consumed at speed each Easter Sunday.

Special Interests

FARM PARKS

St Augustine's Farm
Arlingham
Working farm where you can walk amongst the animals and watch the cows being milked; there is also a craft shop.
☎ 0452 740277

FESTIVALS AND FAIRS

April
Elver Eating Contest – held at the village green; the aim is to eat a pound of baby eels in the shortest time.

August
Frampton Deer Roast

HISTORIC HOUSES

Frampton Court
Off the M5 at jctn 13
Georgian stately home built in 1732 with original furniture, ornamental canal and orangery. Strawberry Hill Gothic style with Dutch influence. Octagonal tower and dovecote.
☎ 0452 740267

Frampton Manor
Manor Farm
Old walled garden with special plants; 12th to 16th century house. Viewing by appointment only.
☎ 0452 740698

Frampton Court

Gloucester

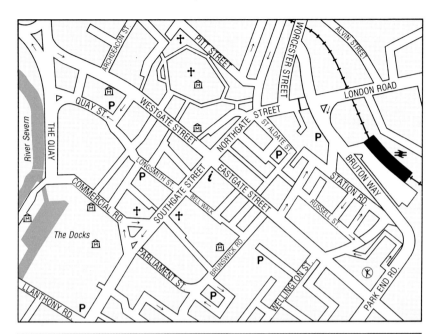

Gloucester Docks and Cathedral

Gloucester, once the site of the Roman town of Glevum, was guardian of the routes to Wales at the lowest Severn crossing point. A fortified town during the time of Alfred the Great, it had its own royal mint, and it was here that Edward the Confessor held winter court. This tradition was continued by William the Conqueror who gave the order for the commencement of the Domesday survey after the Parliament in Gloucester in 1085. The magnificent cathedral reflects all the periods of history that have passed since the Abbey Church of St Peter's was founded by the Saxons over one thousand years ago and can count the ornate tomb of the murdered King Edward II as one of its treasures. There are several interesting mediaeval buildings and many excellent museums covering fields as diverse as the history of our rivers and canals at the National Waterways Museum of packaging and advertising from the Victorian era onwards in the unique Robert Opie collection housed in a Dock warehouse.

The opening of the Gloucester and Sharpness Canal in 1827 made the city an important inland port until the early 1900s when ports such as Avonmouth overtook Gloucester in importance. The port and dock area went into a decline until the 1980s when the Victorian Docks underwent a rejuvenation; a variety of attractions are now housed within the warehouses and they are a must to visit whilst in Gloucester.

i St Michael's Tower, The Cross
☎ 0452 421188

Market days Monday, Thursday
Population 93,000

Aerial Sports

BALLOONING

ACP Nationwide
SE27 Staverton Airport
Banner towing, ballooning, blimps, activity days.
☎ 0452 857431

FLYING

Cotswold Aero Club
Staverton Airfield
Qualified instructors, choices of aircraft flying techniques. Well equipped clubhouse and lounge, briefing rooms and a club shop.
☎ 0242 36770
☎ 0452 713924 for a brochure

Staverton Airport
Gloucester and Cheltenham Joint Airport
Channel Island Service, flying schools, clubs, business and commercial flying; private and group aircraft, helicopters, hangarage.
☎ 0452 712005/713095

Indoor Sports

LEISURE CENTRES

Gloucester Leisure Centre
Burton Way
Large sports hall, wide range of sports and three pools.
☎ 0452 306498

SQUASH

Gloucester Leisure Centre
☎ 0452 306498

Gloucestershire Squash Rackets Association
Information on the association and affiliated clubs in Gloucestershire from J Row, 4 Hawk Close, Abbeydale.

Mutli-Activity Holidays

MULTI-ACTIVITY CENTRES

Gloucester Hotel and Country Club
Robinswood Hill
Situated in 220 acres of Cotswold countryside the hotel offers extensive leisure facilities including golf and swimming.
☎ 0452 25653

SPECIAL INTEREST CENTRES

Hatton Court
Upton Hill, Upton St Leonards
Occasional 'Who Done It'? weekends.
☎ 0452 617412

Outdoor Leisure

CRICKET

Gloucestershire County Cricket Club
☎ 0272 246743

FISHING

Coarse Fishing
Fishing in the River Severn at Hawbridge and Lower Lode.

Allsports
Eastgate Street
☎ 0452 22756

Gloucester United Anglers Association
☎ 0452 413972

River Severn at Wainlode
Permits available from The Red Lion,
Wainlode Hill, Norton
☎ 0452 730251

Tredworth Tackle
☎ 0452 23009

Special Interests

ANTIQUES

Gloucester Antique Centre
Gloucester Docks, Severn Road
Four floors holding 68 shops and
showcases which offer a wide variety of
antiques. Restoration department and
restaurant.
☎ 0452 29716

ART GALLERIES

**Nature in Art International Centre for
Wildlife Art**
Wallsworth Hall, Twigworth
World's first museum dedicated entirely
to the exhibition of wildlife art from all
periods, all nations and in all media.
Housed in a 1740 Georgian mansion.
☎ 0452 731422

ARTS AND CRAFTS

Gloucester Pottery
3 College Street
A comprehensive range of collectables;
porcelain, fine arts, antique maps and
prints.
☎ 0452 25792

COUNTRY PARKS

Robinswood Hill Country Park
280 acres of greenery with panoramic
views of Gloucester and across the
Malverns; plenty of wildlife, nature
trails, picnic area and a tourist
information centre.
☎ 0452 413029

FESTIVALS AND FAIRS

June
Gloucester Cricket Festival - two
County Championship games and one
Sunday league match.

July/August
Gloucester Carnival Festival - street
carnival, with floats. Various events held
in the Park over two weeks from
concerts to funfairs.

September
Barton Fair - revival of an ancient hiring
fair with fairground attractions,
handicraft stalls and an annual
procession of the Mayor of Barton.

Three Choirs Festival - famous
triennial festival held for one week.
Music concerts in Gloucester Cathedral
and many fringe events; performances by
local and national organisations.

Three Choirs Festival

FOOD AND DRINK

Double Gloucester Cheese
Old Ley Court, Churcham
Working farm where the making of
double and single Gloucestershire
cheeses can be watched.
☎ 0452 75225

HERITAGE

Bishop Hooper's Monument
St Mary's Square
In honour of Bishop Hooper who suffered
death at the hands of Mary I.

HISTORIC BUILDINGS

Blackfriars
A perfectly preserved example of a
Dominican Priory; work on restoration
is now being undertaken, revealing
important remains from later additions.

Churches
There are many fine churches in
Gloucester, for information contact the
Tourist Information Centre.
☎ 0452 421188

Gloucester Cathedral
Founded by the Saxons as St Peter's
Abbey; contains the tomb of the
murdered King Edward II.

Gloucester Cathedral

Fireworks over Gloucester Docks

Gloucester Docks
The last Victorian port, completely overhauled and now a large complex of museums and shops.

Greyfriars
Fine example of an early 16th century Franciscan Friary, ruined after the Dissolution.

Llanthony Priory – Secunda
Distinctive mediaeval building undergoing mass restoration, very important archaeological site.

St Oswalds Priory
Gloucester's oldest building, founded in 909 and dedicated to the martyr King of Northumbria. Now in ruins and within walking distance of the Cathedral.

MUSEUMS

Gloucester Cathedral Treasury
Exhibition of Anglican church plates collected from parishes throughout the diocese.
☎ 0452 28095

Gloucester City Museum and Art Gallery
Brunswick Road
Varied range of displays of local and national importance. Various 18th century luxury items; local wildlife; archaeology; British paintings.
☎ 0452 24131

Gloucester Folk Museum
99–103 Westgate Street
Museum of local history, folklore, crafts and industries. Period room settings and craft workshops.
☎ 0452 26467

The House of the Tailor of Gloucester
Beatrix Potter Centre, 9 College Court
Building behind a small shop front, built into the stone wall of the Cathedral gate chosen by Beatrix Potter for her story of the Tailor; illustrates the author's life through her memorabilia.
☎ 0452 422856

National Waterways Museum
Llanthony Warehouse, Gloucester Docks
The story of 200 years of canals, working models and exhibits, archive film, workshops and historic floating boats.
☎ 0452 307009/25524

Robert Opie Collection
Museum of Advertising and Packaging, Albert Warehouse
History of our consumer society revealed by superb collection of advertising and packaging items.
☎ 0452 302309

Regiments of Gloucester
Custom House, Gloucester Docks
300 years of regimental and social history displays, illustrating the life of soldiering through the centuries.
☎ 0452 22682

Transport Museum
Longsmith Street
Small collection of well preserved vehicles from the 19th century. Housed in a disused fire station.
☎ 0452 26467

ORNAMENTAL PARKS

The Park
32 acres of open space, walks, lawns and flowerbeds. Classic Victorian park complete with bandstand and children's play area, divided by a series of public tennis courts from the Spa area.

THEATRES

Guildhall Arts Centre
23 Eastgate Street
Performances by various groups; exhibitions, workshops, music, film.
☎ 0452 505089

The Kings Theatre
Kingsbarton Street
☎ 0452 300130

The New Olympus Theatre
Barton Street
Various forms of entertainment for all ages by visiting groups.
☎ 0452 25917

Water Sports

BOAT TRIPS

National Waterways Museum
Daily trips on the canal from June.
☎ 0452 307009

SWIMMING

Gloucester Leisure Centre
Three pools, two giant 'turbo twister' water slides.

Winter Sports

SKIING

Gloucester Ski Slope
One of the longest dry ski slopes in Britain, part of the Gloucester Hotel and Country Club complex.
☎ 0452 414300

Great Malvern is a spa town in the Malvern Hills, magnificent walking country with views towards Wales in the west and Warwickshire in the east. They are protected by the Malvern Hills Conservators who plant trees and maintain the footpaths. Famous as Elgar country the town is renowned for its music festival – major symphony concerts and operatic recitals with varied fringe events make it second only to Edinburgh – and its active Festival Theatre. It also has a varied selection of sporting and leisure activities making it an ideal touring centre.

i Winter Gardens Complex
☎ 0684 892289

Market day Friday
Early closing Wednesday

Multi-Activity Holidays

MULTI-ACTIVITY CENTRES

Montrose Hotel
Countryside discovery, heritage, arts and crafts, painting, sports and other holidays.
☎ 081 905 9556

Rainbow Action Holidays
Uphill House, Wyche Road
Malvern Hills adventure centre for the under 14s; abseiling; arts and crafts; orienteering; boating, camping, fishing, hiking, archery, animal tracking and more.
☎ 0684 567888

Outdoor Leisure

HORSE RIDING

The Avenue Riding Centre
Hanley Road
Lessons, holidays, escorted hacks.
☎ 0684 310731

TENNIS

The Manor Park Tennis Club
Albert Road North
☎ 0684 564725

WALKING AND RAMBLING

The Elgar Trail
Circular route through countryside loved by Elgar to buildings associated with him. Leaflet from the Tourist Information Centre.
☎ 0684 892289

The Ramblers Association
☎ 0684 564423

Special Interests

ART GALLERIES

Lismore Gallery
3 Edith Walk
☎ 0684 568610

Malvern Arts
43 Worcester Road
☎ 0684 575889

ARTS AND CRAFTS

The Doll's House Emporium
Gandolfi House, 211-213 Wells Road,
Malvern Wells
☎ 0684 569747

Malvern Workshop
90 Worcester Road
Ceramics, paintings, photography,
knitwear and jewellery.

FESTIVALS AND FAIRS

May/June
The English Festival and Festival Fringe
- major symphony concerts and operatic
events with varied fringe events second
only to Edinburgh.

Three Counties Countryside Show -
agricultural show at the showground.
☎ 0684 892751

September
Malvern Drama Festival at the Festival
Theatre.

FOOD AND DRINK

Stocks Vineyard
The Stocks, Suckley
Producers of English wine.
☎ 0886 884202

GARDENS

Barnards Green House
National Gardens Scheme
☎ 0684 574446

The Picton Gardens
Old Court Nurseries, Walwyn Road,
Colwall
National collection of Michaelmas
daisies in 1½-acre garden; plants for
sale.
☎ 0684 40416

HISTORIC BUILDINGS

Holy Well
Holywell Road, Malvern Wells
The Spa building where visitors can
sample the famous waters bottled at the
spring since 1622.
☎ 0684 562462

Little Malvern Court
Priors Hall and associated rooms, cells of
former Benedictine monastery;
English and European paintings.
☎ 0684 892988

Priory Church
Church Street
15th century church with fine stained
glass windows and monk stalls with
mediaeval tiles.
☎ 0684 561020

HISTORIC HOUSES

Madresfield Court
Worcester Road
Victorian house in impressive grounds;
the site of the annual show. Avenues of
trees and a maze.
☎ 0684 573614

MUSEUMS

Boehm Studios
Tanhouse Lane
Showroom and museum where
dimensional art may be viewed.
Manufacturers of fine porcelain
exhibited in 117 museums, art galleries
and institutions around the world.
☎ 0886 33333

Malvern Museum
Abbey Gateway
Features the history of Malvern, the
conservation of the hills and the life of
Elgar.
☎ 0684 567811

NATURAL HISTORY

Knapp and Paper Mill Nature Reserve
60 acres of woodland, meadow, orchard,
marsh and stream. Nature trail.

Ravenshill Woodland Reserve
Alfrick
Woodland picnic area, information and
sales centre and trails.
☎ 0886 21661

ORNAMENTAL PARKS

Priory Park
Beautiful setting below the hills; elegant
Victorian bandstand and a lake which
was once the monk's fishpool.

THEATRES

Malvern Festival Theatre
Winter Gardens Complex, Grange Road
☎ 0684 892277

WILDLIFE PARKS

Malvern Hills Animal and Bird Gardens
2 miles south of Malvern at Welland
Tropical house, pets corner and reptiles.
Visitors can handle animals.
☎ 0684 310016

Water Sports

SWIMMING

The Splash
Priory Road
Tropical pool, waterslide and
refreshments.
☎ 0684 893423

Ballooning at the Three Counties Show

HEREFORD & / Great Witley / WORCESTER

Great Witley is a small Worcestershire village with an exceptionally fine Baroque church. The richness and splendour of its interior is the result of the second Lord Foley purchasing the contents of the chapel of Canons in Edgware when it was demolished in 1747. The treasures transferred here include numerous Venetian paintings and several fine stained glass windows. There is a music programme held throughout the year at the church to which visitors are welcome. The church is joined to the ruins of what was once Witley Court.

Outdoor Leisure

HORSE RIDING

Rockmoor Stables
Rock
General tuition and hacking.
☎ 029922 556

Special Interests

GARDENS

Sankyns Green
Little Witley
Old-world cottage garden, plants for sale.
☎ 0299 896389

HISTORIC BUILDINGS

Great Witley Church
Fine Baroque church; contact the
warden.
☎ 0299 896761

Wichenford Dovecote
South-east of Great Witley at
Wichenford
17th century half-timbered dovecote.
National Trust.
☎ 0684 850051

Hagley, a large residential village, is notable for Hagley Hall, a Palladian mansion set in a 350-acre deer park. A falconry centre with a newly opened owl park is nearby.

Adventure Sports

CAVING

West Mercia Caving Club
For details contact P Weavers,
6 Wheatmill Close, Blakedown.

Indoor Sports

LEISURE CENTRES

Old Helesonians Club
Multi-purpose club with weight training and fitness facilities.
☎ 0562 883036

Outdoor Leisure

FALCONRY

The Falconry Centre
Kidderminster Road South, West Hagley
Over 120 birds including kestrels, sparrow-hawks, various falcons and 15 pairs of owls; regular flying displays.
☎ 0562 700014

GOLF

Hagley Country Golf Club ⛳
Visitors welcome on weekdays.
☎ 0562 883852

HORSE RIDING

Lea Castle Equestrian Centre
Westhead Park Road, Wolverly
Specialise in disabled work. General lessons, pony trekking, special days out; all abilities catered for. Shop, café, bar.
☎ 0562 850088

ORIENTEERING

Clent Course
Clent Hills, Clent
Map available from the Clent village shop. For details contact A Hempstead.
☎ 021 382 6168

Special Interests

COUNTRY PARKS

Clent Hills Country Park
1½ miles south-east of Hagley
Guided events and walks in 300 acres of wood and grassland.
☎ 0562 710392

HISTORIC HOUSES

Hagley Hall
Grand Palladian mansion built for the first Baron Lyttleton in the years 1754 to 1760 by Sanderson Miller; fine Rococo interior, extensive grounds, restaurant.
☎ 0562 885823

Hanbury has an interesting hilltop house and is noted for Hanbury Hall, a Queen Anne red brick house of classic proportions.

Special Interests

ARTS AND CRAFTS

The Jinney Ring Craft Centre
Old farm buildings converted to individual workshops where craftsmen can be seen working.
☎ 052784 272

HISTORIC HOUSES

Hanbury Hall
Built in 1701, a classic example of Wren architecture. Set in parkland with an orangery and ice-house.
☎ 052784 214

Hay-on-Wye is famous for having the world's largest collection of secondhand books. This small border town has many bookshops of either general or specialist interest – some shops stay open 364 days a year. The town's streets have a distinctly continental atmosphere blended with the historic buildings that recall its turbulent Welsh border past. This delightful town, siutated as it is on the Wye Valley close to the Golden Valley and Offa's Dyke, is an excellent centre for walking, fishing, camping, canoeing and cycling.

i Oxford Road
☎ 0497 820144

Adventure Sports

CAVING

Gagendor Caving Group
For details contact A Lewington,
6 Victoria Terrace, Cusop
☎ 0497 821015

Outdoor Leisure

CAMPING AND CARAVANNING

Radnors End Campsite
20 pitches, range of facilities.
☎ 0497 820780/820233

FISHING

Coarse Fishing
Excellent fishing in the River Wye for grayling, club, dace, roach and pike.

G & B Sports
19 High Street

H R Grant & Son
6 Castle Street

Game Fishing
The River Wye is one of the premier salmon fishing rivers in the country. The Monnow and its tributaries are the best trout fishing waters in the area.

River Wye Information
24-hour recorded information service about river levels and fishing conditions on the Wye.
☎ 0222 796646

Sportfish (Fly)
Lion Street

WALKING AND RAMBLING

The Offa's Dyke Path
168-mile walk along 8th century Offa's Dyke through a great variety of countryside. For twenty smaller circular walks including several based around Hay-on-Wye contact the Offa's Dyke Association.
☎ 0547 528753

Wye Valley Walk
Links Hereford, Chepstow, Hay-on-Wye and Monmouth. Outstanding views and magnificent scenery.

Special Interests

ART GALLERIES

The Kilvert Gallery
Ashbrook House, Clyro
Former home of the diarist, the Revd Francis Kilvert; it houses contemporary art: paintings, sculpture, ceramics and jewellery.
☎ 0497 820831

The Marches Gallery
Lion Street
Paintings and drawings of horses, cattle, landscapes and architecture that reflect the life of the area.
☎ 0497 821242

FESTIVALS AND FAIRS

August
Vintage Rally
Jazz in the Hay

HISTORIC HOUSES

Moccas Court
Moccas
Georgian house built by Anthony Keck, decoration designed by Robert Adam. Situated in parkland laid out by Capability Brown on the banks of the River Wye.
☎ 098 17 381

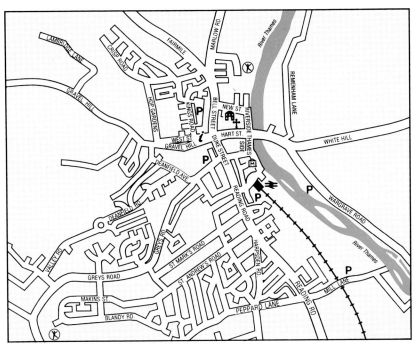

Henley-on-Thames is famous for its boating traditions. It was here that the first Oxford and Cambridge boat race was held in 1829 and since 1839 the Henley Royal Regatta has been held during the first week in July. Crews and visitors come to this event from all over the world. This very elegant Georgian riverside town lies in a beautiful location on the Thames where there has been a bridge since the 13th century. The town contains over 300 listed buildings including the Chantry House, several old inns and one of England's oldest theatres, Kenton Theatre; it is a town of delights for lovers of fine architecture.

Even though Henley is close to London it is becoming increasingly popular as a centre for short and long holidays. Henley's many diverse attractions include scope to pursue most aquatic pastimes, rowing being an obvious choice, but there are also a variety of motor launches for hire for those who wish to explore the Thames the easy way and the wide stream of the Thames at Henley allows all river users including the fishermen ample room.

i * Town Hall
Market Place
☎ 0491 578034

Market day Thursday
Early closing Wednesday
Population 12,000

Indoor Leisure

BADMINTON

Henley Badminton Club
The Indoor Sports Centre
☎ 0491 682057

LEISURE CENTRES

Henley and District Sports Centre
Gillots Lane
Sports hall and pool; facilities for the disabled.
☎ 0491 577909

Outdoor Leisure

FISHING

Coarse Fishing
Good fishing in the River Thames for the usual coarse fish.

111

The Boat Yard
Riverside
Contact M Parrott for tackle and
licences.

Thames Conservancy
Nugent House, Vastem Road, Reading
For permits to fish from the weirs.

GOLF

Badgemore Park Country Club 18
Peppard Road
No restrictions, open to visitors.
☎ 0491 574175

Henley Golf Club 18
Harpsden
Handicap certificate holders only.
Non-members from Monday to Friday.
☎ 0491 573304

Huntercombe Golf Club 18
Nuffield
Open to the public on weekdays; may
need a handicap certificate.
☎ 0491 641207

HORSE RIDING

Turville Valley Stud Riding School
Turville
Instruction for children; general
instruction; jumping and dressage.
☎ 0491 63338

TENNIS

Phyllis Court Club
Overlooking the Royal Regatta course
Temporary membership available;
facilites - putting, snooker, croquet.
☎ 0491 574366

WALKING AND RAMBLING

Riverside Walks
Details from the Chiltern Society or
the Tourist Information Centre.

ART GALLERIES

The Barry M Keene Gallery
12 Thameside
Watercolours, paintings, etchings, maps
and prints.
☎ 0491 577119

Bohun Gallery
15 Reading Road
Specialise in contemporary fine art;
paintings, original prints, jewellery,
sculpture, ceramics.
☎ 0491 576228

Luxters Fine Art Gallery
Hambledon
British contemporary painting,
sculpture and modern design furniture.
☎ 0491 63330 for appointment

Special Interests

ARTS AND CRAFTS

Henley Arts and Crafts Guild
☎ 0734 722512

Henley Exhibition Centre
Upper Market Place

FESTIVALS AND FAIRS

Swan Upping at Cookham – the beaks
of the new cygnets are marked to
identify their ownership by the Queen,
the Dyers or the Vintners, who own all
Thames swans.

June
Henley Royal Regatta – world famous
rowing festival. It starts from Temple
Island and provides five days racing.
☎ 0491 572153

July
Henley Festival of Music and the Arts
Open air concerts, soloists, art
exhibitions, music recitals and various
side entertainments throughout the
festival site during the week following
the Henley Regatta. For details contact
Henley Festival, Festival Yard, 42 Bell
Street.
☎ 0491 410414

FOOD AND DRINK

Brakspears Brewery
New Street
Established in 1779, Henley Ales are
notably fine, and available in 116 pubs
in and around the town.
☎ 0491 573636

Chiltern Valley Wines
Old Luxters Vineyard and Winery,
Hambledon
Producers of single vintage estate
bottled English wines and winner of
Best English wine of the years 1986/87.
☎ 0491 63330 for appointment

The Hambledon Brewery
Old Luxters Farm Brewhouse,
Hambledon
Producers of traditional farmhouse cask
conditioned ales.
☎ 0491 63330 for appointment

GUIDED TOURS

Country Ways
Mearfield, Crocker End Common
Horse and cart excursions, starting
from the old brick kiln, Nettlebed.
☎ 0491 641364

HISTORIC BUILDINGS

The Chantry House
Hart Street
Connected to the church by a porch;
overhanging timber-framed building,
originally built as a school for poor
boys in 1420, now the Church Hall.
☎ 0491 577340

St Mary's Church
Hart Street
16th century square chequerboard
tower, a landmark made of flint and
stone; fine monuments and good views
of the countryside from the tower.

HISTORIC HOUSES

Fawley Court
1 mile north of Henley
House built in 1684, designed by Sir
Christopher Wren and set in parkland
laid out by Capability Brown, now a
public school. Museum of Polish
memorabilia.

Greys Court
3 miles west of Henley on the A423
Jacobean manor house amongst the
ruins of a 14th century fortified house.
Tudor well-house with large donkey
wheel and an Archbishop's Maze in a
lovely garden. National Trust.
☎ 049 17 529

ORNAMENTAL PARKS

Mill Meadow Park
The Promenade
☎ 0491 576564

Water Sports

BOAT HIRE

Hobbs & Sons Ltd
Station Road
Day and weekly hire specialists;
passenger boat hire and river trips; also
boat equipment and engineering.
☎ 0491 572035

J S Hooper
Booking office near Little White Hart
during the summer.
☎ 0491 576867

Salter Bros Ltd
Folly Bridge
Passenger boats for party hire.
☎ 0865 243421

BOAT TRIPS

Salter Bros Ltd
Folly Bridge
Daily services from mid-May to mid-
September. Special packages for Henley
Royal Regatta.
☎ 0865 243421

DINGHY SAILING

Henley Sailing Club
☎ 0491 572500

PUNTING

Henley Riverside
Punts for hire from the riverside during
the summer months.

ROWING

Henley Rowing Club
Walgrave Road
Open to all, must be able to swim.
☎ 0491 573943

SWIMMING

Henley & District Sports Centre
Heated pool.
☎ 0491 577909

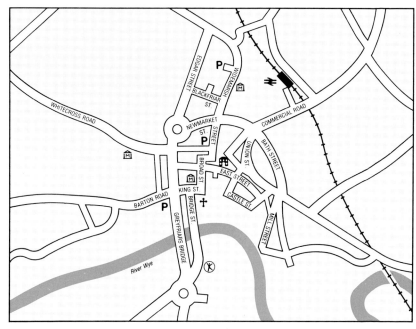

Hereford, 'City of the Marches', was once the Saxon capital of West Mercia. Steeped in history and once the military base for the English in their battles against the Welsh it was later bombarded and beseiged during the Civil War. Today it is a peaceful market town surrounded by beautiful orchards and rich pasturelands grazed by herds of the famous red-and-white Hereford cattle. Hereford's present cathedral is largely Norman but a cathedral has stood on the same site since Anglo-Saxon times. The cathedral is famous for its unique and internationally famous 13th century Mappa Mundi, a large map of the world dating from about 1290. It was recently saved from being sold to raise funds for the restoration of the cathedral. Amongst its many other treasures the cathedral houses the largest chained library in the world with books and manuscripts dating from the 8th century.

The town has much to offer the visitor, who can browse around the antique shops enjoying the historic buildings as they stroll, or visit one of the museums which offer interests ranging from cider production methods to steam railways, and when weary, can refresh themselves with a glass of the golden cider for which the region is also famous.

i St. Owens Street
☎ 0432 268430

Market days Wednesday, Saturday

Adventure Sports

CAVING

Hereford Caving Club
☎ 0544 8301

SHOOTING

Hereford Shooting School
☎ 043 271 636

Indoor Sports

BADMINTON

Herefordshire Badminton Association
☎ 0432 263693

LEISURE CENTRES

Hereford Leisure Centre
Holmer Road
Sports hall, fitness unit, multi-gym;
outdoor facilities including golf course.
☎ 0432 278178

Hereford Swimming Baths
St Martin's Avenue
Sauna, solarium, sunbed, squash, pools and cafeteria.
☎ 0432 272512

SQUASH

Herefordshire Squash Rackets Association
☎ 0432 274183

Multi-Activity Holidays

MULTI-ACTIVITY CENTRES

Acorn Activities
5A King Street
Organised activity days and breaks throughout Herefordshire. Many different hobbies and interests catered for, from watersports to Murder Mystery tours, aerial sports and crafts.
☎ 0432 357335

Western Adventure
2 Wye Terrace, Bridge Street
Activity days for all ages in climbing, abseiling, canoeing and caving; all equipment provided.
☎ 0432 279030

Outdoor Leisure

CAMPING AND CARAVANNING

Hereford Racecourse Holiday Caravan and Campsite
Roman Road
60 pitches, extensive facilities.
☎ 0432 273560

CYCLING

Coombes Cycles
94 Widemarsh Street
☎ 0432 354373

FISHING

Coarse Fishing
Excellent fishing in the River Wye; there is a fishing platform for disabled anglers in the bank of the River Wye at King George V Playing Fields.

Hattons
64 St Owens Street
☎ 0432 272317

Hereford and District Angling Association
☎ 0432 356584

Perkins of Hereford Ltd
23 Commercial Road
☎ 0432 274152

Game Fishing
The River Wye is a renowned salmon river.

Hereford Fly Fishing Club
☎ 0432 276744

FOOTBALL

Hereford United
Edgar Street
☎ 0432 276666

GOLF

Belmont House Golf Club ⛳₁₈
Belmont
☎ 0432 352666

Herefordshire Golf Club ⛳₁₈
Ravens Causeway, Wormsley
☎ 0432 71219

Hereford Municipal Golf Course ⛳₉
Holmer Road
Equipment for hire.
☎ 0432 271639

HORSE RACING

Hereford Racecourse
Roman Road
$1^1/_2$ mile oval racecourse hosting up to ten national hunt days each year.
☎ 0432 273560

HORSE RIDING

Greenbank Riding School
Marden
Lessons, hacking, jumping, cross country, stable management.
☎ 0432 72460

TENNIS

Whitecross Tennis Club
☎ 0432 357281

King George V Playing Fields
☎ 0432 268121

WALKING AND RAMBLING

Hereford Visitor Trail
Waymarked trail starting from the Tourist Information Centre, the leaflet illustrates Hereford's history.
☎ 0432 268430

Nature Trails
Leaflets from the Tourist Information Centre.
☎ 0432 268430

Special Interests

ANTIQUES

Antique Tea Shop
5A St Peters Street
Specialise in Japanese antiques.
Morning coffees and afternoon teas
served.
☎ 0432 342172

I and J L Brown
58 Commercial Road
Specialise in antique English and
French country furniture.
☎ 0432 58895

Stephen Cousins Antiques
Berrows House, Bath Street
Antique furniture restorer.
☎ 0432 268822

Edwin Waring
43 St Owen Street
19th century furniture and antiques.
☎ 0432 276241

ART GALLERIES

Hatton Gallery
Churchill Gardens Museum
Devoted to work of local artist, Brian
Hatton, killed in WWI.
☎ 0432 267409

FACTORY TOURS

Bulmers Cider
The Cider Mills, Plough Lane
Tour the famous Bulmers Cider Mills;
view all the processes of traditional cider
making; tastings.
☎ 0432 352000

FESTIVALS AND FAIRS

April/May
Riverside Fete and Regatta – racing and
fairs held on the Spring Bank Holiday.

May
St Ethelberts Fair, three day May Fair –
street carnival; annual event for 900
years.

July
Carnival Parade

August
Three Choirs Festival – hosted in
Hereford every three years for over 300
years, an international event with the
cathedral choirs of Hereford, Worcester
and Gloucester at its centre.

GARDENS

Fragrant Garden
Churchill Gardens
Raised beds of wide varieties of fragrant
shrubs and plants. Suitable for the blind
and disabled.

Redcliffe Gardens
Castle Green
Flower gardens, bandstand, 60 foot
column of Lord Nelson.

GUIDED TOURS

Hereford Guild of Guides
Details from the Tourist Information
Centre.
☎ 0432 268430

HERITAGE

Chained Library
Hereford Cathedral
Largest in the world; books and
manuscripts dating from the 8th century
onwards.

Mappa Mundi
Hereford Cathedral
Unique map of the world drawn in 1289
by an honorary canon of Hereford
Cathedral, Richard de Bello of
Haldingham. Recently had its home in
Hereford Cathedral secured after it was
put up for sale to raise funds for the
cathedral restoration.

HISTORIC BUILDINGS

Hereford Cathedral
Norman cathedral standing on the site of
Anglo-Saxon church with 13th century
Lady Chapel, 15th century College of
Vicars Choral; contains shrine of
Ethelbert, the 8th century King of the
East Angles murdered near Hereford by
King Offa of Mercia, and later canonized.
Its many treasures include the largest
chained library in the world and the
Mappa Mundi.

The Old House
High Town
1621 house, a fine example of Jacobean
architecture. Once part of Butchers Row;
now a Museum.

MUSEUMS

The Broomy Hill Engines
Herefordshire Waterworks Museum
Victorian pumping engines in 19th
century pumping station.

The Bulmer Railway Centre
Standard gauge steam railway museum,
home of the ex-GWR, 6000 'King George
V' and ex-LMS 6201 'Princess Elizabeth';
industrial locomotives and rolling stock.
☎ 0272 834430

Churchill Gardens Museum
Venns Lane, Aylestone Hill
18th and 19th century furniture,
costumes and paintings; costume
exhibition; Victorian rooms and Hatton
Gallery.
☎ 0432 267409

Cider Museum
Pamona Place, Whitecross Road
Story of traditional cider-making
through the ages.
☎ 0432 354207

Hereford City Museum and Art Gallery
Broad Street
☎ 0432 268121 extn 207

St John Mediaeval Museum
Coningsby Hospital
13th century building with exhibits of
the Ancient Order of St John and its wars
during the 300 years of the crusades.
☎ 0432 272837

THEATRES

The New Hereford Theatre
Edgar Street
☎ 0432 59252

Water Sports

CANOEING

Hereford Kayak Club
☎ 0432 275521

DIVING

Hereford Sub-Aqua Club
☎ 0432 277277

ROWING

Hereford Rowing Club
☎ 0432 273915

SWIMMING

Hereford Swimming Baths
St Martin's Avenue
Main, learner and diving pool.
☎ 0432 272512

Winter Sports

SKIING

Hereford Ski Club
☎ 0432 353209

Hook Norton can be found near the Warwickshire border, once a weaving centre now
it is known for its pottery and its family-brewed 'Hookey' ales.

Indoor Sports

LEISURE CENTRES

Hook Norton Sports and Social Club
Playing Fields, The Bourne
Various indoor and outdoor sports, all
ages welcome.

Outdoor Leisure

GOLF

Tadmarton Heath Golf Club ⛳₁₈
Wigginton
Visitors with handicap welcomed.
☎ 0608 737278

HORSE RIDING

Turpins Lodge
☎ 0608 737033

Special Interests

ARTS AND CRAFTS

Pottery and Craft Gallery
East End Farmhouse
Showrooms with hand-thrown
stoneware and other craft items.
☎ 0608 737414

FOOD AND DRINK

Hookey Ales
Family-brewed since 1849.

117

HISTORIC BUILDINGS

Church
Norman church with later additions, it has rare wall-paintings, a peal of eight ancient bells and a mediaeval font.

NATURAL HISTORY

BBONT Reserve
Reserve incorporating disused railway line; wide range of habitats.
☎ 0865 775476

Hope-under-Dinmore is a quiet village. Its church, largely rebuilt in the 19th century, has some older fitments and there is a grand monument to an infant who choked on a cherry stone in 1708. Hampton Court, built in 1434 and older than its famous London namesake, is nearby – privately owned, it is worth a glance whilst passing by. On Dinmore Hill the Queenswood country park offers wonderful riding, fishing and walking amongst its 170 acres. Dinmore Manor is a fascinating building enclosing a world of gardens and pools that will enchant and the local vineyard will provide their wines for you to sample.

Multi-Activity Holidays

SPECIAL INTEREST CENTRES

Campus Centre
Residential and day holidays for children. Outdoor pursuits including climbing; abseiling; archery; canoeing and horse riding.
☎ 0586 611412

Outdoor Leisure

FISHING

Coarse/Game Fishing
Fishing in the River Lugg.

Walking in Queenswood Country Park

Humber Brook
☎ 056 882 224

Marlbook Water
☎ 0568 3371/5942

Special Interests

COUNTRY PARKS

Queenswood Arboretum and Country Park
Dinmore Hill
170 acres with waymarked walks; 400 varieties of trees; picnic areas; exhibitions; riding and fishing facilities.
☎ 0568 84 7052

FOOD AND DRINK

Broadfield Vineyard
Broadfield Court Estate, Bodenham
Vineyards and gardens, wine tasting and light refreshments.
☎ 0568 84 483

HISTORIC HOUSES

Dinmore Manor
16th century house, 12th century chapel dedicated to Saint John of Jerusalem and cloisters; all enclosing superb lawns, rock gardens, winding pools and bridges. Headquarters of the Knights Hospitaller of Saint John of Jerusalem from 1170 until the dissolution of the monasteries 400 years later.
☎ 0432 71322

Inkberrow, a small Worcestershire village, has a pub that is thought to be 'The Bull' of Ambridge in The Archers, the radio programme about a farming community that has become so familiar to so many over the years. Ambridge is thought to be based on the nearby village of Ashton-under-Hill and Lakey Hill on Bredon Hill. The whole world of the Archers is set in this part of the heart of Worcestershire.

Outdoor Leisure

HORSE RIDING

Broadclose Farm
General tuition and hacking.
☎ 0386 792266

TENNIS

Inkberrow Tennis Club
Sands Lane
☎ 0386 792791

Special Interests

GARDENS

White Cottage Garden
2 acres of gardens; stream and bog garden; wildflower garden and nursery.
☎ 0386 792414

HISTORIC BUILDINGS

Moat Farm Dovecote
Dormston

Islip is situated at the meeting point of the Rivers Cherwell and Ray. It has a notable history being the birthplace of Edward the Confessor and was a Royalist garrison during the Civil War. It lies at the edge of Otmoor, for centuries a derelict marshland where isolated communities lived by fishing, fowling and peat cutting. From the mid-1800s drainage has reclaimed much of the area for agriculture but its central part remains remote and wild, a shelter for rare plants and insects and a delight for the naturalist. The Oxfordshire Way also passes through Islip, it provides a delightful way of discovering the countryside on foot.

Outdoor Leisure

FISHING

Coarse Fishing
Fishing in the Rivers Ray and Cherwell. For permits and information contact the National Rivers Authority.
☎ 0865 749400

WALKING AND RAMBLING

The Oxfordshire Way
Long distance footpath across Oxfordshire between Bourton-on-the-Water and Henley.

Special Interests

NATURAL HISTORY

Otmoor
East of Islip
Once derelict marshland, much of which was reclaimed in the 1800s. 6 acres remain, a habitat for rare insects and plants.

Kidderminster is the largest town in the Wyre Forest area, one of Britain's most important broadleaved woodlands, a National Nature Reserve covering 6000 acres. Once the carpet manufacturing capital of the British Empire, Kidderminster with its majestic Victorian mills and decorative chimneys is better known today for its award winning 'old' station, a recreation of the railway architecture of yesteryear and the home of the Severn Valley Railway that follows the Severn Valley for most of its route – a must for railway enthusiasts everywhere.

i Severn Valley Railway Station
Station Approach
Comberton Hill
☎ 0562 829400✳
☎ 0299 404740

Indoor Sports

LEISURE CENTRES

Wyre Forest Glades Leisure Centre
Multi-gym, leisure pool, squash courts, sunbed suite, bar and restaurant.
☎ 0562 746533

SQUASH

Wyre Forest Glades Leisure Centre
Five squash courts.
☎ 0562 746533

Outdoor Leisure

FISHING

Coarse Fishing
Fishing in the River Stour and local pools.

Hurcott Pool
Permits available from the east side of the pool.

Kidderminster and District Angling Association
☎ 0562 753471

Ladies Pool
Blakedown
Permits from Mal Storey Tackle Shop, Station Road.
☎ 0562 745221

HORSE RIDING

Acre Farm
Far Forest
☎ 0299 266434

Far Forest Stables
Far Forest
BHS approved.
☎ 0299 266438

Lea Castle Equestrian
Lea Castle, Wolverly
☎ 0562 850088

Sokum Livery Stables
Blakefall, Wolverly
☎ 0562 850009

West Midlands Equitation Centre
Debdale Farm, Cookley
☎ 0562 850662

Special Interests

GARDENS

Stone House Cottage Gardens
2 miles north-east at Stone
Walled garden with towers, many unusual wall shrubs, climbers and herbaceous plants. Adjacent to a retail nursery.
☎ 0562 69902

GUIDED TOURS

County Museum and Stone House Cottage Gardens
☎ 0299 250416/250560

Royal Doulton Crystal and Harvington Hall
Tour of the Royal Doulton Crystal factory to see the centuries-old process of handmade lead crystal manufacture, then lunch at Harvington Hall with a tour of the hall.
☎ 0384 440442

HISTORIC BUILDINGS

St George's Church
Radford Avenue
A 'Waterloo' church, built in 1822 as a thanks offering for the victory at Waterloo. Interior refurbished by Sir Gilbert Scott; an acknowledged masterpiece.
☎ 0562 66717

120

St Mary's Parish Church
St Mary's Ringway
Grade I listed building, protected for its special architectural and historic interest. Some parts of the church date back to 1315; crenellated tower; 15th century monuments; brasses.
☎ 0562 823265

HISTORIC HOUSES

Harvington Hall
Harvington
Moated Elizabethan manor with Elizabethan wall paintings and a fine collection of secret priest holes.
☎ 0562 777267

MUSEUMS

Hereford and Worcester County Museum
Hartlebury Castle, Hartlebury
The castle has been the home of the Bishops of Worcester for over 1000 years. Exhibits illustrate social life in the 19th and 20th centuries; collections of toys, costume, domestic artefacts, period rooms, furniture, horse-drawn vehicles. Picnic area, refreshments. Events through the summer.
☎ 0299 250416/250560

RAILWAYS

Severn Valley Railway
Station Approach, Comberton Hill
Fine steam railway; 16 miles; six stations; runs through magnificent riverside scenery from Bridgenorth to Kidderminster. Gala events and Santa trains.
☎ 0299 403816

THEATRES

Rose Theatre
Chester Road North, Broadwaters
181-seated modern theatre with resident amateur company – The Nonentities; visiting companies.
☎ 0562 743745

Water Sports

SWIMMING

Wyre Forest Glades Leisure Centre
Leisure pool – Mediterranean environment, palm trees, warm waves, 40 metres of flume, two slides.
☎ 0562 746533

Hartlebury, near Kidderminster

Kidlington is situated between Oxford and Banbury beside the canal and the River Cherwell. It is a Garden City built in the 1930s around an old greystone village and although a seemingly modern town in appearance it retains reminders of its ancient settlement in two 16th century houses and the 13th century church noted for its soaring spire, stained glass and rood screen.

The town is primarily residential serving Oxford as a dormitory town having good shopping centres and leisure facilities. It also has the Oxford Canal passing through offering towpaths to walk along, fish from or sit on watching the gaily painted narrowboats drift by.

Market days Friday, Saturday
Early closing Monday, Wednesday
Population 13,826

Aerial Sports

FLYING

Oxford Air Training School
Oxford Airport
Flying training ranging from Private Pilot's licence to advanced levels; helicopter charter.
☎ 086 75 4321

Indoor Sports

LEISURE CENTRES

Kidlington and Gosford Sports Centre
Gostard Hill
Large sports hall, squash courts, floodlit games area and swimming pool, technogym, clubs, coaching and equipment hire.
☎ 086 75 6368

SQUASH

Kidlington and Gosford Sports Centre
☎ 086 75 6368

Outdoor Leisure

FISHING

Coarse Fishing
Fishing in the River Cherwell and the Oxford Canal. For details and permits contact the National Rivers Authority.
☎ 0865 749400

GOLF

North Oxford Golf Club ⛳
South of Kidlington off the A423
☎ 0865 53977

Special Interests

HISTORIC BUILDINGS

Church
13th century in part with a soaring spire, mediaeval glass, tub font and wall paintings.

Water Sports

INLAND WATERWAYS

Oxford Canal
90-mile inland waterway between Oxford and Coventry; narrow-boat cruising, sailing and fishing; walking along the towpath. For information contact the British Waterways Board.
☎ 0923 226422

Oxford Canal

SWIMMING

Kidlington and Gosford Sports Centre
☎ 086 75 6368

Kingston Bagpuize

Kingston Bagpuize is south-west of Oxford and is notable for Kingston House, a superb Charles II manor house with interesting gardens. Nearby is Pusey House Gardens, a manor given to William Pewse by King Canute and now the site of an exceptionally fine garden that is open to the public. For the sportsman there is a golf course or a water skiing club both of which welcome visitors.

Outdoor Leisure

GOLF

Frilford Heath Golf Club ⛳
Visitors with a handicap certificate welcome.
☎ 0865 390864

Special Interests

FARM PARKS

Millets Farm
2 miles east on the A415 near Frilford Large pick-your-own fruit and vegetable farm; farm shop; garden centre; pets corner; trout fishery; refreshments and picnic area.
☎ 0865 391555

GARDENS

Kingston House Garden
Large garden with flowering shrubs, bulbs, herbaceous borders and fine trees.
☎ 0865 820259

HISTORIC HOUSES

Kingston House
Beautiful Charles II manor house with panelling and a magnificent cantilevered staircase; fine furniture and pictures.
☎ 0865 820259

Water Sports

WATER SKIING

Standlake Barefoot Ski Club
Aston Road, Standlake
Slalom, jump and barefoot; visitors welcome.
☎ 0865 300621

Pusey House, near Kingston Bagpuize

Kington, a maze of narrow streets between the bridge over the River Arrow and the church, dates from Saxon times and possibly earlier. It is marvellous walking and touring country, the hills of Bradnor and Hergest Ridge rise to 1400 feet on either side of the town; magnificent open countryside with breathtaking views and an excellent stretch of the Offa's Dyke footpath runs nearby. A large stone known as the Whetstone is to be found near the summit of Hergest Ridge. It is believed to have been a trading stone used in the 14th century when, because of fear of the Plague, farms would place their wheat on the stone and retreat while buyers approached to test it.

Kington Golf Course at 1284 feet is the highest 18 hole course in the country affording panoramic views and nearby are the Hergest Croft Gardens.

i Mill Street
☎ 0544 230202
☎ 0544 230778✳

Population 2123

Multi-Activity Holidays

MULTI-ACTIVITY CENTRES

Cantry Village Weekend Breaks
Cruck House, Eardisley
Walks, talks, crafts, history and entertainment, bed and breakfast or all meals.
☎ 054 46 529

Outdoor Leisure

FISHING

Game Fishing
Trout are preserved in the Rivers Arrow and Trothy. Contact the Regional Rivers Division.
☎ 0222 770088

GOLF

Kington Golf Course
Bradnor Hill
The highest 18 hole course in England and Wales.
☎ 0544 230340

WALKING AND RAMBLING

The Offa's Dyke Path
168-mile walk along the 8th century dyke that follows the Welsh border. Good views of the Dyke at Kington. For shorter walks and information contact the Offa's Dyke Association.
☎ 0547 528753

Special Interests

ART GALLERIES

Brobury House Gallery
Brobury
Gallery houses over 100,000 antique prints and a collection of old and contemporary watercolours, all for sale.
☎ 09817 229

FESTIVALS AND FAIRS

June
Kington Festival
Kington Eisteddfod – Vale of Arrow Choir and district Operatic Society

September
Kington Horse and Agricultural Show

GARDENS

Brobury House Gardens
Brobury
7 acres of semi-formal gardens on the banks of the Wye; gallery.
☎ 09817 229

Hergest Croft Gardens
Wide variety of rare plants, shrubs and trees set in the grounds of an Edwardian house; old fashioned kitchen garden and hidden valley. Plants for sale and home-made teas available.
☎ 0544 230160

HISTORIC HOUSES

Cwmmau Farmhouse
Brilley
Early 17th century half-timbered farmhouse. National Trust.

MUSEUMS

Kington Museum
Displays of local finds; exhibitions.

Ledbury is an attractive market town, south-west of the Malvern Hills and equidistant from Hereford, Worcester and Gloucester. It has several historic half-timbered buildings including a magnificent Market Hall which stands on sixteen chestnut pillars and, a short walk away, up a delightful lane is a delightful church. The poet John Masefield was born here and his work displays the influence of his Herefordshire roots. It was also a favourite place of the poets Wordsworth and Browning. Ledbury offers both interest and atmosphere to the visitor and nearby is Eastnor Castle, a flamboyant 19th century folly set in an extensive deer park.

i Church Lane
☎ 0531 6147

Market day Thursday
Early closing Wednesday
Population 6000

Indoor Sports

SQUASH

Feathers Hotel
High Street
Contact D Elliston.
☎ 0531 2600

Outdoor Leisure

FISHING

Coarse Fishing
For information contact F Allsop, the local angling representative.
☎ 0531 2768

TENNIS

Ledbury Lawn Tennis Club
Gloucester Road
☎ 0684 40047

WALKING AND RAMBLING

Circular Trails
Details of these and various other interesting walks are available from the Tourist Information Centre.
☎ 0531 6147

Special Interests

ANTIQUES

John Nash Antiques
1st Floor, Tudor House, 17C High Street
☎ 0531 5714

York House Antiques
155 The Homend
☎ 0531 4687

ART GALLERIES

The Biddulph Gallery
21, High Street
Water colours of local landscapes.
☎ 0531 2976

Collection Gallery
The Southend
Contemporary fine arts, ceramics, glass, wood, jewellery, basketry; exhibitions held regularly.
☎ 0531 4641

Shell House Gallery
36, The Homend
Contemporary fine art; paintings and prints.
☎ 0531 2557

ARTS AND CRAFTS

Homend Pottery
205 The Homend
Quality hand-thrown and decorated terracotta for the house and garden.
☎ 0531 4571

Ledbury Craft Centre
1 High Street
Specialise in English craftwork; products for sale.
☎ 0531 4566

FESTIVALS AND FAIRS

April
Fayre and Folk Events - street festival.

August
Carnival Day - music, dancing, fun fair, shows.

Bosbury Vineyards and Gardens
The Slatch, Bosbury
9-acre English vineyard, wine for sale.
Water feature rose garden. Wine tasting
in 16th century oast house.
☎ 053186 226

HISTORIC BUILDINGS

Eastnor Castle
Mediaeval-looking castle, 200 years old;
armour, pictures, Italian furniture,
arboretum, refreshments, deer park.
☎ 0531 2302

Old Grammar School
Church Lane
Restored timber-framed building now a
Heritage Centre tracing the development
of the town.
☎ 0531 6147

MUSEUMS

Butcher Row House Museum
Church Lane
History and folk museum.
☎ 0531 2040

NATURAL HISTORY

Ledbury Naturalists Field Club
☎ 0531 2515

Water Sports

SWIMMING

Ledbury Swimming Pool
Lawnside Road
☎ 0531 2890

Church Lane

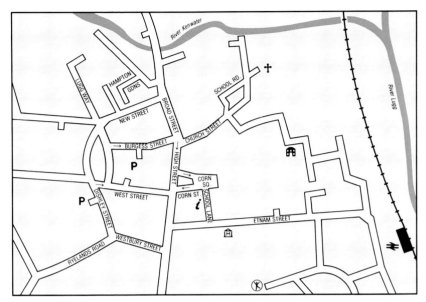

Leominster dates from the 7th century, its importance as a religious centre is reflected by the Priory Church. A great wool market of England for 500 years, the high quality of the wool brought it the name 'Lemster Ore' or gold. The prosperity of this period is seen in the fine Georgian houses that surround the mediaeval market place with its half-timbered buildings and narrow streets that follow the mediaeval grid pattern layout.

Leominster has become a noted antiques centre amongst collectors, an enjoyable town to browse around. There are several small, diverse and welcoming historic houses in the surrounding area.

i 6 School Lane
☎ 0568 6460/611100

Population 8693

Adventure Sports

SHOOTING

Leominster Gun Room
49 Etnam Street
Shotguns, country clothing, fishing tackle. Clay shooting by appointment (guns provided).
☎ 0568 5652

Indoor Sports

BADMINTON

Leominster District Leisure Centre
Coningsby Road
☎ 0568 5578

LEISURE CENTRES

Leominster District Leisure Centre
Sports hall, studio gym, weight training, squash, badminton and bar.
☎ 0568 5578

SQUASH

Leominster District Leisure Centre
☎ 0568 5578

Outdoor Leisure

FISHING

Coarse/Game Fishing
For fishing in Dinsley Brook, Ridgemore Brook, Humber Brook, Duddleston Brook and the Rivers Arrow and Trothy contact the Welsh Water Regional Rivers Division.
☎ 0222 770088

127

GOLF

Leominster Golf Club ⛳
Ford Bridge
☎ 0568 2863

HORSE RIDING

Meadow Bank Riding Centre
Hamnish
Versatile riding school; hacking
trekking, day rides, driving, side saddle,
learning how to make tack.
☎ 0568 82 267

TENNIS

Leominster Tennis Club
☎ 0568 2673

WALKING AND RAMBLING

Circular/Woodland Walks
Detailed leaflets of the many walks in
this beautiful countryside are available
from the Tourist Information Centre.
☎ 0568 6460

Special Interests

ANTIQUES

Jeffery Hammond Antiques
Shaftesbury House, 38 Broad Street
17th, 18th and early 19th century
furniture.
☎ 0568 4876

Hubbard Antiques
Bridge Street
Specialising in 17th and 18th century
period oak and country furniture.
☎ 0568 4362

ARTS AND CRAFTS

The Lower Hundred Craft Workshop
4 miles north of Leominster off the A49
Handmade candles, fabric boxes, inkle
weaving and tatting; crafts by local
craftsmen.
☎ 0584 72 240

FESTIVALS AND FAIRS

June
Leominster Festival (alternate years)

August
Leominster Agricultural Show

HISTORIC BUILDINGS

Berrington Hall
North of Leominster on the A49
Late 18th century neo-Classical house
built by Henry Holland for Thomas
Harley (Harley Street, London). Gardens
designed by Capability Brown. Full
programme of events.
☎ 0568 5721

Grange Court
Beautifully carved 17th century building
sold and re-erected on the present site in
1855. Purchased by Leominster District
Council in 1938/9 to prevent its
shipment to America, now council
offices.

Priory Church
A nunnery in the 7th century, rebuilt as
a monastery in the 11th. Unique tower,
14th century chalice and England's last
used ducking stool.

MUSEUMS

Leominster District Folk Museum
Etnam Street
Local exhibits on display.
☎ 0568 5186

Littledean, a village in the Forest of Dean, commands splendid views across the Severn River. There is evidence of Roman roads that once served the nearby iron mines. The 14th century church has some interesting carvings and Littledean Hall has ancient forest trees, a Roman temple and Saxon remains to investigate.

Outdoor Leisure

HORSE RIDING

Littledean Trekking Centre
Wellington Farm, Sutton Road
Horseriding in the Forest of Dean;
beginners welcome. Trekking holidays
for children.
☎ 0594 823955

WALKING AND RAMBLING

Blaize Bailey
Great scenic views from high ridge east
of the Forest.

Special Interests

HISTORIC HOUSES

Littledean Hall
Hall claimed to be the oldest
continuously inhabited house in Britain,
also claimed to be haunted; Saxon
cellars; 50 acres of grounds with water
gardens and Roman remains.
☎ 0594 824213

Long Hanborough lies in the Evenlode Valley west of Oxford. It is home to a newly opened Bus Museum that is being developed and a restored steam engine, water wheel and working forge nearby holds steam days with link-ups to the museum.

Outdoor Leisure

FISHING

Coarse Fishing
For fishing in the River Evenlode contact
the National Rivers Authority.
☎ 0865 749400

Special Interests

HISTORIC BUILDINGS

Church of St Lawrence
West at Combe
14th century church, largely unrestored
with remnants of a 15th century wall
painting.

Combe Mill
On the River Evenlode at Combe
Restored, working 19th century beam
engine on the Blenheim estates sawmill;
steam days in the summer.

MUSEUM

Oxford Bus Museum Trust
BR Station Goods Yard
Over 40 vehicles from Oxford horse
trams to 1960s buses; some
roadworthy, some being restored.
☎ 0867 74080

Lydney can be found on the south-east border of the Forest of Dean. It is possible to take a training course in caving, abseiling, canoeing and survival or take a trip around the Forest by horse, on foot, with a local guide or try the remaining 4-mile stretch of a steam railway network that once served the whole Forest.

Adventure Sports

CAVING

Marches Caving Club
☎ 0594 841038

Wye Pursuits
Carpenters Farm, Woolaston
Training courses or days out from introductory to advanced level.
☎ 0594 52782

CLIMBING

Wye Pursuits
Climbing and abseiling courses catering for a wide range of abilities.
☎ 0594 52782

Multi-Activity Holidays

MULTI-ACTIVITY CENTRES

Wye Pursuits
Residential training courses in canoeing, caving, climbing, orienteering and survival throughout the Forest of Dean area.
☎ 0594 52782

Outdoor Leisure

CYCLING

Riders of Lydney
17 High Street
Cycle hire in the Forest of Dean; local accommodation arranged.
☎ 0594 841777

FISHING

Coarse Fishing
Fishing in Lydney lake and canal. Licences and permits available from Peter James Sports.
☎ 0594 842515

Lydney and District Angling Club
☎ 02912 71402

HORSE RIDING

Woodside Equestrian Centre
Woodside Farm, Woolaston
Hacks, day rides and jumping lessons.
☎ 0594 52454

ORIENTEERING

Wye Pursuits
Survival and overnight bivouac.
☎ 0594 52782

Special Interests

GARDENS

Lydney Park Gardens
Extensive woodland garden and deer park; Roman temple site and museum.
☎ 0594 842844

GUIDED TOURS

Royal Forest of Dean and Wye Valley Educational Tours
Highclere, High View Way, Bream
Packaged education tours of the Forest.

MUSEUMS

Dean Forest Railway
Norchard Steam Centre
Large collection of steam and diesel locomotives; signs and signals on display in museum. Steam rides.
☎ 0594 843423

Lydney Park Museum
West of Lydney on the A48
Display of Roman items excavated from the Lydney Park Roman temple.
☎ 0594 842844

Water Sports

CANOEING

Wye Pursuits
Canoe days out; canoe/camping trails; BCU training courses arranged.
☎ 0594 52782

130

Mapledurham

Mapledurham is situated right on the River Thames, a quiet hamlet set in woods amongst rolling hills. A small cluster of red-brick almshouses surround the superb Elizabethan mansion in which Elizabeth I was entertained. An ancient watermill and weir make this a delightful spot to stop and take a picnic in the riverside park.

Special Interests

HISTORIC BUILDINGS

Mapledurham Watermill
Restored 15th century mill with original machinery and mill stones, one of last working examples of the many mills that once lined the river.
☎ 0734 723350

St Margaret's Church
Small church with remarkable tomb of Richard Blount and his wife.

HISTORIC HOUSES

Mapledurham House
Elizabethan mansion, the Blount family home since it was built; paintings; moulded plasterwork; family chapel; riverside picnic park.
☎ 0734 723350

Minchinhampton

Minchinhampton, originally Nun's Hampton, was named after the nuns of Caen who lived there in Norman times. A perfect example of a small Cotswold town it has a fine 17th century Market House standing on a series of pillars.

Aerial Sports

GLIDING

Cotswolds Gliding Club
Aston Down Airfield
☎ 0285 76473

GOLF

Minchinhampton Common Old Course ⁱ⁸
Open to visitors, tuition available.
☎ 0453 83 2642

Minchinhampton Golf Club New Course ⁱ⁸
Visitors with handicaps or members of other clubs welcome.
☎ 0453 83 3866

Outdoor Leisure

FESTIVALS AND FAIRS

August
Gatcombe Horse Trials - at Gatcombe Park.

Special Interests

GUIDED TOURS

Pathfinder Tours
Stag House, Gydynap Lane, Inchbrook, Woodchester
Special train excursions touring the countryside; executive trains with full dining service. Pick-ups at Cheltenham and Worcester.
☎ 0453 83 5414

Minchinhampton Common

131

HERITAGE

Minchinhampton Bulwarks
Minchinhampton Common
Remains of ancient earthworks.
National Trust.

HISTORIC BUILDINGS

Market House
Market House for wool originating from
1698; connections with Sarah Siddons.
By appointment only.
☎ 0453 883241

Special Interests

NATURAL HISTORY

**Rodborough and Minchinhampton
Commons**
High, open grassland and woods; wide
variety of birds and other wildlife;
interesting flowers and archaeological
sites. National Trust.

Moreton-in-Marsh is a small Cotswold town that straddles the Roman Fosse Way. Its
high street is flanked by attractive stone houses and inns. The town has an
interesting Curfew tower complete with its bell and there are two notable historic
houses nearby, one of which was the inspiration for Brighton Pavilion. The
exceptionally lovely Batsford Park is north-west of the town – 50 acres of rare and
common trees.

Special Interests

ANTIQUES

Anthony Sampson
Dale House, High Street
☎ 0608 50763

ARTS AND CRAFTS

Evenlode Pottery
Evenlode
'Slipware' pottery (decorated with liquid
clay); visitors welcome to see potter at
work.
☎ 0608 50804

COUNTRY PARKS

Batsford Park Arboretum
1¹/₂ miles north-west at Batsford
50 acres of gardens with over 1200
species of rare and common trees; views
of the Vale of Evenlode; seasonal
flowering plants, refreshments.
☎ 0608 50722
☎ 0386 700409 (weekends)

GARDENS

Sezincote Garden
Sezincote
Oriental water garden with mature trees
surrounding the Indian-style house.
☎ 0386 700444

Batsford Park

HERITAGE

Curfew Tower
16th century tower in which the 17th
century curfew bell still hangs.

Four Shires Stone
1¹/₂ miles east of the town
18th century monument inscribed with
the names of the four counties that meet
here.

HISTORIC HOUSES

Chastleton House
South-east off the A44
Jacobean manor with fine panelling,
tapestries, furniture and embroideries;
17th century topiary garden.
☎ 060 874 355

Sezincote House
1¹/₂ miles west off the A44
Regency manor house in Indian-style,
the inspiration for the Brighton Pavilion.
☎ 0386 700444

Much Marcle is a tranquil village near the Gloucestershire border. It is the home of
good cider, Hereford beef cattle and Hellen's, a well known mansion.

Multi-Activity Holidays

MULTI-ACTIVITY CENTRES

Lower House Farm
Kempley, Dymock
Riding holidays for children, nature
trails and walks.
☎ 0531 85301

Outdoor Leisure

TENNIS

Woolhope Tennis Club
Berryfield, Woolhope
☎ 0432 860371

WALKING AND RAMBLING

Dymock Daffodil Way
8-mile circular path through the wild
daffodil countryside.
☎ 0594 36307

Poets Paths
8-mile circular path through countryside
associated with the Dymock poets.
☎ 0594 36307

Special Interests

FOOD & DRINK

Lyne Down Farm
1 mile from Much Marcle on the A449
Producers of strong ciders for
generations; tastings; cider and perry for
sale.
☎ 0531 84 691

Weston and Sons
The Bounds
Traditional cider and perry makers since
1880.
☎ 0531 84 233

HISTORIC HOUSES

Hellen's
Mansion begun in 1292, still occupied by
the descendants of the family who built
it; pictures, tapestries, furnishings,
armour and carriages. Great Hall has
stone table where Edward the Black
Prince dined.
☎ 0531 84 668

Nailsworth, inhabited since Saxon times, can be found by turning off the Stroud to Bath road. Important for its cloth mills during the 16th and 17th centuries, it remains today a thriving community and shopping centre. Many of the former mills have been converted for use by commerce or industry and one Ruskin Mill, has become a working arts and crafts centre. There is a cycle trail along the former railway track to Stonehouse that will give a quiet view of the delightful surrounding countryside.

Aerial Sports

GLIDING

Bristol and Gloucester Gliding Club
Nympsfield
Gliding tuition.
☎ 0453 860342

Outdoor Leisure

CYCLING

Cycle Trail
Signposted from the A46 and the A419
Route follows former railway track from Nailsworth to Stonehouse.

Special Interests

ARTS AND CRAFTS

Ruskin Mill
Horsley Road
Craft workshops, coffee shop and water wheel in Ruskin Mill, one of this unique set of 17th century mills standing along the valley bottoms.
☎ 0453 762571

FESTIVALS AND FAIRS

April
Nailsworth Spring Festival

Newent is a lively little town on the fringe of the Forest of Dean. It has a well-preserved 16th century timbered market hall, many 18th century houses and a mediaeval spired church. The town has a host of interesting attractions that include a museum of Victorian life, a glass workshop where the processes of blowing and fashioning glass can be seen in action; a gold and silversmiths who welcome visitors, a falconry centre where this ancient art is being revived, the birds can be seen at work in regular displays, and a butterfly park. Two local vineyards invite visitors to sample their wines, a welcome break after climbing nearby May Hill to enjoy the panoramic views from the summit.

i Newent Library
High Street
☎ 0531 822145

Early closing Wednesday
Population 5680

Outdoor Leisure

FALCONRY

The National Birds of Prey Centre
Free-flying eagles, hawks, vultures, falcons and owls; regular displays. Aviaries for nesting, breeding and rearing chicks; falconry museum; guided tours; play area; shop and coffee shop.
☎ 0531 820286

Market Hall, Newent

HORSE RIDING

Huntley School of Equitation
Wood End Farm, Huntley
Instruction in riding and jumping;
preparation for horse trials.
☎ 0452 830440

WALKING AND RAMBLING

Forest Walks
For details of the many walks, contact
the Forest of Dean Tourist Information
Centre.
☎ 0594 36307

Special Interests

ANTIQUES

The Mushrooms
10 Church Street
Curiosity shop and second hand
bookshop; antiques and collectors items.
☎ 0531 821734

ARTS AND CRAFTS

Cowdy Glass Workshop
31 Culver Street
Showroom of handmade goods, seconds
shop and gallery. Watch craftsmen
blowing and fashioning glass.
☎ 0531 821173

Newent Silver
15 Broad Street
Gold and silversmiths; designer
jewellery; craftsman Ken Knowles
welcomes visits to the studio to watch
work in progress.
☎ 0531 822055

FOOD AND DRINK

St Annes Vineyard
Wain House, Oxenhall
Wines and vines for sale; tastings.
☎ 0989 82 313

Three Choirs Vineyard
Rhyle House, Welsh House Lane
Production of English wine reviving the
ancient tradition of Gloucestershire
wine making. Casual visits and
accompanied tours. Ploughman's
lunches with wine tasting. Wines for
sale.
☎ 0531 85 223/555

MUSEUMS

The Shambles
20 Church Street
A four-storey house set out to illustrate
Victorian family life, set in gas-lit
cobbled street and square with Victorian
shops.
☎ 0531 822144

NATURAL HISTORY

Betty Daw's Nature Reserve
2 miles north of Newent
An ancient wood renowned for its
spectacular display of wild daffodils.
Many species of trees; shrubs and wild
flowers.
☎ 0453 822761

**Newent Butterfly and Natural World
Centre**
Springbank, Birches Lane
Tropical butterfly house, insect gallery,
natural history exhibition, reptile house
and aquatic display.
☎ 0531 821800

Newent Butterfly Centre

Northleach has remained almost unchanged since the Middle Ages when it was a prosperous wool trading centre. There are several interesting old buildings including the particularly fine 15th century church. Its attractions include an award winning museum of mechanical musical instruments, a collection of exhibits of rural life in the Cotswolds and a Roman Villa – an unexpected and interesting selection of places to visit.

i ✳ Cotswold Countryside Collection Museum of Rural Life
☎ 0451 60715

Special Interests

FESTIVALS & FAIRS

June
Northleach Charter Festival – morris dancing, carnival procession

July
Northleach Steam and Stationary Engine Show

HERITAGE

Chedworth Roman Villa
4th century mosaics and two bath houses are among the remains of this Romano-British villa; museum houses smaller finds and video guide to the site. Shop, picnic area in nearby woodland. National Trust.
☎ 0242 89256

HISTORIC BUILDINGS

Northleach Church
A fine Cotswold wool church, perpendicular style with a notable collection of woolmerchant's brasses.

MUSEUMS

Cotswold Countryside Collection
Cotswold rural life and tradition displayed in a House of Correction (country prison) with restored cell block and courtroom. Agricultural history exhibits, 'seasons of the year' exhibits; audio and video sequences; weekend events.
☎ 0451 60715
☎ 0285 655611

Keith Harding's World of Mechanical Music
Oak House
Award winning museum of antique clocks, musical boxes and mechanical musical instruments in an old wool merchants house; also leading restorers of clocks and musical boxes; shop.
☎ 0451 60181

Chedworth Roman Villa

Cotswold Countryside Collection

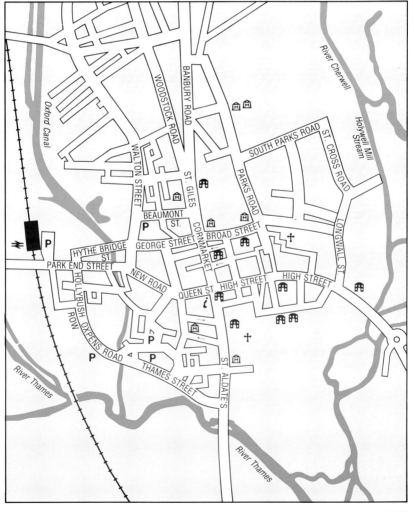

Oxford, 'city of dreaming spires', the oldest university in the world apart from the Sorbonne and perhaps the most famous seat of learning. A city of great architectural distinction there are over 600 listed buildings in the centre square mile alone. Its museums and art galleries are amongst the finest in Britain and it has one of the largest and most distinguished libraries in the world. There is an interesting challenge for the visitor to Oxford – no one building dominates the town, there is no one Cathedral or castle that will give a short-cut view of the city. All its treasures are spread throughout the city including the University which has a tangle of 35 buildings intermingling with shops and offices, entrances hidden away down narrow alleyways where cameos of Oxford's exquisite architecture might also be hiding for the unsuspecting to discover and the persevering to be rewarded. To make your sightseeing easier and to ensure you don't miss anything there are guided tours including the open-top bus tours and official two-hour walking tours but you can be sure that wherever you go in this beautiful city, guided or alone, you will find something to delight.

Oxford's appeal does not rest just in her buildings and streets or the immaculate gardens that have recently won the 'Britain in Bloom' contest, but also in her riverside location. The city stands on the River Thames, known here as the Isis, and the Cherwell, the two rivers meet below Folly Bridge providing a whole range of water-based enjoyment including excellent punting, rowing, boating and fishing that can be enjoyed amongst the willow lined banks.

i St Aldate's
☎ 0865 726871

Population 116,000

Indoor Sports

BADMINTON

Blackbird Leys Leisure Centre
Pegasus Road, Blackbird Leys
☎ 0865 777871

East Oxford Sports Centre
5 Collins Street
☎ 0865 242486

Northway Centre Gymnasium
Maltfield Road, Northway Estate
☎ 0865 742048

ICE SKATING

Oxford Ice Rink
Oxpens Road
☎ 0865 248076

LEISURE CENTRES

Douglas Bader Sports Centre
☎ 0865 53547

Blackbird Leys Leisure Centre
Sports hall, fitness room, pool, bar and refreshments.
☎ 0865 777871

East Oxford Sports Centre
Indoor and outdoor facilities.
☎ 0865 242486

Ferry Sports Centre
Pools, squash courts, spectator area.
☎ 0865 510330/310978

Northway Sports Centre
Gymnasium, playing fields, multi-gym fitness room.
☎ 0865 742048

Oxrad Centre
☎ 0865 240169

Temple Cowley Pools
Temple Road, Cowley
Fitness room with multi-gym, sauna suite, sunbed, exercise studio, pools.
☎ 0865 749449

SQUASH

Ferry Sports Centre
☎ 0865 510330/310978

Multi-Activity Holidays

SPECIAL INTEREST CENTRES

Oxford Heritage Study Visits
20 Warnborough Road
Arts, antiques and architecture.
☎ 0865 57502

Stained Glass Activities
Courses in stained glass techniques tutored by Paul San Casciani, Oxford's stained glass artist.
☎ 0865 727529

Outdoor Leisure

CAMPING AND CARAVANNING

Cassington Mill Caravan Park
Eynsham Road, Cassington
Site on banks of the River Evenlode,
fishing and permits; extensive facilities.
☎ 0865 881081

Oxford Camping International
426 Abingdon Road
Modern site with extensive facilities.
☎ 0865 246551

CRICKET

Oxfordshire County Cricket Association
For details contact the secretary,
P Salway.
☎ 0865 812738/252125

CYCLING

Cycle Touring Club
For details contact Eileen Johnson, 27
St Swithuns Road, Kennington.
☎ 0865 739997

Dentons Cycle Hire
Banbury Road
☎ 0865 53859

Pennyfarthing Cycle Hire
5 George Street
☎ 0865 249368

FISHING

Coarse Fishing
For permits and details of fishing in and
around Oxford contact the National
Rivers Authority.
☎ 0865 749400

National Federation of Anglers
For details contact D Capon, the
secretary.
☎ 0844 291863

FOOTBALL

Oxford United Football Club
Manor Ground, Headington
☎ 0865 61503

GOLF

North Oxford Golf Club
Banbury Road
☎ 0865 54415

Southfield Golf Course
Hill Top Road
☎ 0865 242158

HORSE RIDING

British Horse Society (Oxford)
Knowle Cottage, North Place, Old
Headington
☎ 0865 62813

Field Study Riding Centre
Tetworth
☎ 084 428 494

ORIENTEERING

South Central Orienteering Association
For details contact D Stubbs.
☎ 0734 65829

WALKING AND RAMBLING

Thames Path
163-mile long distance route following
the River Thames.

Towpath Walks
Thames, Isis or Oxford Canal towpath
walks.

Special Interests

ANTIQUES

The Jam Factory
Park End Street
Numerous independent dealers under
one roof covering a wide variety of
antique collections from toys to
textiles.
☎ 0865 251 075

The Oxford Antique Trading Company
☎ 0865 793927

ART GALLERIES

Christ Church Picture Gallery
Oriel Square
Fine collection of Old Master paintings
and drawing includes works by
Tintoretto, Van Dyck, Leonardo da Vinci
and Michaelangelo.

Museum of Modern Art
30 Pembroke Street
Highly acclaimed exhibitions of
international contemporary painting,
sculpture, drawing, photography film,
design, architecture; workshops and
seminars.
☎ 0865 728608

Oxford Gallery
23 High Street
Changing exhibitions of contemporary
works.

ARTS AND CRAFTS

Alice's Shop
83 St Aldate's
Sweet shop used by the real Alice of
Lewis Carroll's Adventures in
Wonderland, woven into the story and
now a gift shop.
☎ 0865 723793

Oxford Gallery Ltd
23 High Street
Contemporary British applied art and
limited edition artists' prints.
☎ 0865 242731

COUNTRY PARKS

Shotover Country Park
Headington
Shotover Plain, Brasenose and Magdalen
Woods are all included in the park;
extensive walks; panoramic views of the
Thames valley; natural sandpit with
huge boulders; orienteering course and
nature trails. For details contact the
Countryside Officer.
☎ 0865 715830

FESTIVALS AND FAIRS

February
Torpids – a bump race between rowing
crews from the colleges.

May
Eights Week – a bump race where
rowing crews from the colleges try to
catch and bump the boat ahead, the
winner of the knockout competition is
declared 'Head of the River'.
May Morning – Magdalen College
Choristers sing madrigals and carols
from the tower from 6.00am; bell ringing
and morris dancing follow to celebrate
May Day.

July
The Sheriff's Races – amateur riders
carry on a flat-racing tradition that took
place for 200 years, now held on
Wolvercote Common as a charity event.

September
St Giles Fair – Street fair with rides,
stalls and exhibits.

December
Morris Dancing – the Headington
Quarry side perform their sword dance
and mummers play.

FOOD AND DRINK

**Frank Cooper Shop and Museum of
Marmalade**
84 High Street
Frank Cooper started selling his wife's
marmalade at these premises in 1874.

Morris Dancers

Halls Oxford & West Brewery Company
Dates back to 1795 and runs 300 pubs in
the south and south-west of England.
☎ 0865 882255

Morrells Brewery
Founded in 1782 and reputedly the only
independent family-run brewery with a
history of over 200 years of continuing
production on the original site; a range of
popular beers available at 136 public
houses within a 40-mile radius of
Oxford.
☎ 0865 792013

GARDENS

Botanic Garden
High Street
Over 8000 species of plants in the garden
and greenhouses; collections of
carnivorous plants, tropical water lilies,
rose and variegated plants plus
herbaceous borders, rock and bog
gardens.
☎ 0865 276920/276921

Worcester College Gardens
Beaumont Street
Exquisite college gardens with a large
lake, spreading lawns and stately trees.
☎ 0865 278300

GUIDED TOURS

Guide Friday
Regular circular routes run by open-top
double decker bus from the railway
station and points around the city.
☎ 0865 790522

The Oxford Guild of Guides
Blue Badge Guides conduct tours from
the Tourist Information Centre. Group
and foreign language tours can be
arranged.
☎ 0865 726871

Spires and Shires Minibus Tours
Tours of Oxford, Blenheim Palace and
Oxfordshire.
☎ 0865 513998

Whites of Oxford Ltd
Chauffered tours of the Cotswolds and
Oxfordshire.
☎ 0865 61295

HISTORIC BUILDINGS

Oxford has over 600 listed buildings in
the centre square mile alone.

Oxford Colleges
Most colleges open their quadrangles
and chapels to visitors in the afternoons.
For details of the colleges and their
opening times contact the Tourist
Information Centre for their leaflet
Welcome to Oxford.
☎ 0865 726871

Carfax Tower
City centre
Remains of the 14th century city Church
of St Martin, demolished to widen the
roadway; clock on the east side has
'Quarter Boys' chiming every quarter
hour; superb views.
☎ 0865 250239

Christ Church
One of largest colleges founded in 1546
by Henry VIII; notable for its quad, Tom
Quad, the largest in Oxford; its tower,
Tom Tower, designed by Wren; its
cathedral hall and picture gallery.
☎ 0865 276172

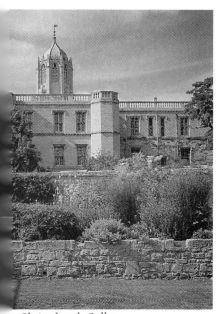
Christchurch College

Church of St Michael at the North Gate
Cornmarket Street
The Saxon tower dates from the early
11th century and is Oxford's oldest
building; church treasure displays of rare
silver and documents; mechanisms and
bells of the clock are open to view.
☎ 0865 240940

Sheldonian Theatre
Broad Street
Built in 1663, one of Sir Christopher
Wren's earliest works; used for
University ceremonies.
☎ 0865 277299

University Church of St Mary the Virgin
New College Lane
Late mediaeval church; magnificent
tower with good views; centre for
mediaeval university. Weekly academic
sermon still preached on Sundays.

St Hugh's College

MUSEUMS

Ashmolean Museum
Beaumont Street
Britain's oldest public museum, founded
in 1683, 60 years before the British
Museum. Now housed in a classical
1840s building it contains the
University's outstanding and priceless
collections including Pre-Raphaelite and
French impressionist works; major
collection of Michaelangelo drawings;
British, Roman, Egyptian and Greek
antiquities.
☎ 0865 278000

**Bate Collection of Historical
Instruments**
Faculty of Music, St Aldate's
The most comprehensive collection of
European woodwind, brass and
percussion instruments in Britain.
☎ 0865 276139

Bodleian Library
Broad Street
Founded in 1602 with six million books it is one of the world's greatest libraries; notable collection of manuscripts and early printed books. The Divinity School, off the main entrance, is noted for its exquisite fan vaulting.
☎ 0865 277000

Museum of the History of Science
Broad Street
Scientific and medical equipment, clocks, cameras and scientific apparatus.
☎ 0865 277280

Museum of Modern Art
Pembroke Street
Changing exhibitions by contemporary artists.
☎ 0865 728608

Museum of Oxford
St Aldate's
History of Oxford depicted by graphics, models and reconstructed period rooms.
☎ 0865 815559

The Oxford Story
Broad Street
Eight centuries of Oxford life depicted by audio-visual techniques.
☎ 0865 728822

Pitt Rivers Museum
Parks Road
World prehistory and ethnography; Balfour Building's collection of musical instruments.
☎ 0865 270927

University Museum
Parks Road
University's natural history collections including gemstones, fossils, dinosaurs and Alice's dodo housed in soaring Victorian-Gothic building.
☎ 0865 272950

NATURAL HISTORY

Aston Eyot
Off Iffley Road
Spacious fields rich in local wildlife and vegetation.
☎ 0865 715830

BBONT
3 Cowley Road, Rose Hill
Naturalists' Trust promoting conservation and education; owns and leases over 100 reserves.
☎ 0865 775476

Chilswell Valley
Off the A34 in South Hinksey
Steep sided gulley with varied insect life, butterflies and flowers in summer; magnificent views of Oxford.
☎ 0865 715830

Lye Valley Nature Reserve
Access off Girdlestone Road
Reed beds, fen vegetation, sedge warblers and other birdlife; walks.
☎ 0865 715830

Port Meadow
Access from Walton Well Road
Extensive urban common, meadowland leading to the River Thames, used for local grazing, unchanged for centuries.
☎ 0865 715830

Raleigh Park
North Hinksey
Meadow with pond and marsh area rich in wildflowers.
☎ 0865 715830

Rock Edge
Headington
Small disued limestone quarry, cliff face has only remaining exposure of coarse coral limestone, Coral Rag, from which many of Oxford's buildings constructed.
☎ 0865 715830

ORNAMENTAL PARKS

Bury Knowle Park
London Road, Headington
Large children's playground; also tennis, hockey and putting.

Cutteslowe Park
Banbury Road
City's largest park; facilities include play area, aviary and duck pond, model railway, putting green; provision for football, tennis, cricket and bowls; the City Council's nurseries – previous winners of Britain in Bloom, tours can be arranged.
☎ 0865 774911

Florence Park
Florence Park Road
Formal flower beds with facilities for tennis, bowls, croquet and putting.

Headington Hill Park
Headington Road
Formal park, woodland garden with over 150 specimen trees and ornamental shrubs.

Hinksey Park
Abingdon Road
Park with large lake used for fishing and windsurfing; swimming pools; boating ponds; facilities for tennis and football.

South Park
Morrell Avenue
Open park with views over Oxford's 'dreaming spires'.

142

Oxford Canal, near Oxford

THEATRES

Apollo Theatre
George Street
☎ 0865 244544

Burton Taylor Theatre
Gloucester Street
☎ 0865 798229

The Old Fire Station Arts Centre
George Street
☎ 0865 794494

Water Sports

BOAT HIRE

Boat Enquiries
Hoseasons Brochure, 43 Botley Road
Hire cruisers on the Thames and canals.
☎ 0865 727288

The Thames Hire Cruiser Association
19 Acre End Street, Eynsham
20 members and 500 holiday cruisers;
minimum standards for quality of boats;
mutual assistance to cover mechanical
breakdown; mooring overnight in
members' yards.
☎ 0865 880107

BOAT TRIPS

Salter Bros Ltd
Folly Bridge
Passenger boats on the Thames.
☎ 0865 243421

CANOEING

Riverside Canoe Club
☎ 0865 248673

DINGHY SAILING

Oxford Sailing Club
Farmoor Reservoir
RYA sail training, racing.
☎ 0295 86604

DIVING

British Sub-Aqua Southern Region
For details of local clubs contact
J Maddocks.
☎ 0705 588621

INLAND WATERWAYS

Oxford Canal
Narrow-boat cruising, fishing or walking
along the towpaths.

PUNTING

Salter Bros Ltd
Folly Bridge
☎ 0865 243421

ROWING

Oxon Rowing Association
For details contact J Rosewell.
☎ Kidlington 3620

SWIMMING

Blackbird Leys Pool
Blackbird Leys Road
☎ 0865 779843

Ferry Sports Centre
25-metre pool, 12-metre learners pool.
☎ 0865 510330/310978

Temple Cowley Swimming Pools
Temple Road, Cowley
25-metre pool, diving pool, 10-metre
learner pool.
☎ 0865 749449

WINDSURFING

Hinksey Park Lake
Hinksey Park, Abingdon Road
☎ 0865 68359

Painswick, an old wool town, is considered to be one of the most beautiful towns in Gloucestershire. Even its newer houses blend in well with the older heart of the town. It has four streams, one of which supported twelve mills – the earliest, Tocknell's Mill, dates from the late 16th century. The 14th century church is of particular interest, as is its churchyard in which there are over 100 imposing clipped yew trees many of which were planted in the early 18th century.

i The Library
Stroud Road
☎ 0452 813552

Outdoor Leisure

GOLF

Painswick Golf Club
Golf Course Road
Visitors welcome.
☎ 0452 812180

WALKING AND RAMBLING

Cotswold Walks
Various circular walks from 2 to 6 miles long. For details contact the Cotswold Warden Service.
☎ 0452 425674

Cotswold Way
Walk part of the 90-mile long-distance route from Chipping Camden to Bath along the Cotswold scarp slope.

Special Interests

FESTIVALS AND FAIRS

Whit Sunday
Cheese rolling at Cooper's Hill.

September
Clipping Ceremony – mediaeval custom in which children join hands around the church whilst a hymn is sung, once an ale-swilling dance.

Cheese rolling at Cooper's Hill

GARDENS

Painswick Rococo Garden
The Stables, Painswick House
6-acre garden of formal vistas and winding walks is being restored to its original Rococo design; it is the only complete survivor of this period.
☎ 0452 813204

HERITAGE

Cooper's Hill
3 miles north of Painswick
Ancient Iron Age Camp; good views; nature reserve.

Haresfield Beacon
3 miles west of Painswick
Ancient rampart with earthworks on open edge of Cotswold ridge; good views of the Severn Vale.

HISTORIC BUILDINGS

St Mary's Church
15th century church with over 100 clipped yews in the churchyard, some have been there since 1714; very fine peal of 12 bells; pair of iron stocks by the churchyard wall.

HISTORIC HOUSES

Castle Godwyn
Small 18th century manor house. Viewing by written appointment only, contact Mrs Milne.

NATURAL HISTORY

Cooper's Hill
3 miles north of Painswick
Nature reserve; nature trail; location for annual cheese rolling event; Iron Age Camp site.

Frith Wood Nature Reserve
1 mile south-east of Painswick
Ancient woodland of mature beech, oak and ash; woodland flowers, birds, butterflies, snails and funghi; a Site of Special Scientific Interest.
☎ 0453 822761

Pembridge is an attractive village of black-and-white half-timbered houses with a 600-year-old church that once served as a place of refuge for the villagers when the Welsh raided the area. It boasts an unusual Scandinavian style tower. The Market Hall is a Tudor building set on the base of an old stone cross. The New Inn, built in 1311, was once a major stop on the coach route to Aberystwyth.

Special Interests

ART GALLERIES

Old Chapel Gallery
East Street
Art, crafts, country furniture and textiles made on the premises. Paintings and prints by local artists.
☎ 0544 78842

FESTIVALS AND FAIRS

May
Hiring Fair -celebration of the old hiring market where the local farmers used to hire workers for the next year.

September
Art and Craft Festival

FOOD AND DRINK

Dunkertons Cider Company
Luntley

Ciders and perry made from local, unsprayed apples.
☎ 054 47 653

HISTORIC BUILDINGS

Church of St Mary
14th century church built on the site of an older church with a pyramidic detached bell tower in Scandinavian style, one of only seven in the country.

Market Hall
Tudor hall once the trading centre for the area; notches can be seen where traders set planks to use as counters. Later the 'hiring' market where local farmers took on their workers for the next year. The north-east corner is set on the base of an old stone cross.

The New Inn
Built in 1311, once a major stop on the Aberystwyth coach route.

Pembridge village street

145

Pershore grew up around the old Benedictine abbey, the monks of the abbey built the 14th century bridge across the River Avon. Today it is a peaceful market town with elegant Georgian buildings and arched coach entrances leading off the High Street. The town has had a dessert plum named after it and is surrounded by orchards; the spring blossom can be enjoyed in April and May.

i Wanderers World
19 High Street
☎ 0386 554262

Population 6850

Aerial Sports

GLIDING

RSRE Flying Club
RSRE Pershore
☎ 0386 552123

Outdoor Leisure

FISHING

Coarse Fishing
Fishing on the River Avon at Wick Grange. For licences and information contact the National Rivers Authority.
☎ 021 711 2324

Kinver Freeliners Angling Club
Permits and information from Christine Johnson.
☎ 0384 270244

TENNIS

Fladbury Tennis Club
Contact J Lister for details.
☎ 0386 870072

Pershore and District Sports Club
The Bottoms, Defford Road
☎ 0386 552856

WALKING AND RAMBLING

Riverside Walks
Access from River Meadows
Walks along the River Avon from Pershore and Eckington bridge.

Spring Blossom Trail
Trail to follow in April and May through the Vale of Evesham.

Tiddesley Woods
Off the A44

Special Interests

GARDENS

Bredon Springs
8 miles south-west of Pershore near Ashton-under-Hill
1½ acres of gardens in a lovely setting.

Fladbury Mill, near Pershore

Pershore Abbey

The Priory
8 miles south of Pershore at Kemerton
4-acre garden, herbaceous borders,
stream, sunken garden; plants for sale.

HERITAGE

Bredon Hill
5 miles south-east of Pershore
Outcrop of Cotswold stone; site of an
Iron Age hill fort, now Parson's Folly
crowns the hill; magnificent views; the
'Lakey Hill' of *The Archers* radio
programme.

Pershore Bridge
Eastern edge of Pershore town
Solid 14th century six-arched bridge over
the Avon built by the monks of Pershore
Abbey.

HISTORIC BUILDINGS

Pershore Abbey
Benedictine Abbey of local limestone
with 14th century buttressed lantern
tower; Norman nave, transept and
crossing; fine vaulted roof.
☎ 0386 552071

Tithe Barn
7 miles south of Pershore at Bredon
14th century stone tithe barn with fine
porches and chimney with cowling.
National Trust.

Wick Church
1 mile east of Pershore at Wick
12th century arcade and 15th century
wagon roof.

HISTORIC HOUSES

Perrott House
High Street
Built in 1760 with Adam-style ceilings.

Wick Manor
1 mile east of Pershore at Wick
Elizabethan-looking manor around a
courtyard; timber frame dates from 1924
– a deceptive fake.

ORNAMENTAL PARKS

Abbey Park
West of the High Street

WILDLIFE PARKS

Domestic Fowl Trust
Honeybourne
Over 150 varieties of ducks, geese, hens
and turkeys. Childrens farm, adventure
playground, tearoom.
☎ 0386 833083

Water Sports

SWIMMING

Pershore Indoor Swimming Pool
☎ 0386 552346

HEREFORD & / Peterchurch / WORCESTER

Peterchurch is situated in the middle of the beautiful Golden Valley, ten miles of
orchards, cornfields and rich meadows through which the River Dore winds between
Dorstone and Pontrilas. The village has a fine Norman church and in the surrounding
countryside the ruins of a mediaeval castle and a Neolithic chambered tomb can be
found. The latter represents one of the earliest traces of human habitation in the area.

Outdoor Leisure

FISHING

Coarse Fishing
For details and permits contact the
National Rivers Authority.
☎ 021 711 2324

WALKING AND RAMBLING

There are delightful walks along the
Golden Valley and in the hills
surrounding Peterchurch.

Special Interests

HERITAGE

Arthurs Stone
2½ miles north-west of Peterchurch
Notable chambered tomb dating from
Neolithic times, 3rd millenium BC, one
of the earliest traces of human
habitation in the area.

Snodhill Castle
2 miles north-west near Dorstone
Ruins of a mediaeval castle.

HISTORIC BUILDINGS

Peterchurch Parish Church
Fine Norman church.

Vowchurch Parish Church
2 miles south-east of Peterchurch
14th century with a fine Jacobean screen
and an unusual roof supported by oak
posts in the building instead of the walls.

MUSEUMS

Clothiers Farm
Urishay near Peterchurch
Museum and tearoom.
☎ 0981 550359

HEREFORD & Pontrilas WORCESTER

Pontrilas, a hamlet at the southern end of the Golden Valley, offers not only wonderful walks in this idyllic valley but also fishing as well as a country pottery and the beautiful garden at Abbey Dore to enjoy. There are two interesting houses to visit in the area, Pontrilas Court and Kentchurch Court, the seat of the Scudamore family which was remodelled by Nash in 1795.

Outdoor Leisure

FISHING

Coarse Fishing
For permits, licences and information
contact the National Rivers Authority.
☎ 021 711 2324

WALKING AND RAMBLING

The Golden Valley and the Black
Mountains offer wonderful walking
options.

Special Interests

ARTS AND CRAFTS

The Village Well
Ewyas Harold
Variety of crafts for sale. Contact
Patrick Ahern
☎ 0981 240711

GARDENS

Abbey Dore Court Garden
2 miles north-west of Pontrilas at Abbey
Dore
4-acre garden with wooded area, pond,
rock garden, shrub and hardy perennial
borders, old walled gardens, teas, served
in a conservatory, gift gallery.
☎ 0981 240419

HISTORIC HOUSES

Kentchurch Court
2 miles south-east of Pontrilas
The seat of the Scudamore family since
the 11th century; remodelled by John
Nash in 1795; fine 17th century wood
carving.

Pontrilas Court
17th century gabled stone house.

Walking in the Golden Valley

Redditch, designated a new town in 1964, is not just another modern industrial town but has a history dating back to the 12th century. Reminders of its past can be seen at the Bordesley Abbey archaeological site and the history of its famous needle and fish hook industry, 90 per cent of the world's needles were once made here, is displayed at the National Needle Museum. The town has large country parks including the Arrow Valley Park that runs through the centre of town, excellent shopping facilities and a wide variety of indoor, outdoor and water sports and leisure attractions.

i Civic Square
Alcester Street
☎ 0527 60806

Market days Monday to Saturday

Arrow Vale Sports Centre
☎ 0527 500010

The Leys Sports Centre
☎ 0527 29724

Indoor Sports

BADMINTON

The Leys Sports Centre
☎ 0527 29724

St Augustines Sports Centre
☎ 0527 500010

LEISURE CENTRES

Abbey Stadium Sports Centre
Birmingham Road
Large sports hall, multi-gym, indoor and outdoor sports facilities.
☎ 0527 60206

Arrow Vale Sports Centre
Greenswood Lane, Matchborough
Sports hall, gym, squash courts, indoor and outdoor sports facilities.
☎ 0527 500010

The Leys Sports Centre
Woodrow Drive
Sports hall, gym, squash courts, indoor and outdoor facilites, café and bar.
☎ 0527 29724

St Augustines Sports Centre
Windmill Drive
Multi-gym, badminton and table tennis.
☎ 0527 500010

SQUASH

Abbey Stadium Sports Centre
☎ 0527 60206

Arrow Squash
Battens Drive
Private club facilities for local players.
☎ 0527 20414

Outdoor Leisure

FISHING

Coarse Fishing
For permits and licences contact the National Rivers Authority.
☎ 021 711 2324

Arrow Valley Lake
For details contact the Warden.
☎ 0527 68337

GOLF

Abbey Park Golf & Country Club ⚑18
Dagnell End Road
Visitors welcome.
☎ 0527 63918/584140

Pitcheroak Municipal Golf Course ⚑9
Plymouth Road
Undulating course adjoining Pitcheroak Wood.
☎ 0527 541054

Redditch Golf Club ⚑18
Lower Grinsty Lane
☎ 0527 546372

TENNIS

Abbey Stadium Tennis Club
Abbey Stadium, Birmingham Road
6 hard and 3 grass courts.
☎ 0527 60206

Arrow Vale Sports Centre
6 tennis courts.
☎ 0527 500010

Redditch Tennis Club
Bromsgrove Road
☎ 0527 62807

For details contact the Tourist Information Centre.
☎ 0527 60806

Arrow Vale Countryside Group
Alvechurch Village Hall
☎ 0527 27087

Special Interests

COUNTRY PARKS

Arrow Valley Park
900-acre park with a 30-acre lake offering diverse watersports facilities and excellent fishing; numerous footpaths and bridlepaths.
☎ 0527 68337

Morton Stanley Park
Access off Windmill Drive
50-acre landscaped park with nature trail, fitness trail, play area, footpaths and ornamental ponds.

FESTIVALS AND FAIRS

June
Water Fiesta – held at Arrow Valley Lake.

One Act Plays Festival – held at the Palace Theatre.

September
Redditch Carnival

FOREST PARKS

Foxlydiate Woods and Pitcheroak
160 acres of woodland, remnants of the huge forest which once covered most of the area where Redditch now stands.

Oakenshaw Wood
South of the town centre
Attractive woodland with interesting bird and animal life.

Walkwood Coppice
South-west of the town centre
Nature trail through woodland.

HISTORIC BUILDINGS

Bordesley Abbey
Bordesley Lane
Excavated remains of 12th century Cistercian Abbey destroyed by Henry VIII in the dissolution of 1538. First excavated in 1864; later excavations have revealed the timber remains of a watermill, the Gateway Chapel and graveyard; finds are on display.
☎ 0527 62509

MUSEUMS

Midland Bus and Transport Museum
Chapel Lane, Wythall
Large collection of buses and coaches; historic buses operate a service between museums in the area.
☎ 0564 826471

Forge Mill Museum
Needle Mill Lane
Home of the National Needle Museum displaying processes involved in needle manufacture housed in an 18th century mill, the only surviving water-driven needle mill in the world.
☎ 0527 62509

NATURAL HISTORY

Ipsley Alders Nature Reserve
Access off Alders Lane
Area of marsh and peat fen of unique scientific interest for its rare plant and bird life; it is administered by the Worcestershire Nature Conservation Trust.

Mill Pond
Nature conservation area and nature trails.

THEATRES

The Palace Theatre
Alcester Street
☎ 0527 68484

Water Sports

BOAT HIRE

Arrow Valley Park Lake
☎ 0527 68337

CANOEING

Arrow Valley Park Lake
☎ 0527 68337

SWIMMING

Hewell Road Swimming Pool
☎ 0527 64189

The Leys Swimming Pool
Woodrow Drive
☎ 0527 29724

WINDSURFING

Arrow Valley Park Lake
☎ 0527 68337

HEREFORD & **Ross-on-Wye** WORCESTER

Ross-on-Wye stands on red sandstone cliffs overlooking the beautiful Wye Valley. A quaint market town focused around its 17th century arcaded market hall it has some fine Georgian buildings and owes much to a local philanthropist John Kyrie, immortalised by Alexander Pope as the 'Man of Ross'. Ross is renowned as a touring centre for the Wye Valley, it also has a wide selection of adventure centres to cater for many sports. The more adventurous can see the town from the air, there are two ballooning companies based in the town.

i 20 Broad Street
☎ 0989 62768

Market days Friday and Monday
Early closing Wednesday
Population 8500

Aerial Sports

BALLOONING

Ross Balloons
Springfield Walford
Flights in and around the Wye Valley area.
☎ 0989 66034

Wye Valley Aviation
45A Edde Cross Street
Ballooning in the Wye Valley;
champagne flights.
☎ 0989 763134

Multi-Activity Holidays

MULTI-ACTIVITY CENTRES

PGL Adventure Ltd
Alton Court, Penyard Lane
Wide range of activities offered.
☎ 0989 764211

PGL Drummonds Dub Watersports Centre
Alton Court, Penyard Lane
Windsurfing and sailing; residential and day courses.
☎ 0989 764211

SPECIAL INTEREST CENTRES

Pedalaway
Trereece Barn, Llangarron
Weekly and weekend cycling holidays,
guided tour programmes to suit all tastes
including off-road rides; high quality all-
terrain bikes.
☎ 0989 84357

PGL Adventure
Court Farm, Hole-in-the-Wall
Canoeing from the River Wye canoe
centre.
☎ 0989 763149

Outdoor Leisure

CYCLING

Little and Hall
48 Broad Street
☎ 0989 62639

Pedalaway
Cycling holidays and hire.
☎ 0989 84357

FISHING

Coarse Fishing
Fishing for grayling, roach, pike, chubb
and dace in the River Wye.

Game Fishing
Excellent salmon and trout fishing in the
River Wye. The Garron, Gamber and
Monnow are all good trout streams. For
details of river levels and fishing
conditions on the River Wye there is a
24-hour recorded information service.
☎ 0222 796646

G B Sports
10 Broad Street
For permits and information.
☎ 0989 63723

GOLF

Ross-on-Wye Golf Club
Two Park, Gorsley
☎ 0989 822667

HORSE RIDING

Lea Bailey Riding School
5 miles from Ross-on-Wye
Holidays, competitions, side saddle,
hacking, jumping and livery.
☎ 0989 81360

TENNIS

Ross-on-Wye Tennis Centre
Walford Road
☎ 0989 66607

WALKING AND RAMBLING

The Wye Valley Walk
Fully waymarked trail along the Wye
Valley linking Hereford to Hay-on-Wye.
Magnificent scenery; full colour map-
pack available from the Hereford &
Worcester Countryside Service. For
further details contact the Rangers at
Goodrich.
☎ 0600 890610

Special Interests

ANTIQUES

Trecilla Antiques
36 High Street
☎ 0989 63010

ARTS AND CRAFTS

Ross-on-Wye Candlemakers
Old Gloucester Road
Shop and workshop open to the public
with regular evening demonstrations.
☎ 0989 63697

FESTIVALS AND FAIRS

May
100-mile Raft Race on the River Wye
Ross Festival of the Arts

July
Steam Rally
Carnival Week

August
Ross Regatta

GARDENS

The Hill Court Gardens
3 acres of ornamental gardens set in the
grounds of a William and Mary
mansion; rose gardens, water garden,
yew walk, garden centre and tea rooms.
☎ 0989 763123

How Caple Court
On the B4224 Ross to Fawnhope road
Edwardian gardens under restoration
with old English roses and herbaceous
plants.
☎ 0989 86626

Countryside Touring
Ross Travel, 27 High Street
Small groups taken on accompanied tours of the Royal Forest of Dean and the Golden Valley.
☎ 0989 62147

HERITAGE

Wilton Bridge
16th century bridge across the River Wye with six stone arches and a large sundial mounted in the central parapet.

HISTORIC BUILDINGS

Bockhampton-by-Ross Church
5 miles north of Ross-on-Wye
An unusually attractive modern church built in 1901 by a follower of William Morris; interior tapestry by Burne-Jones. Interesting thatched lychgate in the churchyard.

How Caple Church
On the B4224 Ross to Fawnhope Road
Notable stained glass and 16th century diptych.

How Caple Church

St Mary's Church
208-foot spire, lovely stained glass and many monuments of interest.

MUSEUMS

The Lost Street Museum
Palma Court, 27 Brookend Street
Ten authentic shops spanning the years 1885 to 1935; all contents and fittings are original – a 'time capsule' to walk into and enjoy.
☎ 0989 62752

ORNAMENTAL PARKS

The Prospect
Town centre
Walled public garden funded in the 18th century by John Kyrie, 'The Man of Ross', the town's philanthropist. Elegant gates and beautiful views over town and countryside.

Water Sports

CANOEING

PGL Adventure
Court Farm, Hole-in-the-Wall
☎ 0989 763149

SWIMMING

Ross-on-Wye Swimming Pool
☎ 0989 62883

WINDSURFING

Hartleton Lake
North-east of Ross-on-Wye off the B4224

How Caple Court

St Briavels

St Briavels is situated high up in the Forest of Dean between the Severn and the Wye valleys. Its mediaeval castle is used as a youth hostel affording fine views over the Wye Valley and the town provides a splendid walking and activity centre.

Multi-Activity Holidays

MULTI-ACTIVITY CENTRES

Cinderhill House
Country guest house offering varied activity breaks; walking, golf, painting, fishing, birdwatching and the industrial history of the Royal Forest of Dean.
☎ 0594 530393

Outdoor Leisure

FISHING

River Wye
Excellent coarse and game fishing on the River Wye, contact the 24-hour information service for details about the river levels and fishing conditions.
☎ 0222 796646

WALKING AND RAMBLING

Circular Walks
5 circular walks from 2¹/₂ to 8 miles long around the parish of St Briavels. For details contact the Tourist Information Centre requesting the St Briavels Footpath Group leaflets.
☎ 0594 36307

Offa's Dyke Path
168-mile national trail along the 8th century dyke; circular walks around the path are available from bookshops. For more information contact the Offa's Dyke Association.
☎ 0547 528753

Wye Valley Walk
Magnificent views; for details and colour map-pack contact the Rangers at Goodrich
☎ 0600 890610

Special Interests

ARTS AND CRAFTS

McCubbins
The Craft Shop
Pots, silver jewellery and other selected crafts.
☎ 0594 530297

St Briavels Pottery
Makers of a wide range of decorative and domestic stoneware pottery.
☎ 0594 530297

HISTORIC BUILDINGS

St Briavels Castle
13th century castle; magnificent views over the Forest of Dean; now houses a Youth Hostel.

St Briavels Church
Good Norman and early English features.

St Briavels Church

Shobdon

Shobdon is a small Herefordshire village which surprises the visitor with its exquisite church built in 1756 to a design by Horace Walpole. It is also surprising for the range of aerial sports available at its airfield which was built in 1940 to train glider pilots. At the time it was the second largest runway in the country growing by the end of World War II to be an airfield of some size and importance.

Aerial Sports

FLYING

Herefordshire Aero Club
Shobdon Airfield
Flights and lessons available.
☎ 0568 81 723/724

GLIDING

Herefordshire Gliding Club
Shobdon Airfield
☎ 0568 81 723/724

MICROLIGHT FLYING

Microflight
Shobdon Airfield
☎ 0568 81 723

PARACHUTING

Herefordshire Aero Club
Shobdon Airfield
☎ 0568 81 723/724

Outdoor Leisure

BIRDWATCHING

Pearl Lake
Home to a wide variety of water fowl.

Shobdon Airfield
Large flocks of golden plover can be found on the airfield.

FISHING

Coarse Fishing
For fishing in Pearl Lake and the River Arrow contact the National Rivers Authority for licences and permits.
☎ 027 711 2324

Special Interests

HERITAGE

Sessile Oak
Opposite East Hampton Farm
Reputedly the largest sessile oak in the country, estimated to be 300 to 400 years old, 32 feet in circumference and 80 tons in weight.

HISTORIC BUILDINGS

Shobdon Church
Remarkable church, the finest of its kind, designed by Horace Walpole in the style of Strawberry Hill, his Twickenham house, and built in 1756 by the Bateman family to replace a notable Norman church, the Norman font remains. The present Gothic interior is a visual extravaganza of light blue and white stucco panelling with an enormous pulpit and Gothic furnishings.

Shobdon Folly
The Norman church interior arches were re-erected outside but the soft stone has not weathered well.

GLOUCESTERSHIRE / **Slimbridge** / GLOUCESTERSHIRE

Slimbridge is one of the showplaces of this part of Gloucestershire. It is known internationally for the Wildfowl Trust, the world's largest wildfowl collection, set up here by Sir Peter Scott in a natural setting of over 800 acres. The village has an exceptionally fine 13th century church which is well worth including in your visit.

Outdoor Leisure

BIRDWATCHING

The Wildfowl and Wetlands Trust
Berkeley Estate
The world's largest and most varied selection of wildfowl; more than 2500 swans, geese and ducks of over 180 species and six flocks of flamingoes; founded in 1946 by Sir Peter Scott. Wild geese can be seen feeding from towers on the Trust land.
☎ 0453 890333

FISHING

Coarse Fishing
Good fishing on the nearby Sharpness and Avon Canal.

WALKING AND RAMBLING

Circular Walk
Level circular walk taking in Slimbridge Church and the Gloucester and Berkeley Canal. A leaflet is available from the Stroud Tourist Information Centre.
☎ 0453 765768

Stanway is a typical Cotswold village distinguished by Stanway House, a Jacobean manor house of golden limestone standing in planted parkland in its centre. A Cistercian abbey, a Tudor mansion and Gloucestershire's largest steam railway are nearby.

Outdoor Leisure

WALKING AND RAMBLING

The Cotswold Way
Join part of the 90-mile route that follows the Cotswold escarpment passing near Stanway en route from Chipping Campden to Bath.

Special Interests

HISTORIC BUILDINGS

Buckland Rectory
3 miles north-east of Stanway at Buckland
Oldest mediaeval parsonage in Britain still in use; fine mediaeval great hall with open timber roof.

Hailes Abbey

Hailes Abbey
2 miles south-west of Stanway
Picturesque ruins of a Cistercian abbey founded by Edward III's brother in 1246, a place of pilgrimage until Dissolution; excavation has revealed an extensive plan of the monastic buildings, museum, shop. English Heritage.

HISTORIC HOUSES

Snowshill Manor
2 miles north-east of Stanway
Tudor mansion set in beautiful terraced gardens; once the home of Katherine Parr, Henry VIII's wife; collection of toys, musical instruments, clocks and Japanese armour. National Trust.
☎ 0386 852410

MUSEUMS

Hailes Abbey Museum
Hailes Abbey
Interesting range of archeological finds. National Trust.

RAILWAYS

Gloucestershire and Warwickshire Steam Railway
$^1/_2$ mile west of Stanway at Toddington
Steam railway, largest in Gloucestershire, runs a 6-mile round trip with wonderful views; refreshments.
☎ 0242 621405

Steeple Aston lies between Oxford and Banbury beside the Oxford Canal and the River Cherwell in a rural and sparsely populated district. Its main attraction is nearby Rousham House, a Jacobean mansion which contains beautiful paintings and furnishings, as well as letters from Alexander Pope, Jonathan Swift and Charles II. It stands in 30 acres of landscaped gardens designed by William Kent, featuring cascades and statues, ponds and vistas. There are pleasant walks along the canal and opportunities to ride and fish as well as a nature reserve, part of an old quarry, where interesting geology and wildlife can be discovered.

Outdoor Leisure

FISHING

Coarse Fishing
Fishing in the River Cherwell and the Oxford Canal. For permits and information contact the National Rivers Authority.
☎ 021 711 2324

HORSE RIDING

Westfield Farm Riding Centre
Fenway
Hacking in woodland and bridleways; general instruction in riding and jumping.
☎ 0869 47421

Special Interests

GARDENS

Rousham Landscaped Garden
30 acres of gardens and only remaining unaltered landscape garden designed by William Kent; cascades, statues, dovecote, bordered rose garden, decorative ponds and beautiful views; set beside the River Cherwell.
☎ 0869 47110

HISTORIC HOUSES

Rousham House
Original Jacobean house transformed by William Kent in the 1730s; outstanding 30-acre gardens.
☎ 0869 47110

NATURAL HISTORY

BBONT Reserve
Ardley
Part of an old quarry with notable geology, flora and fauna.
☎ 0865 775476

Water Sports

BOAT HIRE

Black Prince
Lower Heyford
☎ 0869 40348

INLAND WATERWAYS

Oxford Canal
Original wooden lift bridges and humped wagon bridges over the 90-mile waterway between Oxford and Coventry. Fishing and cruising; walking along the towpaths. For information contact the British Waterways Board.
☎ 0923 226422

Stonehouse was noted in the Domesday book as having two mills and a vineyard and it experienced considerable prosperity with the advent of the railway and the Stroudwater Canal. The canal today offers good fishing, is an excellent option for boat trips and sailing and the towpaths provide delightful walks. In the 19th century the town had some reputation as a spa but was never to rival Cheltenham.

In the area there is an interesting tithe barn to see, the Cotswold Way to follow and the beautiful parish church of Stonehouse is one of only a few dedicated to the child martyr, St Cyr. Stonehouse Court dates from 1600, later destroyed by fire and rebuilt in 1908 in the Tudor style. For those who enjoy an aerial perspective there is a ballooning centre nearby.

Aerial Sports

BALLOONING

Jon Langley and Co, Aeronauts
3 Holly Tree Garden, Bridge Road, Ebley
Air trips over the Cotswolds.
☎ 0453 82 5447

Outdoor Leisure

FISHING

Coarse Fishing
Fishing in the Stroudwater Canal. Contact the National Rivers Authority for information and licences.
☎ 021 711 2324

WALKING AND RAMBLING

Cotswold Way
Passes through Stonehouse on its 90-mile journey along the Cotswold scarp from Chipping Campden to Bath.

Special Interests

COUNTRY PARKS

Jardinerie Countryside Centre
3 miles north of Stonehouse on the B4008
Conservation oriented wildlife and countryside park with gardens, pond, meadow, butterfly tunnel; birds and animals.
☎ 0452 728338

HISTORIC BUILDINGS

Frocester Tithe Barn
2 miles south-west of Stonehouse
Late 13th century tithe barn and exterior of a 16th century gatehouse and courthouse.
☎ 0453 823250

Water Sports

INLAND WATERWAYS

Stroudwater and Thames-Severn Canal
Constructed in 1779 to transport wool into Stroud and take finished cloth away; fishing, sailing and walks along the towpaths. For details of craft licences contact the British Waterways Board.
☎ 0923 226422

Stonor

Stonor is situated north of Henley-on-Thames in the beautiful Chiltern Hills. It is notable for Stonor Park, a house of considerable architectural and historical interest built on what was once the site of a prehistoric stone circle and surrounded by a secluded deer park. It houses an exhibition on the life of Sir Edmund Campion as well as furniture and works of art belonging to the Stonor family. An unusual oriental well can be found nearby and there are several enjoyable walks in the area to discover the local hills and heathland.

Outdoor Leisure

WALKING AND RAMBLING

Christmas Common
1¹/₂ miles north-west of Stonor
Ridge of the Chilterns, good walking country.

Icknield Way
Join the ancient route.

Turville Heath
¹/₂ mile north of Stonor
Heathland in the heart of the Chilterns.

Special Interests

HISTORIC BUILDINGS

Maharajah's Well
South-west of Stonor on the B481
Exotic well given to Mr E A Reade by the Maharaja of Benares in appreciation of work he carried out on the water supply system in Benares in 1863.

HISTORIC HOUSES

Stonor Park
5 miles north of Henley-on-Thames
Historic home of the Stonor family for over 800 years; house built from 1190 and developed over many centuries, it remains a family home with many rare and unusual pieces of furniture, family portraits and sculptures. Exhibition of life and work of Sir Edmund Campion. Centre for Catholicism; mediaeval chapel is still used to celebrate Mass, using the pre-Reformation licence. A secluded deer park surrounds the house.
☎ 049 163 587

Stonor Park

158

Stourport-on-Severn is the only town in Britain to be built solely as an 18th century canal port. It is clustered around the wharves at the confluence of the Severn, the Stour, and the Staffordshire and Worcestershire Canal and once bustled with activity when this was a busy Midlands port and commercial centre. The advent of the railways saw the decline of the canals and Stourport's role changed from inland port to inland resort. It is now a centre for boating and river trips, walking and riverside amusements and its well-preserved Georgian centre houses a museum documenting its unique past.

i ✳ The Library
County Buildings
Worcester Street
☎ 02993 2866

Indoor Sports

BADMINTON

Stourport Sports Centre
☎ 02993 2308/9

LEISURE CENTRES

Stourport Sports Centre
Harold Davies Drive
Sports hall, multi-gym suite, sunbed, facilities for a wide range of indoor sports and a pool.
☎ 02993 2308/9

SQUASH

Stourport-on-Severn Squash Club
Tan Lane
☎ 02993 2673

Worcestershire Squash Rackets Association
For information about where to play and affiliated clubs contact M Burton.
☎ 0299 402221

Multi-Activity Holidays

MULTI-ACTIVITY CENTRES

Organisation Unlimited
Central Building, Worcester Road
Entertainment programmes arranged for visitors to the Wyre Forest area.
☎ 0299 827197

Outdoor Leisure

FISHING

Coarse Fishing
Good fishing at the confluence of the Rivers Stour and Severn and in the Staffordshire and Worcester Canal.

John White Tackleist
Raven Street
For permits and information.
☎ 02993 71735

HORSE RIDING

Hartlebury Stables Ltd
Waresley Manor Stables, Hartlebury
General riding instruction only; no hacking.
☎ 0299 250710

Manor Farm Riding School
St Johns Road
Qualified instructors offer private lessons to people of all ages. Trekking, hacks and group lessons also available.
☎ 02993 2403

TENNIS

Stourport-on-Severn Tennis Club
Tan Lane
☎ 02993 2673

Special Interests

COUNTRY PARKS

Hartlebury Common and Leapgate Country Park
South of Stourport on the A4025
Worcester Road
Over 200 acres of sandy heath; important Nature Reserve; ideal for walking and cycling.
☎ 0562 829400

159

August
Stourport-on-Severn Regatta

September
Carnival

FUN PARKS

Shipleys Riverside Amusement Park
Roller coaster rides, children's Grand
Prix track, dodgems, Astroglide, play
area. River boat trips and boat hire.
☎ 0299 827755

ORNAMENTAL PARKS

Riverside Meadows
Extensive riverside recreational area.

Water Sports

BOAT TRIPS

Severn Steamboat Company
Riverside Walk
2 twin-decked passenger boats, each can
hold 200 passengers, bars, refreshments,
full catering service, entertainments,
group hire available.

River Severn

INLAND WATERWAYS

Staffordshire and Worcestershire Canal
Wharves and warehouses surround the
canal; good for fishing, sailing and
walking along the towpaths. For details
and craft licences contact the British
Waterways Board.
☎ 0923 226422

SWIMMING

Stourport Sports Centre
☎ 02993 2308/9

GLOUCESTERSHIRE **Stow-on-the-Wold** GLOUCESTERSHIRE

Stow-on-the-Wold is the highest town in the Cotswolds, standing at about 800 feet in
a hilltop position. The 15th century parish church is a local landmark. Its great
market square was once the scene of two annual sheep fairs, it still has its mediaeval
market cross and wooden stocks and is surrounded by elegant Cotswold stone houses
and old coaching inns. Now the square abounds with antique shops and art galleries
to browse around.

i Hollis House
The Square
☎ 0451 31082

Population 1596

Multi-Activity Holidays

SPECIAL INTEREST CENTRES

Grapevine Hotel
Short breaks featuring antiques, painting
and wine.
☎ 0451 30344

Old Stocks, Stow-on-the-Wold

Outdoor Leisure

FISHING

Game Fishing
Donington Fish Farm
Condicote Lane, Upper Swell
Working trout farm with farm shop
selling top quality fresh and smoked
trout; day tickets for fly fishing.
☎ 0451 30873

HORSE RIDING

Cromwell Stables
Church Street, Bleddington
Full instruction for beginners and
experienced riders.
☎ 0608 658191

Special Interests

ANTIQUES

Acorn Antiques
Sheep Street
☎ 0451 31519

The Cotswold Antiques Centre
Market Square
☎ 0451 31585

Lynn Greenwold Antiques
Digbeth Street
☎ 0451 30398

Stow Antiques
Market Square
☎ 0451 30377

ART GALLERIES

John Blockley Galleries
Church Street
☎ 0451 31371

Fosse Gallery
Market Square
☎ 0451 31319

Peppercorns House Gallery
Sheep Street
☎ 0451 31821

Talbot Court Galleries
Talbot Court
☎ 0451 32169

ARTS AND CRAFTS

Langston Priory Workshops
East of Show at Kingham
Several craftsmen at work; large
selection of crafts on display.
☎ 0608 658645

Walton House Studio
Sheep Street
Pottery for sale; please telephone before
visiting.
☎ 0451 31782

FESTIVALS AND FAIRS

May
Fair – continuation of a fair authorised
in 1476 by King Edward IV to celebrate
the feast day of St James and St Edward
the Confessor.

October
Fair – continuation of the traditional
celebration of St Philip's feast day.

FOOD AND DRINK

Wye Organic Foods
First privately owned shop in the UK to
sell Soil Association produce.
☎ 0451 31004

GARDENS

Abbotswood Gardens
1 mile south-west of Stow at Upper
Swell

HERITAGE

Long Barrows
Several Neolithic burial mounds have
been found near Stow.

The Wells
Well Lane
Ancient spring that has supplied Stow
with water since man first settled there.

HISTORIC BUILDINGS

Lower Swell Parish Church
1 mile west of Stow
Superb Norman carving.

Parish Church of St Edward
15th century Cotswold wool church
with an 88-foot tower, a local landmark;
all styles of architecture from Norman to
Tudor, many notable features including
a 17th century painting of The
Crucifixion. Used as a prison by
Cromwell's men during the Civil War,
later restored.

HISTORIC HOUSES

Upper Swell Manor
1 mile north-west of Stow at Upper
Swell
18th century manor house.

Stroud

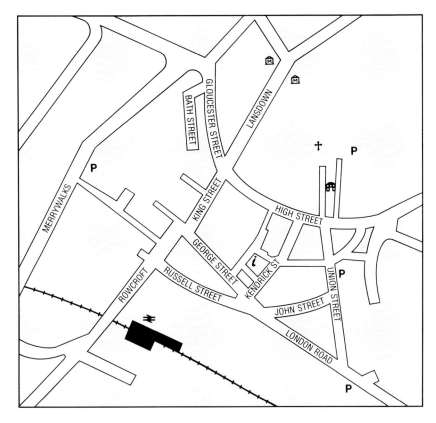

Stroud stands at the junction of five valleys, its steep hills and narrow streets retaining a quaint charm. An old and prosperous wool town it was an important centre for the production of broadcloth and the dyeing trade – military uniforms were usually made from 'Stroudwater Scarlets'. The cloth industry has declined since 150 mills produced cloth around Stroud in 1824 but several mills still operate producing cloth of quality for Royal uniforms and Papal robes.

The town retains several historic buildings, notably The Shambles, the recently restored Mediaeval Hall which is the oldest building in Stroud and an imposing building called the Subscription Rooms. There are two museums to visit with displays of local history and crafts of the area including farming, brewing and rope manufacture.

There are many walks in the area either along the canal or the old Midlands branch lines, or join the Cotswold Way for some of its length. There is also a cycle trail to follow or for a real taste of adventure try a balloon flight or an aero-tow gliding tour as part of a short break.

i Subscription Rooms
☎ 0453 765768

Market day Wednesday
Early closing Thursday
Population 108,900

Aerial Sports

BALLOONING

John M Albury
Jasmine Cottage, The Pitch, Brownshill
Ballooning holidays and flights.
☎ 0453 885187

Indoor Sports

LEISURE CENTRES

Stratford Park Leisure Centre
Stratford Park
Large and small halls, sauna, solarium, indoor and outdoor pools and sports facilities, bar and cafeteria.
☎ 0453 766771

SQUASH

Stratford Park Leisure Centre
☎ 0453 766771

Multi-Activity Holidays

SPECIAL INTEREST CENTRES

Amberley Inn
Two night break with an aero-tow gliding tour.
☎ 0453 872565

Ashleigh House
Bussage, near Stroud
Short break holidays featuring painting and sketching.
☎ 0453 883944

Outdoor Leisure

CYCLING

Stroud Valleys Cycle Trail
Runs along the Stonehouse and Nailsworth valleys, an illustrated guide is available from the Tourist Information Centre.
☎ 0453 765768

HORSE RIDING

Camp Riding Centre
Camp
Hacking in beautiful countryside; indoor facilities.
☎ 028 582 219

WALKING AND RAMBLING

Circular Walks
A range of walks for the casual and energetic walker. Leaflets available from the Library or the Tourist Information Centre.
☎ 0453 765768

Coaley Peak Picnic Site
4 miles south-west of Stroud
12 acres of grassland with panoramic views, picnic site, circular walks, site of an ancient burial ground.
☎ 0453 765768

Cotswold Way
90-mile waymarked route along the Cotswold escarpment, good views over the Severn Vale.

Stroud Valleys Pedestrian Trail
Trails along the old Midlands railway branch lines, an illustrated guide is available from the Tourist Information Centre.
☎ 0453 765768

Stroudwater Canal Towpath
A guide to the canal towpath with its locks, bridges, mills and wildlife is available from the Tourist Information Centre.
☎ 0453 765768

Special Interests

FESTIVALS AND FAIRS

July
Stroud Show – includes the brick and rolling-pin throwing contest.

September
Stroud Brass Band Festival

October
International Arts Festival
Half Marathon

HISTORIC BUILDINGS

Mediaeval Hall
The oldest building in Stroud; restored hall and well, good stonework.

The Shambles
Tudor town hall once the meat market.

St Laurence's Church
Rebuilt in the 19th century; it retains a 14th century tower.

MUSEUMS

Stroud (Cowle) Museum
Lansdown, north-east Stroud
Local and industrial archaeology; geology; prehistoric remains; replica dinosaur.
☎ 0453 763394

Lansdown Hall
Lansdown, north-east Stroud
Display of local history and crafts tracing the history of cloth, mills, brewing, farming, and rope manufacture.
☎ 0453 762782

NATURAL HISTORY

Coaley Peak Nature Reserve
4 miles south-west of Stroud
Sloping grassland, scrub and disused
quarry supports a variety of wild flowers.
☎ 0453 822761

Elliot Nature Reserve
2 miles north-east of Stroud at Swift's
Hill
Site of Special Scientific Interest; small
quarry with excellent variety of orchids
and wild flowers; butterflies and
grassland birds.
☎ 0453 822761

ORNAMENTAL PARK

Stratford Park
56-acre park with ornamental lake,
picnic area, children's playground,
miniature railway and leisure centre.

THEATRES

The Cotswold Playhouse
Parliament Street
☎ 0453 764545

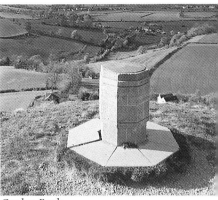

Coaley Peak

Water Sports

INLAND WATERWAYS

Stroudwater Canal
Good for fishing, sailing and towpath
walks. For details of craft licences
contact the British Waterways Board.
☎ 0923 226422

HEREFORD & / Symonds Yat / WORCESTER

Symonds Yat is where the River Wye twists into a large horse-shoe for over five miles
and Yat Rock, a limestone pillar over 400 feet high, provides breathtaking views, a
challenge to rock-climbers and a home to nesting peregrine falcons. Every sort of
adventure sport is catered for here, there are good facilities for canoeing and there are
a wide selection of other interesting leisure attractions. There are many sites for
camping and caravanning which are good bases for walking and birdwatching.

Multi-Activity Holidays

MULTI-ACTIVITY CENTRES

Holly Barn
Group accommodation in a converted
barn completely refurbished to provide
full accommodation for organised
groups; indoor climbing wall and drying
room. Contact Paul and Jane Howells.
☎ 0600 890129
☎ 0594 33238

SPECIAL INTEREST CENTRES

Wyedean Canoe and Adventure Centre
Penny Royal Cottage, Symonds Yat East
Qualified instruction in canoeing and
other watersports.
☎ 0600 890129

Outdoor Leisure

BIRDWATCHING

Symonds Yat Rock
Breeding place of wild peregrine falcons;
RSPB protected; superb views over the
Wye valley; steep climb.

CAMPING AND CARAVANNING

Blackthorne Farm
Hillersland, near Symonds Yat
Campsite next to the forest in a flat field
with superb views.
☎ 0594 32062

Eastville Static Caravan Park
Coopers Read, Christchurch
Luxury caravans with all mod cons.
☎ 0594 34956
☎ 0272 510082

Symonds Yat East Campsite
Penny Royal Cottage, Symonds Yat East
Small, level river bank site; beautiful
scenery, river access, camp shop,
showers, canoe hire and outdoor
activities. Ideal centre for walking,
climbing and canoeing.
☎ 0600 890129

FISHING

Coarse Fishing
River Wye
Excellent coarse and game fishing, some
of the best in the country.

Newport Angling Association
For details contact B Small.
☎ 0633 263517

WALKING AND RAMBLING

Wye Valley Walk
Access from Kerne Bridge picnic site
Wonderful views of the Wye Valley. For
details and map-pack contact the
Rangers at Goodrich.
☎ 0600 890610

Special Interests

FARM PARKS

Wye Valley Farm Park
Goodrich near Symonds Yat
Many rare breeds of traditional farm
animals; children are especially
welcome; riverside walks; woodlands;
picnic spots and a courtyard tearoom.
☎ 0600 890296

FOREST PARKS

Symonds Yat Rock
Forest trail, walks in Highmeadow
Woods, peregrine falcons, view point,
picnic areas, shop and site rangers.
☎ 0594 33057

GUIDED TOURS

Wyedean Archaeological Tours
Old Post Office, Lower Lydbrook
Tours catering for personal tastese,
many artefacts to handle, a tour
through 7000 years. Contact Alf Webb.
☎ 0594 843548

HERITAGE

Goodrich Castle
North of Symonds Yat at Goodrich
Magnificent 12th to 14th century castle
ruins on rocky hill overlooking the Wye
Valley; destroyed by Cromwell's army
during the Civil War.

Promontory Fort
Symonds Yat Rock
An ancient monument.

MUSEUMS

Herefordshire Rural Life Museum
Doward, near Symonds Yat
Large collection of historic farm
machinery, vintage tractors and rural
bygones in an award-winning museum.
☎ 0600 890474

THEME PARK

The Jubilee Maze
Symonds Yat West
Traditional hedge maze, museum of
mazes describing 5000 years of the
history of mazes, puzzle shop.
Illuminated by night; no pets.
☎ 0600 890360

WILDLIFE PARKS

Symonds Yat Bird Park
Symonds Yat West
160 species of rare and exotic birds in
one of Britain's largest breeding
collections. Picnic area, gift shop, access
for the disabled.
☎ 0600 890989

The World of Butterflies
The Wye Valley Visitor Centre,
Symonds Yat West
Free-flying tropical butterflies in exotic
indoor garden; craft workshops; tearoom;
garden centre; walk to riverside church.
☎ 0600 890360

Water Sports

BOAT TRIPS

Kingfisher River Trips
Saracen Head Hotel, Symonds Yat East
Regular trips on luxury river cruiser;
available for parties and evening trips.
☎ 0600 890435

CANOEING

Monmouth Canoe Hire
Dixton Road, Monmouth
Travel along the Wye in a canoe; week
and day hire from Symonds Yat.
Instruction also available.
☎ 0600 3461

Wyedean Canoe and Adventure Centre
Penny Royal Cottage, Symonds Yat East
Qualified instruction in canoeing and
various adventure sports.
☎ 0600 890129

Tenbury Wells lies on the banks of two rivers and is joined to Shropshire by an elegant bridge across the river Teme. It has an unusual round market and the Royal Oak provides a fine example of intricate black-and-white timber framing. Mineral springs were discovered here in 1839 and it was hoped that Tenbury would become a fashionable spa town, it did not and the abandoned pump rooms are only now being restored. A town with much to discover and plenty to do, it is surrounded by unspoilt undulating countryside.

i   *   21 Teme Street
☎ 0584 810118

Market days Tuesday, Thursday
Early closing Thursday

Indoor Sports

LEISURE CENTRES

Tenbury Sports Club
☎ 0584 810456

Multi-Activity Holidays

SPECIAL INTEREST CENTRES

Fabric Craft Centre
Woodstock House, Brimfield
Fabrics, patchwork, quilting and embroidery. Residential and non-residential courses.
☎ 058 472 445

Outdoor Leisure

FISHING

Coarse Fishing
Fishing in the River Teme. For permits, licences and information contact the National Rivers Authority.
☎ 0584 810794

Game Fishing
For permits for the River Teme contact Mrs Goddard.
☎ 0584 70411

TENNIS

Tenbury Tennis Club
Burgage Recreation Ground
For details contact S West.
☎ 0584 811747

WALKING AND RAMBLING

Local Walks
Ideal walking country, undulating and unspoilt. Contact the Tourist Information Centre for details.
☎ 0584 810118

Tenbury Rambling Club
☎ 0584 79454

Special Interests

ART GALLERIES

Forge House Gallery
Local arts and crafts, pictures and gifts.
☎ 058 472 500

ARTS AND CRAFTS

Fabric Craft Centre
Woodstock House, Brimfield
Fabric, patchwork, quilting and embroidery.
☎ 058 472 445

FESTIVALS AND FAIRS

August
Tenbury Agricultural Show

FOOD AND DRINK

Hyde Farm Cheese
Stoke Bliss
Interesting cheeses of quality made from goats milk.
☎ 0885 410408

GARDENS

Burford House Gardens
West of Tenbury Wells
4-acre garden designed by John Treasure, garden museum, plant centre, specialist grower of clematis and herbaceous plants and tea rooms.
☎ 0584 810777

HERITAGE

Saxon Preaching Cross
Displayed in the parish church.
Unearthed during 18th century
restoration work.

HISTORIC BUILDINGS

Newnham Bridge Watermill
2 miles east of Tenbury Wells
Working watermill.

Pump Rooms
Built in 1862 after discovery of mineral
springs with intention of making
Tenbury a spa town; an unsuccessful
attempt; pump rooms being restored.

The Royal Oak
Market Place
Spectacular 16th century black-and-
white timber-framed building now a
pub.

Teme Bridge
Elegant bridge over the River Teme
rebuilt by Thomas Telford in the 18th
century.

HISTORIC HOUSES

Burford House
West of the town
Elegantly proportioned house built in
1728; small museum and exhibitions.
☎ 0584 810777

MUSEUMS

Tenbury Museum
Pembroke Avenue
Local history and artefacts.
☎ 0584 810118

Water Sports

CANOEING

Teme Bridge
Launching site, the River Teme offers
excellent waters for canoeists.

SWIMMING

Tenbury Swimming Pool
Palmer's Meadow
☎ 0584 810448

GLOUCESTERSHIRE / **Tetbury** / GLOUCESTERSHIRE

Tetbury, a southern Cotswold town, has a recorded history of over 1300 years since
Tetta's Monastery was recorded in 681. An important mediaeval centre for the wool
trade its town centre has many fine wool merchants' houses and a fine Market Hall. It
is now famous for its many antique shops and is a centre for the trade. Attractions for
visitors include a museum depicting the history of the Tetbury Police, and a working
watermill producing stoneground flours.

i Old Court House
63 Long Street
☎ 0666 53552

The Old George
3 The Chipping
☎ 0666 503405

Special Interests

ANTIQUES

Brakespeare Antiques
☎ 0666 503122

Bristow Antiques
28 Long Street
Furniture and clocks.
☎ 0666 52222

ART GALLERIES

Long Street Gallery
50 Long Street
☎ 0666 53722

FOOD AND DRINK

Shiptons Stoneground Flour
Off the B4014
Riverside mill, first recorded in the
Domesday book; working watermill;
flours for sale.

HISTORIC BUILDINGS

Market Hall
17th century stone building with interesting features including Tuscan columns, stone slate roof and cupola with gilded dolphin weathervane.

St Mary's Church
Early Gothic revival style, completed in 1781.

HISTORIC HOUSES

Chavenage House
2 miles north of Tetbury off the B4014 Elizabethan manor house with Cromwellian associations; 17th century tapestries and furnitures; fine mediaeval barn.
☎ 0666 52329

Livestock auction at Tetbury

MUSEUMS

Tetbury Police Bygones Museum
63 Long Street
Displays in cells below former magistrates court; items on loan from the Gloucestershire Constabulary.
☎ 0666 503552

Tewkesbury, a picturesque town of black-and-white, half-timbered buildings, is sited at the confluence of the Rivers Avon and Severn making it the perfect centre for a boating holiday or river trip. The town grew around its abbey which dominates the town and it was here that the last decisive battle of the Wars of the Roses was fought in 1471. There are several walks around the town which give a fascinating reminder of the town's history.

i Museum
64 Barton Street
☎ 0684 295027

Population 9500

Adventure Sports

CLIMBING

Tewkesbury Sports Centre
Ashworth Road
Climbing wall.
☎ 0684 293953

SHOOTING

Severn Sporting Agency Ltd
Skep Cottage, Forthampton
Well established agents dealing with all aspects of field sports.
☎ 0684 293021/297904

Indoor Sports

BADMINTON

Tewkesbury Sports Centre
☎ 0684 293953

LEISURE CENTRES

Cascades
Oldbury Road
Health suite, spa bath, steam room, sunbeds, gym, two pools, geysers and lounge.
☎ 0684 293740

Tewkesbury Sports Centre
Sports hall, gym indoor and outdoor sports facilities, pool.
☎ 0684 293953

SQUASH

Tewkesbury Sports Centre
☎ 0684 293953

Multi-Activity Holidays

MULTI-ACTIVITY CENTRES

Bell Hotel
Church Street
Activity breaks featuring riding, pony-trekking, clay pigeon shooting and windsurfing.
☎ 0684 293293

Outdoor Leisure

CAMPING AND CARAVANNING

Abbey Caravan Club Site
Gander Lane
170 pitches, facilities.
☎ 0684 294035

FISHING

Coarse Fishing
Fishing in the River Avon at various
locations, waters owned by the
Tewkesbury Angling Association.

R Danter Tackle Shop
For membership of the Angling
Association, permits and information.
☎ 0684 299824

GOLF

**Tewkesbury Park Hotel Golf and
Country Club** ▶18
Lincoln Green Lane
Fairly flat course with magnificent
views; visitors welcome weekdays.
☎ 0684 295405

TENNIS

Tewkesbury Sports Centre
☎ 0684 293953

WALKING AND RAMBLING

Alleyways Walk
Fascinating reminder of Tewkesbury's
past, a leaflet will guide you through the
historical associations of the alleyways
and courts.
☎ 0684 295027

Battle Trail
Leaflet guide around the site of the Battle
of Tewkesbury, 1471, available from the
Tourist Information Centre.
☎ 0684 295027

Circular Walks
Several circular walks along the banks of
the Severn and the Avon, leaflets from
the Tourist Information Centre.
☎ 0684 295027

Special Interests

ARTS AND CRAFTS

Beckford Silk Ltd
The Old Vicarage, Beckford
Watch traditional hand-printing, dye
making and other processes in the
manufacture of silk scarves and ties.
☎ 0386 881507

Conderton Pottery
The Old Forge, Conderton
Handmade domestic pottery using
special saltglazing methods; set in an
orchard.
☎ 0386 89387

Tilly M's
Stables Cottage, Kemerton
Arts studio, events, cookery; details on
request.
☎ 0386 89 283

FESTIVALS AND FAIRS

Summer
Tewkesbury Mediaeval Fayre –
re-enactment of the Battle of
Tewkesbury 1471, dates vary.

October
Mop Fair – the old hiring fair is still
celebrated.

GUIDED TOURS

Intercounty Chauffeur Services
ICS House, Tewkesbury Road
Experienced chauffeur guides covering
15 Cotswold regional itineraries to all
major UK sporting events.
☎ 0242 680223

HERITAGE

Odda's Chapel
4 miles south-west of Tewkesbury at
Deerhurst
Saxon relic built into 16th century
farmhouse, inscribed stone recording the
chapel's erection in 1056 is in the
Ashmolean Museum.

St Mary's Priory
Deerhurst
Anglo-Saxon church with 8th century
Virgin and Child sculpture and 9th
century carved font.

HISTORIC BUILDINGS

Abbey Cottages
Built in 1430, originally 23 shops.

Black Bear Inn
Built in 1308, reputedly the oldest inn in
Gloucestershire.

House of Nodding Gables
High Street
Former ticket office for stagecoaches.

King John's Bridge
Bridge over the Avon, built in 1197.

Mythe Bridge
Bridge over the Severn, built by Telford
in 1824, 170-foot span.

Old Baptist Chapel
Church Street
Reputedly oldest Nonconformist chapel in the south, restored in 1976, some 17th century furnishings and original features.
☎ 0864 295010

Tewkesbury Abbey
12th century; consecrated 1121. Outstanding Norman nave and tower, 132-foot high with twelve bells; notable west front with a 65-foot arch; 14th century choir, eastern chapels and north transept; fine stained glass windows and fan-vaulted roof; numerous mediaeval monuments.

MUSEUMS

The Little Museum
45, Abbey Cottages
Simply furnished mediaeval tradesman's home depicting their lifestyle.

John Moore Museum
41 Church Street
Museum, farm interpretation centre, country garden – of special appeal to children and countryside lovers.
☎ 0684 297174

Tewkesbury Museum
64 Barton Street
Imaginative depiction of local history; archaeological heritage centre and model of the Battle of Tewkesbury housed in two ancient timbered houses.
☎ 0684 295027

THEATRES

Roses Theatre
Film theatre with concerts and plays.
☎ 0684 295074

Water Sports

BOAT TRIPS

Tolsey Lane
Trips on the River Avon.

CANOEING

Croft Farm Leisure and Water Park
Canoe hire; windsurfing facilities.
☎ 0684 72321

DINGHY SAILING

Tewkesbury Marinas
Two large marinas provide facilities for most sailing pursuits.

SWIMMING

Cascades
☎ 0684 293740

WINDSURFING

Croft Farm Leisure and Water Park
Bredans Hardwick
Learn to windsurf; hire boards, canoes, and wetsuits; boardsailing shop.
☎ 0684 72321

Thame, the site of a settlement since Saxon times, has a High Street that has changed little since the 18th century; it has over 100 listed buildings including many old inns. The town hosts an annual one-day Agricultural Show and a colourful street fair. It remains a busy market town with a variety of leisure and sporting facilities.

i Town Hall
☎ 084 421 2834

Market day Tuesday
Early closing Wednesday
Population 9500

Indoor Sports

BADMINTON

Swifts Badminton Club
☎ 084 421 4198

Thame Badminton Club
☎ 084 421 3827

Thame Sports and Arts Centre
☎ 084 421 5607

LEISURE CENTRES

Thame Sports and Arts Centre
Oxford Road
Two halls, variety of sports activities.
☎ 084 421 5607

SQUASH

North Street
Five squash courts.

Outdoor Leisure

FISHING

Coarse Fishing
Good fishing in the River Thame.

Thame Angling Club
For information contact R Neil.
☎ 084 421 6213

TENNIS

Elms Park
Park Street

Thame Sports Club
Oxford Road
☎ 084 421 5607

Special Interests

ANTIQUES

Peter of Thame
81 High Street
Clocks and furniture.
☎ 0844 261966

ARTS AND CRAFTS

Thame Sports and Arts Centre
Varied programme of arts activities, craft
and trade fairs.
☎ 084 421 5607

FESTIVALS AND FAIRS

July
Carnival Week

September
Thame Agricultural Show - held at the
Showground, reputedly the largest one-
day agricultural show in the country.
Show Fair - street fair lasting two days
after the agricultural show.

October
Autumn Charter Fair

FOOD AND DRINK

Le Manoir Aux Quatre Saisons
5 miles south-west at Great Milton
Outstanding French provincial cuisine of
the celebrated Raymond Blanc served in
a lovely Cotswold stone manor set in a
27-acre park.
☎ 0844 278881

HISTORIC BUILDINGS

Brill Windmill
7 miles north-west of Thame at Brill
One of the oldest postmills in England;
parts dating from the 17th century;
working until 1916.

Church of the Blessed Virgin Mary
Church Close
13th century church built on site of
Anglo-Saxon church, extended in the
14th and 15th centuries; monuments;
notable brasses.

Long Crendon Courthouse
2 miles north of Thame
Fine half-timbered 14th century
courthouse.

Rycote Chapel
3 miles south-west of Thame at Rycote
Outstanding 15th century chapel with
mediaeval stalls, fine 17th century pews
and late 17th century ornamental screen;
only surviving part of the Quatermayne
family estate, ruined mansion is nearby.

HISTORIC HOUSES

Prebendal House
Priestend
House reconstructed in 1837 from the
ruins of a mediaeval ecclesiastical
building, may be viewed from the
outside.

Thame Park
1 mile south-east of town
18th century mansion altered in 1920
but remaining part of the 13th century
monastic building and the Abbots
Parlour built by Thame's last abbot;
mediaeval chapel preserved in the
grounds.

NATURAL HISTORY

Boarstall Duck Decoy
5$^1/_2$ miles north-west of Thame
18th century duck decoy in extensive
woodlands; nature trail and exhibition.

ORNAMENTAL PARKS

Elms Park
Park with tennis courts and children's
playground.

Uffington, a chalkstone village, is surrounded by ancient sites and legends – 900 feet above the village is the towering white horse carved into the chalk downs, above that is the spot where George is said to have slain the dragon. Nearby is a prehistoric burial place where legend has it that horses will be shod by a Saxon god and more recently the village has been home to the author of the book *Tom Brown's Schooldays*.

Outdoor Leisure

WALKING AND RAMBLING

The Ridgeway
85-mile long-distance path following the ancient Wessex Ridgeway, rich in archeological remains and chalk lowland flora and fauna.

Special Interests

HERITAGE

Blowing Stone
1 mile south-east of Uffington at Kingston Lisle
Large perforated Sarsen stone that produces a fog-hornlike sound when blown; tradition associated it with King Alfred.

Dragon Hill
Below White Horse Hill
Legendary site where Saint George is said to have slain the dragon.

Uffington Castle
Above the White Horse
Ancient Iron Age hill fort.

Wayland's Smithy
3 miles south-west of Uffington at Ashbury
Prehistoric burial place consisting of a long earthern mound containing a chamber made of large blocks of stone; legend has it that any horse left tethered at the entrance will be shod by Wayland, the smith of the Saxon gods, if a coin is left on the lintel as a fee.

White Horse
South of Uffington on White Horse Hill
Famous horse carved into the chalk of the hillside; may have been carved by the Saxons to celebrate their victory over the Danes in the 9th century or carved by Iron Age men much earlier; local people have kept the horse free of grass by traditional 'scourings'.

White Horse Hill
South of Uffington
Highest point of the Downs, 856 feet, with several ancient monuments.

HISTORIC BUILDINGS

St Marys' Church
Imposing, complete 13th century church; 18th century octagonal tower replaces the original spire that was lost in a storm.

Holy Cross Church
South-east of Uffington at Sparsholt
Notable for three oak tomb figures of about 1300 depicting a knight and two ladies; early wooden screen; brasses; old glass and old woodwork.

HISTORIC HOUSES

Ashdown House
South-west of Uffington near Ashbury
Unusual four-storey mansion built in 1663 by the first Earl of Craven; 17th century portraits; good views of the chalk downs from the cupola; formal gardens.

Kingston Lisle Park
1 mile south-east of Uffington at Kingston Lisle
17th century mansion with imaginative interior including dramatic flying staircase, interesting plasterwork and attractive gardens.

MUSEUMS

Tom Brown's School Museum
Broad Street
Displays depicting the life and works of Thomas Hughes, author of *Tom Brown's Schooldays* with other historical material; shop; guided tours by arrangement.
☎ 036 782 675

Upton-upon-Severn is a riverside town with an unusual landmark that now houses its Heritage Centre, known as the Pepperpot it is the town's oldest building, a 14th century tower with a later cupola.

i ✳ The Pepperpot
Church Street
☎ 068 46 4200

Early closing Thursday
Population 2518

Outdoor Leisure

BIRDWATCHING

Birdsmorton Waterfowl Sanctuary
Feed and walk amongst the birds in natural surroundings.

CAMPING AND CARAVANNING

Riverside Caravan Park
Little Clevelode
☎ 0684 310475

FISHING

Coarse Fishing
Fishing in the River Severn from locations on the Waterside and The Ham. For details contact the Tourist Information Centre.
☎ 068 46 4200

HORSE RACING

Fish Meadow
Point to point and quarter horse racing, contact the Croome Hunt for details.

Special Interests

ART GALLERIES

Arteria Galleries
Coach House, Old Street
☎ 068 46 4638

Highway Gallery
40 Old Street
☎ 068 46 2645/2909

ARTS AND CRAFTS

Midsummer Weavers
Old Drill Hall, London Lane
Craft weaving workshop.
☎ 068 46 3503

FESTIVALS AND FAIRS

May
Upton Folk Festival
Oak Apple Day Celebrations

June
Oliver Cromwell Jazz Festival
☎ 06846 3254

July
Upton Steam Rally – held at the Riverside.

August
Water Carnival – held at the Riverside.

HISTORIC BUILDINGS

Dunstall Castle
Dunstall Common, east of Upton
A mock Norman castle ruin built as a folly.

Hill Croome Dovecote
Near Upton-upon-Severn
Restored 15th century dovecote open during daylight hours. National Trust.

MUSEUMS

Upton Heritage Centre
The Pepperpot
Exhibitions of the town's history and the story of the Battle of Upton, 1651, during the Civil War. Housed in the town's oldest surviving building and a local landmark – a 14th century tower with an 18th century copper cupola once attached to the parish church. Also the Tourist Information Centre.
☎ 068 46 4200

Water Sports

BOAT TRIPS

Severn Leisure
Waterside
Regular boat trips on the *MV Conway Castle*; riverboat shuffles and party nights; private charter.
☎ 068 46 3112/2988

Wallingford, one of the oldest Royal boroughs in the country, has been an important riverside crossing place since Saxon times and today a superb 900-foot bridge spans the Thames. There are many interesting historic buildings both in the town and the nearby villages as well as a wide variety of leisure attractions to enjoy – it is a rewarding region to explore.

i 9 St Martin's Street
☎ 0491 35351 extn 3810

Market day Friday
Early closing Wednesday
Population 6500

Indoor Sports

BADMINTON

The Regal Sports & Social Centre
St Martin's Street
☎ 0491 35303/35373

LEISURE CENTRES

The Regal Sports & Social Centre
Hall, roller skating, indoor sports, multi-gym and sunbed.
☎ 0491 35303/35373

SQUASH

Wallingford Sports & Social Club
Apply for membership to Wallingford Sports Trust, Hithercote Road.
☎ 0491 35044

Wallingford Squash Rackets Club
High Street
☎ 0491 35072

Outdoor Leisure

CAMPING AND CARAVANNING

Bridge Villa International Caravan and Camping Site
Crowmarsh
Approved by camping and automobile associations.
☎ 0491 36860

Maidboats Camping Site
Off the A423 at Benson
30 pitches and caravans for hire.
☎ 0491 38304

Riverside Caravan and Camping Site
Swimming and paddling pools; South Oxfordshire District Council Site.
☎ 0491 35351

FISHING

Coarse Fishing
Good fishing in the River Thames and its tributaries. For information and permits contact the Thames Water Authority at Reading.
☎ 0734 593333

Jolly Anglers Club
Wallingford Sports and Social Club, Hithercroft Road
☎ 0491 35044

HORSE RIDING

Blenheim Riding Centre
North of Wallingford at Benson
General instruction in riding and jumping, show centre and livery.
☎ 0491 36057/35474

TENNIS

Bull Croft
High Street
☎ 0491 34707

Wallingford Sports & Social Club
Hithercroft Road
For membership apply to Wallingford Sports Trust.
☎ 0491 35044

WALKING AND RAMBLING

Historic Town Walk
A guide to a walk around the historic places in Wallingford is available from the museum.
☎ 0491 35065

The Ridgeway
85-mile path that follows the ancient Wessex Ridgeway; rich in historical and natural interest.

Riverside Walks
Access from Wallingford Bridge
Footpaths run on the east bank downstream and the west bank upstream from the bridge providing delightful riverside walks.

174

Special Interests

ANTIQUES

Summers
Calleva House, High Street
☎ 0491 36284

ARTS AND CRAFTS

The Lamb Arcade
Castle Street
Crafts and antiques arcade in restored
16th century inn, the King's Hedde; it
later became the Lamb Hotel with a
Georgian facade, and then fell into
dereliction before its present conversion
into an award-winning arcade.

Roland Haycraft
Lamb Arcade
Furniture and musical instrument
maker; antique restorer.
☎ 0491 39622

Village Fabrics
30 Goldsmith's Lane
Reproduction Victorian wooden lamps
and American cotton fabrics.
☎ 0491 36178

FESTIVALS AND FAIRS

May
Wallingford Regatta

June
Wallingford Carnvial
Abbey Festival - held at Dorchester
Abbey.

July
Raft Race

September
Michaelmas Fair - held at Kinecroft.

HERITAGE

The Bridge
900-foot, 13th century bridge with
19 arches spanning the flood plain of the
River Thames, the three arches spanning
the river were rebuilt in 1809. A fording
place in prehistoric times, the earliest
reference to a bridge is in 1141.

Sinodun Hill Fort
North-west near Dorchester
Iron Age earthworks and ramparts
offering splendid views of the Thames
Valley to the Chilterns.

Wallingford Castle
Castle Street
Remains of a mediaeval motte and bailey
castle constructed by order of William
the Conqueror in 1067 and enlarged by
subsequent royal owners. A home of
Princes and Queens, it was a major
Royalist stronghold during the Civil War
causing Cromwell to order its
destruction in 1652.

The Bridge at Wallingford

HISTORIC BUILDINGS

Dorchester Abbey
4¹/₂ north-west of Wallingford at Dorchester
Superb mediaeval abbey church, all that remains of an Augustinian abbey; unusual huge 'Jesse' window in the chancel; wall-paintings, memorials, and modern shrine of Birinus, the saint who made Dorchester a Christian centre in 634.

St Leonard's Church
St Leonard's Lane
Late Saxon herringbone stonework above the north door.

St Mary's Church
2¹/₂ miles north-east at Ewelme
Church, cloisers, almshouses and school were built as a group by Alice, Duchess of Suffolk and granddaughter of Chaucer around 1432; elaborate memorial tomb of Alice is beside the altar; notable old woodwork; brasses and stained glass. Jerome K Jerome's grave is in the churchyard.

St Mary's School
Ewelme
The oldest operating church school in England.

St Peter's Church
Thames Street
18th century church with unusual openwork spire.

Town Hall
Market Place
Built in 1670, with an open ground floor to shelter the market stalls.

HISTORIC HOUSES

Newington House
6 miles north-west at Newington
17th century stately home under restoration, open on Bank Holiday weekends.

MUSEUMS

Benson Veteran Cycle Museum
The Bungalow, 61 Brook Street, Benson
Private museum opened by the owner, Mr Passey, by appointment only; fine collection of 450 veteran bicycles dating from 1818 to 1930.
☎ 0491 38414

Dorchester Abbey Museum
4¹/₂ miles north-west at Dorchester
Small museum displaying artefacts of local history.
☎ 0865 340056

Wallingford Museum
Flint House, High Street
Permanent collection of 1000 years of local history and two special exhibits each year housed in 15th century house.
☎ 0491 35065

RAILWAYS

Cholsey & Wallingford Railway
CWR, Hithercroft Industrial Estate
Wallingford Station site open every weekend; trains run on certain Sundays each month; carnival 'Railfair' gala day in June; shop, museum and model railway.
☎ 0491 35067

THEATRES

The Corn Exchange
Market Place
Theatre housed in a Grade II listed building opened in 1856 with a notable iron-work roof.

Kinecroft Theatre
Kinecroft

WILDLIFE PARKS

Wellplace Bird Farm
3¹/₂ miles south-east of Wallingford at Ipsden
6¹/₂-acre site with over 100 varieties of birds and animals such as lambs, goats, monkeys, otters and racoons some of which can be petted; cafeteria, play area and picnic area.
☎ 0491 680473/680092

Water Sports

BOAT HIRE

Maidboats
Off the A423 at Benson Cruiser Station
Weekly cruiser and day boat hire.
☎ 0491 38304

ROWING

Wallingford Rowing Club
Thames Street

SWIMMING

Wallingford Swimming Pool
Outdoor pool.
☎ 0491 35351

Wantage, former capital of the Saxon kingdom of Wessex, was the birthplace of King Alfred the Great in 849 AD. It is now an attractive market town with several notable period houses of mellow red and local blue-glazed bricks. An unusual feature of the 17th century almshouses is their entrance which is cobbled with sheep's knucklebones. The story of Wantage over the ages can be seen at the Museum Centre which is housed in a converted 17th century cloth-merchant's house.

For those in search of outdoor pursuits, go fishing for trout or walk along part of the ancient route, The Ridgeway, which passes nearby.

FISHING

Game Fishing
Contact the National Rivers Authority for permits, licences and information.
☎ 0865 749400

Clearwater Fish Farm
Ludbridge Mill, East Hendred
Catch your own trout or feed the fish; farm shop selling smoked trout, seafood and salmon.
☎ 0235 833732

Outdoor Leisure

WALKING AND RAMBLING

The Ridgeway
Walk along part of 85-mile path that follows the ancient Wessex Ridgeway; rich in chalk downland flora and fauna and archaeological remains along the route.

Special Interests

ART GALLERIES

Ardington Gallery
Unit 4, Home Farm, Ardington
Frames designed and made; oil paintings, watercolours, fabrics and period frames restored.
☎ 0235 833677

ARTS AND CRAFTS

Ardington Pottery
The Old Dairy, 15 Home Farm, Ardington
Domestic and decorative stoneware displayed in 19th century picture-tiled dairy; commissions and commemorative items made to order; demonstrations by arrangmeent.
☎ 0235 833302

HISTORIC BUILDINGS

St Denys Church
On the A338 at Stanford-in-the-Vale
Spacious Church with mediaeval ceilings, 17th century pulpit and font cover; attractive old headstones in the big churchyard.

Venn Mill
On the A338 at Stanford-in-the-Vale
Mill dating from 1800 but built on an ancient site; currently undergoing restoration.
☎ 0367 718888

MUSEUMS

Champs Chapel Museum
Chapel Square, East Hendred
Displays of local interest housed in an interesting 15th century chapel.

Vale and Downland Museum Centre
The Old Surgery, Church Street
Displays in a converted 17th century cloth-merchant's house tell the story of Wantage and the surrounding areas over the centuries. Reconstructed Downland farm kitchen and dairy; demonstrations temporary exhibitions, events, shop; refreshments and picnic area.
☎ 0235 766838

Weobley is an ancient village; virtually every building is of note and some are over 600 years old. Its wide main street is the result of the demolition of about 40 houses in the 1850s by the Marquis of Bath. Once notorious for the imbibing of ale and the practice of witchcraft, Weobley is now a centre for painting, birdwatching and adventure sports.

Adventure Sports

CAVING

Worlds End Lodge
Youth Hostel, Staunton-on-Wye
☎ 098 17 308

CLIMBING

Worlds End Lodge
☎ 098 17 308

Multi-Activity Holidays

MULTI-ACTIVITY CENTRES

Worlds End Lodge
Pony trekking, caving, climbing, canoeing, orienteering, mountain walking; groups and individuals.
☎ 098 17 308

SPECIAL INTEREST CENTRES

Bob Kilvert's Watercolour Weeks
The Old Corner House, Broad Street
Beginners and experienced painters welcome to tackle the special problems of the watercolour medium and to paint the lovely town and surrounding countryside.
☎ 0544 318548

Outdoor Leisure

BIRDWATCHING

Worlds End Lodge
☎ 098 17 308

GOLF

Herefordshire Golf Club ⛳
3 miles south-east at Wormsley
Converted hunting lodge is used as the clubhouse.
☎ 043 271 219

HORSE RIDING

Worlds End Lodge
☎ 098 17 308

ORIENTEERING

Worlds End Lodge
☎ 098 17 308

TENNIS

Three Counties Lawn Tennis Club
For details contact S Pattison.
☎ 0544 318663

WALKING AND RAMBLING

Country Walks
Several walks around the lovely countryside.

Special Interests

ARTS AND CRAFTS

The Forge Crafts Shop
Local crafts, gifts and toys; morning coffee, home made teas.
☎ 0544 318666

FOOD AND DRINK

Herefordshire Hamper
The Dairy House, Whitehill Park
Quality foods produced by its members.
☎ 0544 318815

HISTORIC BUILDINGS

Cruck Barn
4 miles south-west at Eardisley
14th century cruck-framed barn, former
smithy.

Dilwyn Church
1½ miles north-east at Dilwyn
Large 13th century church with lofty
arcades, added to the tower of previous
building, now demolished; effigy of a
mailed knight from 1300.

Church of Mary Magdalene
4 miles south-west at Eardisley
Fine Norman font dating from 1150 –
perhaps the best and earliest example of
its kind.

Church of St Lawrence
2½ south-east at Canon Pyon
13th and 14th century circular piers,
bays and arches – all out of plumb.

Church of St John The Baptist
South of Weobley off the A480 at Yazor
Ivy covered remains of church dating
from 1300.

Sarnesfield Church
1½ miles south-west on the A4112
Rare tower with 100-nesthole dovecote
and 14th century stained glass figures.

Staunton-on-Wye Church
5½ miles south on the A438
11th century church with fine Jacobean
panelling on walls beneath the tower.

The Throne
16th century inn, once called the
Unicorn, where King Charles I stayed
after the Battle of Laisby in 1645.

Weobley Church
Norman with 12th, 13th and 14th
century additions; massive 14th century
tower linked to church by a later
extension; many interesting statues and
effigies.

HISTORIC HOUSES

Butt House
2 miles south-east at Kings Pyon
Unusual 17th century timber-framed
building with an ornamental dovecote
dated 1632.

GLOUCESTERSHIRE   **Westonbirt**   GLOUCESTERSHIRE

Westonbirt is the location of the famous Westonbirt Arboretum, a tree collection that
was started by the squire of Westonbirt in 1829 and which is now one of the finest in
the country extending to over 116 acres. There are facilities for golf, gliding and
walking as well as a pottery. Highgrove House, home of the Prince and Princess of
Wales, is close by.

Multi-Activity Holidays

MULTI-ACTIVITY CENTRES

Hare and Hounds Hotel
Short breaks including gliding, golf and
riding activities.
☎ 066 688 233

Outdoor Leisure

GOLF

Westonbirt Golf Course
Parkland course, visitors welcome.
☎ 066 688 242

WALKING AND RAMBLING

Cotswold Rambling
Contact Mr Chris Bowyer.
☎ 0666 840478

Special Interests

ARTS AND CRAFTS

Hookshouse Pottery
Handthrown reduction fired stoneware
pottery; showroom; demonstrations on
open days and for group visits; pottery
courses and tuition.
☎ 066 688 297

GARDENS

Westonbirt Arboretum
600 acres containing one of the finest
collections of temperate trees and shrubs
in the world.
☎ 066 688 220

Wheatley is situated to the east of Oxford and is notable for Waterperry House and Gardens and the Saxon village church that is also in the grounds. There is a sports centre nearby and it is possible to join the Oxfordshire Way here.

Indoor Sports

BADMINTON

The Park Sports Centre
Wheatley Park School Grounds
☎ 08677 2128

LEISURE CENTRES

The Park Sports Centre
Large sports hall, conditioning room, weight training, bar and social area; children's holiday programmes.
☎ 08677 2128

SQUASH

The Park Sports Centre
☎ 08677 2128

Outdoor Leisure

WALKING AND RAMBLING

The Oxfordshire Way
65-mile route linking the Cotswolds with the Chiltern Hills; it passes through Wheatley.

Special Interests

ARTS AND CRAFTS

Art in Action
North-east of Wheatley at Waterperry Gardens, Waterperry
Four-day tented craft fair held in July.
☎ 0844 339226

FESTIVAL AND FAIRS

July
Art in Action – four-day craft fair held at Waterperry Gardens.

Waterperry House and Gardens

GARDENS

Waterperry Gardens
North-east of Wheatley at Waterperry
6 acres of ornamental gardens with a year-round display of plants; fine trees, lawns, borders, alpine and shrub nurseries, fruit farms, teashop, garden shop and riverside walks; craft fair held in July.
☎ 0844 339226

HISTORIC BUILDINGS

Conical Lock-up
Town centre
Original conical village lock-up built in 1834.

St Mary's Church
Waterperry Gardens, Waterperry
Remains of a Saxon church with 14th and 15th century stained glass, memorials, Georgian box pews and brasses.
☎ 0844 339226

HISTORIC HOUSES

Waterperry House
North-east of Wheatley at Waterperry
18th century house not usually open to the public. Set in an 83-acre estate part of which is open to the public as Waterperry Gardens.

NATURAL HISTORY

Waterperry Wood
North-East of Wheatley
A woodland nature reserve bordered by the Oxfordshire Way.

Winchcombe, sited along the deep valley of the River Isbourne, was a walled city in Saxon times. It has a fine 'wool' church with an altar cloth worked by Catherine of Aragon; another of Henry VIII's wives, Katherine Parr, is buried nearby.

i * Town Hall
High Street
☎ 0242 602925

Population 4754

Multi-Activity Holidays

SPECIAL INTEREST CENTRES

Thimble Cottage Craft Studio
Old Station House
Residential and non-residential craft courses; lacemaking, willow basket making, painting, sketching and pottery.
☎ 0242 602283

Outdoor Leisure

WALKING AND RAMBLING

The Cotswold Way
97-mile long distance path that follows the Cotswold escarpment through picturesque scenery; it meets the Wychavon Way here.
☎ 0452 425674

Winchcombe Walks
Three walks of varying lengths around Winchcombe.
☎ 0242 602925

The Wychavon Way
Winchcombe is the southern end of this 41-mile middle distance footpath which leads from the Cotswold Way here over Bredon Hill into Worcestershire.
☎ 0684 295027

Special Interests

ARTS AND CRAFTS

Winchcombe Pottery
Broadway Road
Handmade domestic pottery, work of six potters using traditional wood-fired bottle kiln.
☎ 0242 602462

HERITAGE

Belas Knap Long Barrow
2 miles south of Winchcombe
178-foot Neolithic long barrow with a false portal at the north end; dry stone wall surrounds the earthern mound; four burial chambers entered from the sides.
☎ 0272 734472

St Peter's Church
15th century Cotswold wool church with many notable carved heads on exterior.

Sudeley Castle
Magnificent Tudor castle; burial place of Katherine Parr, the last wife of Henry VIII; fine collections of art treasures and antiques; craft centre; Elizabethan gardens.
☎ 0242 602308

MUSEUMS

Simms International Police Collection
Town Hall
Display is part of a huge private collection covering every aspect of law enforcement.
☎ 0242 602925

Winchcombe Folk Museum
Town Hall
Small display of local social history, archaeology and geology.
☎ 0242 602925

Winchcombe Railway Museum and Garden
23 Gloucester Street
Items of railway interest; opportunity to operate signals and other working exhibits; part of collection is laid out in a delightful garden with old rare plants and mediaeval herb garden; play area.
☎ 0242 602257/620641

RAILWAYS

The Gloucestershire Warwickshire Railway
Winchcombe Station 1 mile from the town centre at Gweet
Opened to board trains in March 1990, steam-ride round trips; Santa specials; GWR is based at nearby Toddington.
☎ 0242 621405

181

Witney, an ancient town, has been famous since the 17th century for blanket-making, a local industry that flourished as a result of the high quality of the local wool and the development of mills on the River Windrush. The town continues to grow and develop and has a diversity of places of interest such as the Edwardian working farm at Cogges and the Roman Villa at Northleigh in its surrounding area as well as a wide range of leisure and sporting facilities.

i Town Hall
Market Square
☎ 0993 775802

Market days Thursday, Saturday
Early closing Tuesday
Population 19,000

Aerial Sports

PARACHUTING

POPS UK
37 Fetti Place
☎ 0993 704095

Indoor Sports

BADMINTON

Windrush Sports Centre
Langdale Gate
☎ 0993 778444

LEISURE CENTRES

Windrush Sports Centre
Sports hall, sauna, solarium, weight-training, fitness room, pool and bar.
☎ 0993 778444

Outdoor Leisure

CAMPING AND CARAVANNING

Hardwick Parks Ltd
Downs Road, Standlake
100 pitches, facilities.
☎ 0865 300501

Lincoln Farm Park
Lincoln Farm, High Street, Standlake
☎ 0865 300236

Swinford Farm
6 miles east at Eynsham
☎ 0865 881368

FISHING

Coarse Fishing
Fishing in the River Windrush and the lake at Stanton Harcourt with facilities for the disabled. For permits and licences contact the National Rivers Authority.
☎ 0865 749400

ORIENTEERING

Thames Valley Orienteering Club
Contact D Hicks for details.
☎ 0993 774329

WALKING AND RAMBLING

Windrush Valley Walks
Route through unspoilt villages and delightful river valley scenery.

Special Interests

ANTIQUES

Robin Bellamy Ltd
97 Corn Street
☎ 0933 704793

Anthony Scaramanga
108 Newland
Furniture, pottery, porcelain and fabrics.
☎ 0933 703472

Witney Antiques
96-98 Corn Street
Clocks and furniture.
☎ 0993 703902

ART GALLERIES

The Country Gallery
David Winter Cottages, 35 Acre End Street, Eynsham
Prints and original paintings specialising in the British countryside always in stock. Also picture framing and mount cutting services.
☎ 0865 882014

182

ARTS AND CRAFTS

Robert H Lewin
Overgreen, Alvescot
Handmade wood items.
☎ 0993 842435

The Stable
Kingsway Farm
Ceramic plates.
☎ 0993 850960

Teddy Bears
New and old teddies and teddy-related
items; antique teddies.
☎ 0993 702616

HERITAGE

Buttercross
Church Green
17th century buttercross with sundial
and clock tower resting on a gabled roof
supported by 13 pillars.

Grim's Dykes
3 miles north-east at Northleigh
Earthworks showing evidence of a pre-
Roman settlement.

North Leigh Roman Villa
2 miles north-east at Northleigh
Partially reconstructed excavation of
2nd to 4th century courtyard villa which
had more than 60 rooms; remains of
baths; fine section of mosaic floor.
English Heritage.
☎ 0993 881830

HISTORIC BUILDINGS

Church of St Mary's
Early English architecture with a
magnificent exterior, splendid spire,
table tomb of a 16th century wool
merchant, brasses.

Old Blanket Hall
High Street
18th century building with unusual one-
handed clock built for weighing and
measuring blankets.

St Mary's Church
$1/2$ mile south-east at Cogges
Norman church and vicarage, surviving
part of a small Benedictine priory,
unusual square and octagonal 14th
century tower.

St Mary's Church
$2^1/2$ miles north-east at Northleigh
Notable 15th century Wilcote Chapel
with contemporary stained glass.

St Michael's Church
South-east at Stanton Harcourt
Grand church with central tower,
memorials to the Harcourt family over
500 years, rare wooden chancel screen,
fragments of the Shrine of St Edburg
saved from Bicester Priory during the
Reformation.

HISTORIC HOUSES

Minster Lovell Hall
$4^1/2$ miles west near Minster Lovell
Impressive and romantic ruins of a 15th
century manor house on the banks of the
River Windrush next to the almost
untouched 15th century church;
dovecote; local legends associated with
the manor house.
☎ 0993 775315

Stanton Harcourt Manor
5 miles south-east on the A4449
Manor acquired by the Harcourt family
in the mid-12th century, house is still
occupied by them. Unique Great
Kitchen dates from 1380; fine collection
of pictures, silver, furniture and
porcelain; 15-acre gardens; Pope
translated *The Iliad* here.
☎ 0865 881928

MUSEUMS

Cogges Manor Farm Museum
Eastern edge of Witney
19-acre Edwardian farm museum;
creation of agricultural life in period
reconstructions of the dairy, manor
house, stables, sheds and barns; regular
demonstrations of blacksmithing, hurdle
making, shearing, butter churning and
other skills; breeds of domestic animals
typical of the period; nature and history
trails; Visitor's Centre and picnic areas.
☎ 0993 772602

Water Sports

BOAT TRIPS

Pinkhill Lock
5 miles south-east near Stanton
Harcourt

DINGHY SAILING

Hardwick Leisure Park
South-east of Witney on the A415
☎ 0865 300501

SWIMMING

Windrush Sports Centre
☎ 0993 778444

WINDSURFING

Hardwick Leisure Park
☎ 0865 300501

Woodstock has a Georgian flavour, many fine old buildings and one of England's most popular stately homes, the world famous Blenheim Palace. It is the largest house in the country, was designed by Vanbrugh and its 2000 acres of parkland were landscaped by Capability Brown. It is well known as the birthplace of Sir Winston Churchill.

i Hensington Road
☎ 0993 811038

Early closing Wednesday
Population 3000

Outdoor Leisure

CAMPING AND CARAVANNING

Diamond Farm
Heathfield, Bletchingdon
34 pitches, facilities.
☎ 0869 50909

Special Interests

ANTIQUES

Fox House Antiques
30 Oxford Street
Victoriana antiques and bric-a-brac.
☎ 0993 811377

ARTS AND CRAFTS

Bladon Pottery
1¹/₂ miles south at Bladon
Figurative stoneware sculpture and watercolours.
☎ 0993 811489

Craftsmen's Gallery
1 Market Street
Wide range of crafts portrayed in pottery, porcelain, ceramics, wood, glass, oil paintings, water colours, lithographs and prints.
☎ 0993 811995

Woodstock Leathercraft Ltd
Chaucers Lane
The last manufacturers of handmade Woodstock gloves; full range of fine leather goods. Showroom and factory situated near Blenheim town gate.
☎ 0993 812368

FESTIVALS AND FAIRS

June
Blenheim Horse Trials - at Blenheim Palace.
184

August
Dressage Competition - at Blenheim Palace.

HISTORIC BUILDINGS

St Martin's Church
1¹/₂ miles south at Bladon
Church dates from 1891, notable as the burial place of Sir Winston Churchill who was born at Blenheim Palace.

HISTORIC HOUSES

Blenheim Palace
Queen Anne gave John Churchill, 1st Duke of Marlborough, Blenheim for his services at the Battle of Blenheim 1704. The palace, designed by Sir John Vanbrugh, is set in 2000 acres of parkland landscaped by Capability Brown; it is one of the finest examples of English baroque. Superb collection includes tapestries, paintings, sculpture and fine furniture set in magnificent state rooms; the Long Library is 183 feet long and contains over 10,000 volumes; a small collection is devoted to Sir Winston Churchill. The park incorporates a garden centre, adventure play area, butterfly house, narrow-gauge railway, restaurants, cafeterias and gift shop.
☎ 0993 811325

MUSEUMS

Oxfordshire County Museum
Fletcher's House
16th century stone house containing permanent display galleries telling the story of Oxfordshire through the ages; rural craft and domestic exhibits; lawns, coffee lounge and shop.
☎ 0993 811456

Water Sports

SWIMMING

Woodstock Swimming Pool
Shipton Road
Open air, seasonal.

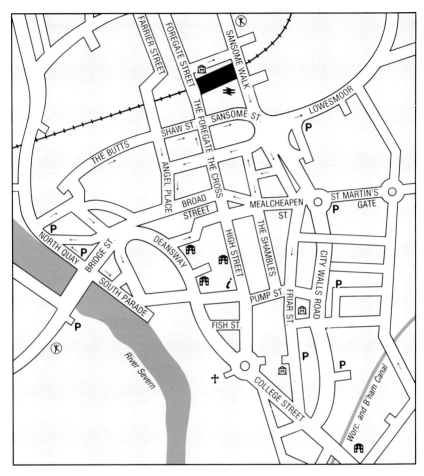

Worcester stands on the banks of the River Severn, an ancient city dominated by its magnificent cathedral that overlooks Worcester's peaceful and beautiful cricket ground. The town is rich in old buildings, historic houses and museums, one of which contains a fine collection of the Worcester porcelain and bone china for which the city is famous worldwide. The city remained faithful to Charles I even after the decisive Battle of Worcester in 1651; relics of this battle can be seen at the Guildhall. The city is well endowed with parks, theatres, art galleries, sports and leisure facilities and is a pleasure to explore.

i Guildhall
High Street
☎ 0905 726311

Market days Friday, Saturday
Early closing Thursday
Population 80,000

Indoor Sports

BADMINTON

Nunnery Wood Sports Centre
Spetchley Road
☎ 0905 357842

Perdiswell Leisure Centre
Bilford Road
☎ 0905 57189

LEISURE CENTRES

Nunnery Wood Sports Centre
Sports hall, fitness room, multi-gym, squash courts and outdoor sports facilities.
☎ 0905 357842

Perdiswell Leisure Centre
☎ 0905 57189

St John's Sports Centre
Swanpool Walk
☎ 0905 429900

Worcester Swimming Pool and Fitness Centre
Sansome Walk
Fitness room, sauna, solarium, two pools, social area.
☎ 0905 20241

SQUASH

Nunnery Wood Sports Centre
Two glass backed squash courts, squash league team and annual tournaments.
☎ 0905 357842

Perdiswell Leisure Centre
☎ 0905 57189

Multi-Activity Holidays

MULTI-ACTIVITY CENTRES

Leisure Leaders Activity Holidays
48 Winchcombe Drive
Courses for children organised on a day-to-day basis.
☎ 0905 58068

Outdoor Leisure

CRICKET

Worcester County Cricket Club
New Road
☎ 0905 748474

CYCLING

Cadence Cycle Hire
Foregate Street Railway Station
Long or short hire, routes recommended.
☎ 0905 613501

FISHING

Coarse Fishing
Fishing in the Avon, Severn, Teme and Worcester Canal. For permits, information and licences contact the National Rivers Authority.
☎ 021 711 2324

GOLF

Perdiswell Municipal Golf Club ⚑₉
☎ 0905 57189

Tolladine Golf Club ⚑₁₈ ⚑₉
The Fairway, Tolladine Road
Visitors welcome on weekdays.
☎ 0905 21074

Worcester Golf and Country Club ⚑₁₈
Boughton Park
Parkland course; visitors welcome with a reservation.
☎ 0905 422555

HORSE RACING

The Racecourse
Pitchcroft
A left-handed, 1 mile 5 furlong, oval course, it hosts 20 national hunt race days each year.

ORIENTEERING

Worcester Woods
Spetchley Road
Novel orienteering course suitable for all ages, no experience necessary.
☎ 0905 766493

Bluebells in Worcester Woods

TENNIS

Gheluvelt Park
Ombersley Road
Six tennis courts.

Nunnery Wood Sports Centre
☎ 0905 357842

Worcester Lawn Tennis Club
Northwick Close
☎ 0905 51092

WALKING AND RAMBLING

The Civil War Trail
Mile walk around the sites associated with the Civil War and the Battle of Worcester.

Worcester Town Trail
A tour of the historic landmarks of
Worcester.
☎ 0905 723471

The Wychavon Way
41-mile waymarked route through
attractive countryside linking
Worcestershire to the Cotswolds.
☎ 0905 723471
☎ 0684 295027

Special Interests

ANTIQUES

A list of twenty antique dealers is
available from the Tourist Information
Centre on request.
☎ 0905 723471

ART GALLERIES

Bevere Vivis Gallery and Pottery Shop
Bevere Knoll
Original paintings, wildlife prints and
pottery by local artists.
☎ 0905 51291

Framed
46 Friars Street
Contemporary picture gallery housed in
Mediaeval timber-framed building;
paintings by local and national artists.

FACTORY VISITS

Royal Porcelain Works
Severn Street
Tours to see the Worcester craftsmen
producing the famous Royal Worcester
porcelain; connoiseur tours can be
arranged. Gift, retail and seconds shop.
☎ 0905 23221

FESTIVALS AND FAIRS

May
May Day Country Fair – at Worcester
Countryside Park.
Worcester Regatta – contact the rowing
club for details.
☎ 0905 726311

July
Worcester Carnival

FOREST PARKS

**Worcester Woods and Countryside
Centre**
Spetchley Road off the A422
Ancient woodland with events and
activities throughout the year; self-
guided trail; snacks; play area. Contact
the Senior Ranger for details.
☎ 0905 766493

GARDENS

Cathedral Gardens
College Green
Gardens stretching down to the River
Severn; remains of a Benedictine priory.

Spetchley Park Gardens
Spetchley Park, Spetchley
30-acres of privately-owned gardens with
rare and unusual shrubs and trees; deer
park with red and fallow deer; plant
centre and tea room.
☎ 0905 65213

Spetchley Park

GUIDED TOURS

Faithful City Guides
Guided walks for individuals, groups or
special interests. Contact the Tourist
Information Centre for details.
☎ 0905 723471

HISTORIC BUILDINGS

Church of St Nicholas
Warndon Court, Old Warndon
Rural church, its history can be traced
back to Roman times.
☎ 0905 52623

Countess of Huntingdon's Hall
Deansway
Converted Methodist Chapel used
mainly for concerts.
☎ 0905 611427

The Guildhall
High Street
Imposing and unusual specimen of early
Georgian-style architecture 1721-23 to a
design of Thomas White; the Assembly
Room is beautifully decorated in Queen
Anne style.
☎ 0905 723471

Worcester Cathedral
College Green
Cathedral was begun in 1084 on a site used as a place of worship since the late 7th century. A landmark with fine perpendicular tower completed in 1375; the crypt is a well-preserved example of classic Norman architecture dating from 1084; the finely vaulted cloisters are a reminder of its monastic past and the chapter house with its ten sides and roof supported by a massive central column is the earliest of a type unique to Britain. Notable tombs, memorials and choir stalls; gift shop and refreshment room.
☎ 0905 28854

HISTORIC HOUSES

The Greyfriars
Friar Street
Mediaeval timber-framed and tiled house with walled garden; museum. National Trust.
☎ 0905 23571

Nash House
New Street
Early 17th century timber-framed town house of an armaments manufacturer.
☎ 0905 21728

The Old Palace
Deansway
House with 13th century interior and 18th century front; connections with Queen Elizabeth I.
☎ 0905 20537/20538

MUSEUMS

City Museum and Art Gallery
Foregate Street
Contemporary art exhibitions; displays of archaeology, natural history and military collections housed in a reconstructed 19th century chemist's shop.
☎ 0905 25371

The Commandery
Notable 15th century timber-framed and tiled house, the Royalist headquarters during the Battle of Worcester and now a museum devoted to the Civil War.
☎ 0905 355071

The Commandery

Dyson Perrins Museum
Severn Street
World's largest collection of Royal Worcester porcelain encompassing the period from the beginning of manufacture in the 1750s to the present day; factory tours and site shop.
☎ 0905 23221

Elgar's Birthplace Museum
Crown East Lane, Lower Broadheath Cottage where Elgar was born in 1857; now houses a collection of manuscripts; scores and Elgar memorabilia.
☎ 0905 66224

The Guildhall
High Street
Restored 18th century house with exhibits and paintings.
☎ 0905 723471

Tudor House Museum
The Greyfriars, Friar Street
Displays of the social and domestic life of Worcester from Elizabethan times.
☎ 0905 20904

ORNAMENTAL PARKS

Cripplegate Park
New Road
Tournament standard bowling greens in formal park.

Fort Royal Park
Overlooking the city
The site of the Duke of Hamilton's stand in the Battle of Worcester 1651 is marked by a lime tree at the top of the park.

Gheluvelt Park
Ombersley Road
Named to commemmorate the stand made by the Worcestershire Regiment in the Great War; bandstand, tennis courts and paddling pool.

Pitchcroft
East bank of the Severn
100-acre recreation area including the Racecourse; tree lined promenade, picnic area and riverside walks.

THEATRES

Swan Theatre
The Moors
Regional theatre with its own professional company.
☎ 0905 27322

Worcester Arts Workshop
21 Sansome Street
Range of fringe activities and arts.
☎ 0905 21095

Water Sports

BOAT HIRE

Pitchcraft Boating Station
Waterworks Road
Boat hire – rowing and motor boats.
☎ 0905 27949

BOAT TRIPS

Ferry Crossing
Ferries run between the Cathedral and
Chapter Meadows.

North and South Quays
River trips are operated from both quays.

ROWING

River Severn Rowing Club
Grandstand House
☎ 0905 22099

SWIMMING

**Worcester Swimming Pool and Fitness
Centre**
Sansome Walk
25-metre main pool, learner pool and
water cannon.
☎ 0905 20241

GLOUCESTERSHIRE / **Wotton-under-Edge** / GLOUCESTERSHIRE

Wotton-under-Edge, an old market town on the edge of the Cotswolds, was a major silk and cloth-making town for over 200 years. A prosperous town over the centuries its architecture is an interesting mix of Cotswold stone and the brick and half-timber styles of the Severn Vale and its narrow streets contain many notable buildings including the house in which Isaac Pitman devised his shorthand system. Today a busy shopping centre, it offers a selection of leisure facilities to the surrounding area.

Indoor Sports

LEISURE CENTRES

Wotton-under-Edge Sports Centre
Katharine Lady Berkeley's School
Sports hall, squash courts, outdoor
facilities.
☎ 0453 842626

SQUASH

Wotton-under-Edge Sports Centre
☎ 0453 842626

Multi-Activity Holidays

MULTI-ACTIVITY CENTRES

Severn Valley Sports
Various different activities.
☎ 0453 842892

The Ram Inn, Wotton-under-Edge

Outdoor Leisure

GOLF

Cotswold Edge Golf Course ⛳18
Upper Rushmire
Fairly flat course with superb views;
visitors welcome weekdays; coaching
available.
☎ 0453 844398

HORSE RIDING

Gin Saddlery
Upper Rushmire Farm
Lessons, hacking, accommodation.
☎ 0453 521203

WALKING AND RAMBLING

Circular Walk
A 5-mile circular Cotswold walk around
Wotton.
☎ 0453 765768

The Cotswold Way
This long-distance route passes through
Wotton as it follows the Cotswold
Escarpment between Chipping Campden
and Bath. Superb views at Nibley Knoll
just north of Wotton of the Severn Vale
and the Black Mountains.
☎ 0452 425674

Special Interests

GARDENS

Alderley Grange Gardens
Gardens with herbs, aromatic plants and old-fashioned roses.
☎ 0453 842161

HISTORIC BUILDINGS

Kingswood Abbey Gatehouse
1 mile south of Wotton
Only remains of Kingswood Abbey.

St Mary's Parish Church
Beautiful 13th century church with a very fine perpendicular tower; a library of historic books previously housed above the porch is now in Christ Church Museum, Oxford.

HISTORIC HOUSES

Newark Park
1 mile east of Wotton
Elizabethan hunting lodge remodelled by James Wyatt in 1790s; built of stones from the demolished Kingswood Abbey; cliff edge location with woodland garden and waymarked walks.
☎ 0453 842644

Tolsey House
Market Street
Ancient brick building with a pyramidal roof, once a market toll house.

OXFORDSHIRE / **Wroxton** / OXFORDSHIRE

Wroxton is a captivating thatch and stone village clustered round its duckpond and mediaeval church. On its outskirts stands Wroxton Abbey, a 17th century mansion standing on the site of an Augustinian priory.

Outdoor Leisure

FISHING

Coarse Fishing
Fishing in Grimsbury Reservoir, for details of licences and permits contact the National Rivers Authority.
☎ 0865 749400

WALKING AND RAMBLING

Rural Walks
Contact the Cherwell District Council for details.
☎ 0295 25235

Outdoor Leisure

HERITAGE

Hornton Stone Quarry
4¹/₂ miles north-west at Hornton
'Hornton Stone', a glowing ironstone used throughout the region, was quarried here.

HISTORIC BUILDINGS

Horley Church
2 miles north-west of Wroxton at Horley
Partly Norman church with well preserved 15th century wall painting.

Hornton Church
4¹/₂ miles north-west of Wroxton at Hornton
Wall paintings include a large 14th century depiction of the Last Judgement.

Wroxton Church
Fine carvings and monuments.

HISTORIC HOUSES

Wroxton Abbey
17th century mansion built on the site of a 13th century priory set in recently restored 18th century park.
☎ 0295 273551

Water Sports

DINGHY SAILING

Grimsbury Reservoir
Details from the Banbury Cross Sailing Club.
☎ 0295 263928

190

Yarpole, a small village north of Leominster, is clustered around its old Manor House. The former bakery and gatehouse are on the banks of a small stream and the 13th century church has a detached bell tower characteristic of many Herefordshire churches. Nearby are excellent walks on wild and elevated commons and there are several important sites and buildings in the surrounding area.

Special Interests

HERITAGE

Croft Ambrey
¹/₂ mile north of Yarpole
Iron Age fort, access via a footpath.

Mortimer's Cross Battlesite
1 mile west on the B4362
The site of the battle that changed the course of history in 1461; the Yorkist Edward won an important victory over Queen Margaret and the Lancastrians which led to his being crowned King Edward IV a month later. The tree topped mound to the south of the B4362 between the crossroads and Lucton is the mass grave for some of the 4000 slain during the battle.

Richard's Castle
4 miles north of Yarpole off the B4361
Site of one of the earliest stone-built Norman castles in Britain, some historians also believe this to be the oldest Norman borough in Britain.

HISTORIC BUILDINGS

Croft Castle
North-west of Yarpole
Mediaeval fortress, home of the Croft family since Domesday; typical castle with corner towers and crenellations; largely refurbished in the 18th century Gothic style. Set in 1036-acre estate of ancient oaks and sweet chestnuts. National Trust.
☎ 0568 85 246

NATURAL HISTORY

Bircher Common
Bircher
Wild common with magnificent views. National Trust.

Fishpool Valley
Yarpole
Area of scientific interest at the southern end of Bircher Common.

Useful Information

MAJOR ROADS

M40   Birmingham to London through Oxfordshire
M5   Birmingham to Bristol through Gloucestershire
M50   Off M5 to Ross-on-Wye
A44   Leominster to Chipping Norton via Worcester, Evesham and Moreton-in-Marsh
A40   Cheltenham to London via Oxford and High Wickham

BUS COMPANIES

Midland Red West
  Hereford and Worcester
  ☎ 0345 212555
Public Transport Section
  Hereford and Worcester County Council ☎ 0905 766800
National Express
  Oxfordshire ☎ 0865 791579
  (calls diverted to Birmingham and N.E. main office)
Public Transport Section
  Gloucestershire County Council
  ☎ 0452 425543
Red & White
  Gloucestershire
  ☎ 0291 622947

MAJOR RAIL ROUTES

Birmingham to Bristol via Worcester, Cheltenham, Gloucester and Bromsgrove
Hereford to Paddington via Worcester and Oxford
Cardiff to Crewe via Hereford and Leominster

Banbury ☎ 262256
Cheltenham ☎ 0452 29501
Evesham ☎ 0452 29501
Droitwich Spa ☎ 0452 29501
Henley-on-Thames ☎ 0734 595911
Hereford ☎ 0432 266533
Gloucester ☎ 0452 29501
Great Malvern ☎ 0452 29501
Kidderminster ☎ 021 643 2711
Ledbury ☎ 0452 29501
Leominster ☎ 0452 29501
Oxford ☎ 0865 722333
Ross-on-Wye ☎ 0452 29501
Redditch ☎ 021 643 2711
Stroud ☎ 0452 29501

COUNTY COUNCIL OFFICES

Gloucestershire County Council
Shire Hall
Westgate Street
Gloucester
☎ 0452 425000

Hereford and Worcester County Council
County Hall
Spetchley Road
Worcester
☎ 0905 763763

Oxfordshire County Council
County Hall
New Road
Oxford
☎ 0865 792422

TOURIST BOARDS

Heart of England Tourist Board
(Hereford & Worcester, Gloucestershire)
2/4 Trinity Street
Worcester
☎ 0905 763436
Thames and Chilterns Tourist Board
(Oxfordshire)
The Mount House
Witney
☎ 0993 778800